George Sheehan

on RUNNING TO WIN

How to Achieve the Physical, Mental & Spiritual Victories of Running

By **George Sheehan, M.D.**

Author, PERSONAL BEST

Medical Editor, ***RUNNER'S*** Magazine

Rodale Press, Emmaus, Pennsylvania

Runner's World is a registered trademark of Rodale Press, Inc.

Printed in the United States of America on acid-free ∞ paper

"Estimating Percentage of Body Fat" on page 94 is reprinted from *Sensible Fitness* (Leisure Press, 1986) by Jack H. Wilmore, Ph.D. Reprinted with permission from the author.

"Rate of Perceived Exertion" on page 125 is reprinted from *Medicine and Science in Sports and Exercise* 14 (1982): 377–81, by Gunnar A. V. Borg, et al.

"Symptoms of Overtraining" on page 135 is adapted from *The Lore of Running* (Leisure Press, 1991) by Timothy D. Noakes, M.D.

Editor: Sharon Faelten
Cover designer: Denise Shade
Book designer: Chuck Beasley
Copy editor: Susan G. Berg
Indexer: Ed Yeager

If you have any questions or comments concerning this book, please write:

Rodale Press
Book Readers' Service
33 East Minor Street
Emmaus, PA 18098

Library of Congress Cataloging-in-Publication Data

Sheehan, George.
George Sheehan on running to win : how to achieve the physical, mental and spiritual victories of running / by George Sheehan.
    p.   cm.
Includes index.
ISBN 0–87596–145–2   hardcover
1. Running—Psychological aspects. I. Title
GV1061.8.P75S54   1992
796.42—dc20   92–19748
                                         CIP

Distributed in the book trade by St. Martin's Press

2   4   6   8   10   9   7   5   3   1   hardcover

To the late Mel Sokolow, squash player, Met fan, and lover of life. Almost two decades ago, Mel took me under his wing and from my first book to this present volume was a constant source of strength and humor and wisdom. He continues to live in the hearts and minds of those fortunate enough to have been his friends.

Contents

Foreword

Dr. George Sheehan is a world-class worrier. He worries that he hasn't written well enough (though he has few peers as a running writer), spoken well enough (though no one on the running clinic circuit speaks better), or run well enough (though he has long been one of the country's fastest men his age).

I've edited George's writing for more than 20 years. He calls me often to say "It's all over, I'm finished" in any one of his three areas of expertise. Then he comes right back to perform well.

So when he called in 1986 to report "bad news," I wasn't too worried. We'd been through this routine many times before.

"I've read through the manuscript again," he said of *Personal Best*, the book that I was editing for him. "It needs more work." George ran through pages of suggested changes, and I thought his requested revision was the bad news. But just when he seemed ready to hang up the phone, he said, "Now I have something bad to tell you. I have a malignancy."

He explained that prostate cancer had been discovered. He outlined his immediate course of treatment.

Then would come the waiting and wondering. How much

had this disease progressed? How fast was it moving? What could be done to stop it?

In 1984, George had gotten his first hint of the trouble to come. He was in Dallas to speak and decided to visit Dr. Kenneth Cooper at the Cooper Aerobics Center. Dr. Cooper couldn't pass up the chance to give George a complete physical exam. The year before, Jim Fixx had gotten away without one, and it might have saved his life. Dr. Cooper wasn't going to let George slip through the net, too.

"That was when he discovered this suspicious area in my prostate," George wrote at the time, before knowing how serious his condition might be. "The news was paralyzing. I was suddenly aware of my mortality."

George had the growth biopsied, then sweated out a week of waiting for the results. "Whether this nodule turns out to be benign or malignant," he said then, "my life has been unalterably changed."

Upon hearing a good report, George noted, "The week of waiting had led me to the truth. This was no pardon I had received. It was a temporary stay. Eventually, I would come to justice. I had been granted a little more time to deal with the inevitable."

It was two more years before George had to face the harsh truth even more directly than before. He would write, "In my lectures on fitness, I have always put forth the argument that it extends life. Now I ask, 'Who runs because of concern about longevity?'

"I answer that question in the next breath: No one. What we are interested in is *performance*. Our consuming concern is getting up in the morning and doing our best the rest of the day."

He added, "What is performance, but our best rebuttal to mortality? Daily, by deed or subterfuge, we make our argument against the essential truth of the human condition."

The day George told me he had cancer, he said he worried about missing speaking, writing, and racing commitments. He wanted to keep performing. Later, he said:

"When I first got my diagnosis, I just gave up. I planned my will and turned down speaking engagements. I wasn't sure I'd be around in three months to fulfill them."

Those months passed. The disease had stabilized, and George had learned to live with it and to work through it.

George once told me that after all he has done as a doctor, runner, writer, and speaker, he still thinks of himself as an "underachiever."

"That's the main reason I'm not just sitting around watching the ocean. I could do that. But I feel I've never achieved all that I could. I haven't run as well as I can, I haven't spoken as well as I can, and I haven't written as well as I can. If you take less than that view, you're finished."

George wasn't finished. Far from it. He resumed his full schedule, writing dozens of articles, giving hundreds of speeches, and running scores of races in the next five years. This book is a product of these years.

Joe Henderson
West Coast Editor
Runner's World Magazine
December 1991

Prologue

The reporter in Anchorage was skeptical. "Is it true," he asked, "that you have called running a religion?" I had come to Alaska feeling insecure, not certain of what I had to offer these pioneer people. My talks were not yet formulated in my mind. To me, it looked as though Alaskans were already fit, and now I was being challenged on the other values I might claim for a running program.

I thought about the question. If I hadn't called running a religion, I had certainly implied it. I had repeated Jim Fixx's story of the woman who described her husband by saying, "Ted used to be a Methodist, but now he's a runner." And I had compared running to Oliver Alden's pursuit of sculling and horseback riding in George Santayana's *The Last Puritan*. "A wordless religion," Santayana had called Alden's regimen.

But Santayana thought of religion not as truth, but as poetry. And he was an observer of athletes, not an athlete himself. He had come up with a poetic phrase and missed the point. And so had I. But fortunately, now I knew the answer. I looked at the reporter and said, "Running is like Alaska. Running is not a religion, it is a place."

This idea had been germinating in my head during the flight from Seattle. I had read an account of a seven-month stay in a Trappist monastery by Father Henri Nouwen, a Belgian priest well known in literary and academic circles. His book

1

A *Genesee Diary* gave me a new insight into the true nature of the running life.

Nouwen's problems are remarkably similar to mine. The things that drove him to retire to the monastery are the same as those that plague me day after day. He was caught in an ascending spiral of activity. Each talk, each article, each book ignited requests for more talks and articles and books, every ring of the phone another demand on his time.

This way of life is addictive. Withdrawal symptoms occur whenever requests and letters and compliments diminish or cease. So the victim has little choice except to continue and even escalate the activity.

"While complaining of too many demands," Nouwen writes, "I felt uneasy when none were made. While speaking of the burden of letter writing, an empty mailbox made me sad. While fretting about my lecture tours, I felt disappointed when there were no speaking invitations. While desiring to be alone, I was afraid to be alone."

The priest who had been teaching and lecturing and writing about the importance of solitude, inner freedom, and peace of mind had become a prisoner, locked into unceasing activity. Finally he made the decision to step back. The time had come, he said, to restore some solitude, some stillness, some isolation to his life. He needed to take a long look at himself and his role in preaching the word of God. So he took a leave of absence and entered the Trappist monastery at Genesee, near Rochester, New York. It was, he found, a perfect place to retreat and restore himself.

The monastery is a place for the body. Father Nouwen was assigned to work in the bakery, helping to make bread, the monks' commercial enterprise. Later, he was chosen to gather stones to build a new chapel.

But the monastery is also a place for the mind. Father Nouwen had his own little sanctum for meditation. Even at work or in the company of others, talking was kept to a minimum. The only demands on his mind were those he made himself.

And of course, the monastery is a place for the soul. "The monastery," says Father Nouwen, "is not built to solve problems, but to praise the Lord in the midst of them."

The monastery is a place for ordinary people, for sinners as well as saints. The work sometimes chafed. Relationships were strained. Thought came slowly. Prayer seemed impossible. Nouwen was still Nouwen. But all the while, he knew he was there because of an inner "must." And he stayed because, he says, "I knew I was in the right place."

And all the while, the priest expected to come out a different person, more integrated, more spiritual, more virtuous, more compassionate, more gentle, more joyful, more understanding. "I hoped that my restlessness would turn into quietude, my tensions into a peaceful lifestyle, my ambivalence into a single-minded commitment to God."

But upon leaving, Father Nouwen knew there had been only a lull in the battle with himself. He was the same man, with the same problems. So he asked the abbot for advice. "You must put 90 minutes aside every day for prayer," the abbot told him. If Father Nouwen was to take Genesee home with him, he would have to take time for this daily dialogue with himself and his God. Without constant renewal, what he had experienced at the monastery would vanish. Otherwise, for the rest of his life, he would awake in the morning with the same tendencies, the same desires, the same sins that he conquered only the day before. Only a return each day to the monastery would save him.

Running, I told the reporter, is just such a monastery—a retreat, a place to commune with God and yourself, a place for psychological and spiritual renewal.

1

What Makes Runners Run?

*If a fitness program is to succeed,
it must be fun.*

WHY I RUN

I've been a distance runner for almost 30 years, and I'm still trying to explain this self-renewing inner compulsion. The more I run, the more I want to run. The more I run, the more I live a life conditioned and influenced and fashioned by my running. And the more I run, the more certain I am that I am heading for my real goal: to become the person I am.

If Francis Bacon had written on running, he would have put it this way: "Running maketh the whole man." I see that whole person as being part animal, part child, part artist, and part saint. Running makes me all of these. It makes me a whole person.

I begin as body. "Be first a good animal," wrote Emerson.

I am. I have that animal energy, that ease of movement, that good tight body, that sense of occupying just the right amount of space. I am pared down to bone and muscle. My skin taut, my eyes clear, I have become my body. I occupy it with delight.

The tests prove what I feel. My biological age is that of a person 30 years younger. I have the oxygen capacity and physical work capacity of a 40-year-old instead of someone over 70. My pulse is slow, my blood pressure normal. My body fat is a mere 5 percent. Yet I am no different from others my age who run with me. Running proves that man at any age is the greatest marvel in the world.

Next comes the child. Running makes me a child, a child at play. That is the aim of life: to become an adult while remaining a child at heart. Play is the key. When we play, we do things because we want to, without thought of payment.

Play is something we would do for nothing, something that has meaning but no purpose. When I run, I feel that. For that hour a day, I am a child finally doing what I want to do and enjoying it. When I do, I realize what happens to the body is simply a bonus. I must first play an hour a day, then all other things will be added on.

One great addition is to make myself an artist. Being an artist is, after all, only seeing things as if for the first time. When we do, we see the real meaning of things, the solutions to our problems. Running gives me that creativity. It provides the meditative setting. It opens up areas in my mind I seem not to use otherwise.

At the minimum, it places me where these things can happen. A physician friend of mine expressed it this way: "I decided to run at a pace that would allow me to (1) enjoy my surroundings; (2) let me think a bit; and (3) be alone for an hour a day." I agree. On the roads at a pace I could run forever, I find what that "forever" is all about.

Finally, running has given me the chance to be a saint, to be a hero. Like everyone else, I want to be challenged. I want to find out whether or not I am a coward. I want to see how much effort I can put out . . . what I can endure . . . if I measure up. Running allows that.

I can run the classic race, the mile, and know the terrible pain that accompanies that third quarter-mile and the almost total oblivion of that final 100 yards to the finish. I can suffer, die, and be born again in a 6-mile race over hills on a cross-country course. And I can compete with myself in the marathon, the race Roger Bannister called the "acme of athletic heroism."

There are as many reasons for running as there are days in the year, years in my life. But mostly I run because I am an animal and a child, an artist and a saint. So, too, are you. Find your own play, your own self-renewing compulsion, and you will become the person you are meant to be.

FIELD OF DREAMS

It was early evening in Eugene, Oregon, and the lights were on at Hayward Field. In the grandstand, 5,000 people watched the VIII World Veterans Championships, still buzzing over the previous race as our group of eight was led to the starting line for the men's 70–74 800-meter final.

Months ago, these championships—short distances, run on a track—were of little interest to me. Over the years, my passion had been road races of 5 miles or more. I was a distance runner and had long since lost any desire to run on a track.

But age and time are not congenial to maintaining the status quo. They do not permit an everlasting present. There are cycles to our life, just as in all of nature. The winter of the 70-year-old yields to the spring of the adolescent.

When I began running at Brooklyn Prep, I ran the half-mile and the mile relay. My running was limited to a few minutes of fear followed by effort, then pain, and then peace. I experienced then what Thoreau had written: "The thrills of joy and those of pain are indistinguishable." The youthful middle-distance runner knows this full well. The 800-meter race is an inextricable mix of joy and pain.

At 70, I returned to the body and play and wisdom of that teenager. In high school, I regarded the cross-country distance of 2½ miles as the ultimate test. Now I think anything over 3 miles is too much for my physical powers. I have returned to the races of my youth.

Instead of getting old, I became young, and in Eugene, I was an adolescent living an adolescent's dream. I was in Hayward Field, the mecca of track and field. The stands, filled with people, loomed high above. The floodlights glistened on the red track, still wet from an earlier rain. The infield was an incredible, improbable emerald green.

The whole scene had an Olympic quality. The finalists included four Americans, an Australian, a New Zealander, a German, and a Swede. I could hear the announcer introducing each of us by name, country, the lane we occupied, and our achievements. One runner, Daniel Bulkley of the United States, was the reigning world champion and the world record holder. The Australian, John Gilmour, an authentic giant and already a legend, was newly in the 70–74 category and setting world records at virtually every distance he raced.

Then I heard the starter say, "Runners! Set!" The gun sounded, and I was running the world championship 800-meter race. It was enough to make anyone lose his wits, and I did. I had gotten in the final by going out slow and picking off four runners with a fast last lap. I had planned to repeat this strategy, but this time the world's best 800-meter runners went out at flank speed, and I went with them. With 400 meters to go, I felt like I was finished, but I held on to pass the German and finish seventh.

Afterwards, as I sat on the box with the big "8" indicating my lane, an official came up and said I had run 2:48.2. A personal best on a personal best evening. So I took that and the memory back to the sweats I'd left on the far side of the field. On the way, the men's 65–69 800-meter qualifiers passed me, bound for a like experience. Eight more adolescents entering their field of dreams.

Later, when I was flying home, still filled with this sense of being an old-young runner, I reviewed the tables that grade running performance with age. How did my 2:48.2 compare with the half-miles I ran years ago as a senior at Brooklyn Prep? A quick calculation showed that my mark in Eugene was equivalent to breaking 2 minutes—1:59.0 to be exact—something I could never do in high school.

And now in a way—in a great and glorious way—I had broken 2 minutes. And somewhere over Iowa my eyes filled with tears.

WHAT GETS *YOU* UP AND RUNNING?

Since 1968, quantum leaps have been made in the study of exercise physiology. The introduction of the needle biopsy enabled physiologists to better study and understand the mechanisms that lead to fitness. The Borg scale of perceived exertion offered a way to train using the body as a guide. (For more on the Borg scale, see chapter 7.) The result was the "fitness formula"—30 minutes of "comfortable" activity four times a week, utilizing many of the activities in Dr. Kenneth Cooper's 1968 book *Aerobics.*

Physicians are now able to offer programs guaranteed to produce fitness. And coupled with attention to diet and living habits, regular exercise can help protect against unnecessary disease and premature death as well. It remained, it seemed, just a matter of getting the word out, and in no time Americans would be on their feet pursuing a life of fitness and health.

Needless to say, no such thing occurred. America was, and still is, a sedentary country. The Centers for Disease Control reports that only 10 percent of Americans exercise up to the recommended guidelines.

The problem isn't any kind of shortcoming in exercise physiology. We know more than we need to know about exercise physiology. The army has no difficulty getting recruits fit. Where we are deficient is exercise *psychology.* We don't know how to motivate people to exercise.

In fact, the question I hear most frequently when I lecture to my medical colleagues on health promotion is "How can I get my patients to exercise?" Most family physicians, internists, and cardiologists want their patients to exercise but have difficulty motivating them to do so. Americans seem willing to obey most of the rules for fitness and heath except one: giving up their sedentary lifestyle.

Dr. J. Michael McGinnis, director of the U.S. Office of Disease Prevention and Health Promotion and a member of the high command in a project setting America's health goals for the year 2000, admits to failure in this area.

"Fitness and exercise—that's proven to be a tough nut to crack," says Dr. McGinnis. "The fitness boom is really a marginal phenomenon. The joggers and bicyclists you see really represent a small proportion of the American public, which for the most part remains sedentary."

Yet the importance of exercise in attaining a long and productive life is only too evident. The United States has a heart attack rate double that of France, Spain, and Italy and higher than all European countries except Finland, despite the fact that Americans smoke considerably less and pay more attention to diet. The deciding factor is lack of exercise, the most prevalent risk factor for heart disease in this country.

How, then, to get a person into a fitness program? Is it enough to list all the ways exercise will change a person's day and life and, indeed, self? I think not. A physician might convince someone to exercise, but unless there is a good match between the person and the activity, it won't take. Unless exercise (and in its higher state, pursuit of some kind of sport) satisfies the personality as a whole, sooner or later the individual will drop out.

I saw a newspaper story that demonstrated this fit between an individual and his exercise activity. A 72-year-old retired football coach had returned to coaching. When asked why, he explained, "My golf game has gone to pieces; my wife won't allow me to fly airplanes anymore; and most of the handball players I used to play with are gone."

There was no photograph of this man in the newspaper. But somehow I knew (and I suspect you do, too) what he looked like. His choice of leisure pursuits suggested he was what could be called a "hitter." He enjoys aggressive, head-to-head sports and likes the tension involved in what he does. And an anthropologist once said, "You can tell by looking at a person whether he is built for fight, flight, or negotiation." So my guess is that this man is big boned and well muscled.

If my guess is right, this man's leisure pursuits fit him to a tee. His primary characteristic is strength; his muscles want to speak. His response to stress is confrontation. So when he seeks an engrossing leisure-time avocation, it involves strength and confrontation. He's a "physical" person. And he has selected pursuits that allow him to express himself physically. It makes him complete.

What separates this man from the great mass of immobile Americans is just this intuitive selection of a sport that is tailored to his body type and personality. The dropout rate in fitness programs is appalling. Almost 70 percent backslide into the sedentary lifestyle. This is a recidivism that matches the failure rate in drug addiction rehabilitation. And these failures come about when little or no consideration is given to a match between the body and personality on one hand and the sport or exercise on the other.

If a fitness program is to succeed, it must be the one for you. Most of all, it should be *fun*. It should *not* remind you of the phys ed classes you hated in school. Success is much more likely to accompany an activity that you were intensely interested in in childhood.

Certain sports appeal to a spectrum of personalities. Tennis enthusiasts, for instance, range from the big hitters to the indefatigable "get everything back" type, to those who simply like the idea of wearing whites and drinking iced tea between matches.

Golfers are equally diverse. The game attracts enthusiasts who exist to whack every ball out of sight and who love to put a bet on every hole just to juice up the excitement. Others enjoy a solitary and precise game, while still others head for home if their foursome (and its socializing) doesn't show up.

So to select the right fitness activity for you, follow the Delphic advice "Know thyself." What's more, there are ways to make an otherwise boring activity interesting. For instance, you could invite an interesting person to join you on your usual daily walk. However, it is much better if your activity is a self-renewing compulsion, something you would do even if it had no other benefit than the joy you felt doing it.

FINDING A LIFETIME SPORT

Exercise psychology includes considerations other than motivation. Psychologists are studying the effect of exercise on many aspects of mental health, such as anxiety, depression, and reactions to stress. They're exploring the role of exercise in improving self-image and building self-esteem. To have any significant impact, however, health promoters will have to solve the problem of motivation.

Let me state from the outset that a large segment of the sedentary public cannot be faulted for lack of trying. The Centers for Disease Control estimates that 50 percent of those who enroll in a program drop out within three months. Indeed, it has been said that health spas expect a majority of their members who sign up for a year or so to drop out.

From what I've read, exercise psychologists can predict fairly well those who will stay in a program and those who won't. What they haven't figured out is how to change that outcome. They've identified who is least likely to succeed, but they're unable to prevent that failure.

Researchers in sports psychology have tended to concentrate on already dedicated athletes. When I asked a well-known sports psychologist how to pick an activity for the people who have a hard time sticking with a sport, he replied, "Ask them what they *like* to do."

Over the years, I have written largely for runners, people who like what they're doing. For them, running is exactly the kind of self-renewing compulsion I mentioned earlier. In fact, the majority of my readers are more than runners; they're *racers*. They see themselves as competitive athletes. They have gone beyond the initial rewards of fitness to those of sport and competition.

While it is true that a certain percentage of runners and even racers drop out, 97 percent of those who read *Runner's World* magazine say they plan to run for the rest of their lives. For them, running fulfills special psychological needs and satisfactions. If it fulfills *your* needs, you'll want to do it the rest of your life.

THINK OF IT AS PLAYTIME

A study by Lise Gauvin, exercise physiologist at Concordia University, Montreal, may help shed further light on the question of why so many people don't stick with their exercise program—or even start one. Gauvin found significant differences in motivation among four groups: self-directed exercisers (runners, cyclists, swimmers, tennis players); fitness program enrollees; fitness program dropouts; and sedentary individuals (who participated in no fitness program of any kind).

The survey concentrated on three elements in motivation:

- Direction—why they worked out, and why they liked it.
- Intensity—how much effort they put into a workout, and what they thought about while doing it.
- Persistence—how they felt about missing a workout, and how they felt after an exercise session.

The study found that self-directed exercisers are committed to attaining health and fitness. They share the attitude expressed by Cristobal Mendez, who wrote the first book on exercise, *Book of Bodily Exercise,* published way back in 1555. Mendez said of exercise: "My life depends upon it."

Also, they like what they do. And they do it at about 75 percent intensity—in other words, a level of perceived exertion rated as "comfortably hard." And during exercise, they think about something other than what they are doing—like family problems, or perhaps nothing at all. And after exercising, they feel energized.

People enrolled in fitness programs *also* said they wanted to be fit. And they want to "look good," too. But even if they stick with it, these people often dislike the exercise, think only about what they are doing, and exercise "hard." After a workout, they feel bushed, not energized.

Fitness program enrollees feel a need to push themselves, and many of those who eventually dropped out had tried "the buddy system," to ensure participation.

The fitness dropouts seem to fight the whole program. Their motive is to have fun, but they don't like the exercise or the setting. And on the perceived exertion scale, they exercise "very hard." During exercise, they force themselves not to quit, telling themselves, "Let's go, don't stop," "I'm doing the best I can," or "I'm such a wimp." They, too, feel fatigued after a workout.

The sedentaries share many characteristics with dropouts. They think exercise should be fun but doubt that it ever is. They dislike exercise and say it takes too much time. And they have any number of reasons as to why they don't exercise. They stand poles apart from those who persist year after year in their selected activity.

When it comes to exercising regularly, runners—like cyclists and other autonomous exercisers—need no prodding or planning. Their attitude is similar to that of veteran marathoner Johnny Kelly: "When I don't run, I feel as if something has been stolen from me."

If you're inactive and would like to exercise regularly, the message is clear. First, take responsibility for your fitness and health. Next, select a form of exercise you enjoy—something you can do comfortably while thinking about other things. When I run, for instance, I put my body on automatic pilot and free my mind to pursue its own thoughts.

The dropouts and sedentaries are correct: Exercise should be fun. Yet for most people, organized programs are drudgery. Dr. Oded Bar-Or, director of a children's rehab program at McMaster Hospital in Hamilton, Ontario, Canada, says that for nonathletic children, organized programs can be an embarrassment as well.

Dr. Bar-Or states that in order to succeed, children must enjoy what they do and feel competent doing it. When it comes to exercise, this means, initially at least, exerting minimal effort, like that required for bowling, baseball, jungle gyms, fishing. Then, as they get back in touch with their bodies, Dr. Bar-Or adds some more demanding exercise.

There is the answer. Go out and play. Fitness and health are bound to follow.

BE YOUR OWN HERO

There are many locker rooms in the house of the Lord. For a certain subset of individuals, sensible, easy-to-perform activities like running hold little appeal. They want sports that require skill. They want an activity that has the possibility of pain. They are looking for danger. How else to understand the appeal of hang gliding, mountain climbing, or riding horses over brush?

These high-risk sports people turn to the martial arts, snowmobiling, and bungee jumping. Racquet sports and rugby are other outlets for their aggressive tendencies.

There are perfectly good reasons for these individual choices. The meaning of sport in a person's life corresponds to the particular needs and satisfactions that such a person requires. Our chosen sport should emphasize our particular strength and allow us to express it in a heroic way. Inside our sport, which is outside the reality of life, we are meant to be heroes.

My message is for those who find heroism in simple, untutored, unremarkable endurance. The marathon is the classic trial for the person void of talent or skill but determined to finish. Risk takers, on the other hand, tend to be highly skilled individuals who like to face death—figuratively and, unfortunately, sometimes literally as well. Whatever the activity, it must require surges of adrenaline to interest them.

People should not have to apologize for finding running a bore and walking worse. There is no disputing taste. This should not be an excuse, however, for ceasing the search. We are meant to be athletes, not spectators. And we must find our sport.

GET OFF THE BENCH

Surveys that presume to keep us up-to-date usually do no more than confirm the fundamentals of human nature. In assuring us of what is *au courant*, they simply validate what we already know.

One poll, for instance, tells us that 90 percent of children would rather play for a losing team than sit on the bench with a winning one. Anyone who is still a child inside would agree with that. Every athlete would wonder why the question had to be asked.

What surprises me is the 10 percent who voted to watch. Not that being a spectator is all bad. I will admit to a certain thrill of seeing history made in sport. I will acknowledge the delight of being present when the best perform at their best. I will not deny that an admired athlete can change one's life. Indeed, many youngsters choose a sport because of the heroes they have seen on TV playing their games.

Nevertheless, spectating should never be a substitute for the actual experience. Sport should not be experienced secondhand. Next to religion, sport is the most important function of man. It teaches us much about who we are, how we should act. Whether pursued in a gymnasium or in a community center, on a track or out on the road, sport introduces us to the limits of our body, the working of our mind, the capabilities of the social self.

Sport, to use the title from John McPhee's book on Bill Bradley, gives you "a sense of where you are." It is a coming-of-age for the young. A renaissance for the adult. A regeneration for the old.

As I write this, I am reminded of a friend of mine, a former mountain climber (now a marathoner) who became interested in the Renaissance. He spent two weeks in Florence and reported back with the essence of the Renaissance movement—competition, creativity, and community. Everyone was an artist. They competed with each other with their art. Theirs was a community of interests and loyalties.

Children at sport have these same three qualities. Sport is a challenge that permits unceasing creativity; a competition in which defeat is washed away before the players reach home; and a community that makes a losing team as close as any winning team could ever be.

Ninety-eight percent of parents queried in the survey mentioned earlier said that they thought effort was more important than outcome. Another classic truth. But one wonders how often these parents tell their children that, even when they win. And how often do they apply that to their own lives? If winning is important to a child, it becomes all-important to an adult. And creativity, competition, and community are no longer positive factors in one's life. Everyone likes to watch their team win. What we have to learn is that the next best thing to playing and winning is playing and losing.

My sport, running, is an individual thing. My opponent is myself. There is never a question of whether I want to run in the race. Only an injury would reduce me to being a spectator. So I seldom go to watch a race. It's too painful not to be part of it. The runner always wants to be in the race. Once a person has entered a race, there is never again a question of watching other people have all the fun.

There's no doubt that runners are a very special breed. And not everyone you see running up the road is a runner. Runners are usually made, not born.

JOGGER, RACER, RUNNER

To the inexperienced eye, the jogger and the runner look much the same. And even people who've been runners for years may be hard pressed to tell the two apart. But in fact, there's a world of difference between the jogger and the runner.

With the current sensitivity to being politically correct, what you call people has become very important. Each age and sex and ethnic group has a favored designation; any other terms may be regarded as pejorative and insulting. So there can be some hesitancy, when faced with someone in running shoes (if you are still calling them "sneakers," you are in real trouble), in choosing his or her correct label.

At one point, I used to define a runner as "a jogger who entered a race." To me, the essential difference between a jogger and a runner was not ability or training; it was an entry blank. After all, I know joggers who train longer and can run faster than runners who compete. It is the attitude, the perception of self, the need for a different expression that leads the jogger to fill out that first entry blank and take the giant step into competition.

Now I'm not so sure about that definition. The jogger who goes into races becomes a competitor, not a runner. The jogger has merely become a racer, a change that may be more sidewise than forward in progressing toward the goal of becoming a runner.

The jogger and the racer are in many ways quite alike. If the jogger is the runner in embryo, so is the racer. If the jogger is a novice, it is also true of the racer.

For each, the growth is first in ability. For the jogger, the yards become miles, the minutes become hours, the days become weeks. The dedicated pursuit of fitness occupies his mind and will. Jogging is the perfecting of the body. It ends there.

Some see the jogger as an automaton. In their groundbreaking book *Type A Behavior and Your Heart,* Ray Rosenman and Meyer Friedman state, "Jogging is a form of exercise in which man transforms himself into a machine, chug-chug-chugging along, looking neither right nor left."

William Zinsser of the *New York Times* described joggers

as "self-contained prisoners of fitness." He could see, he said, no joy on their faces, only duty and pain.

And it is true, of course, that the jogger is looking for results. Joggers expect to firm the body, lose weight, develop their legs, improve their wind. They want to get back into shape. It is also true that it is not easy, particularly at first. The muscles protest. Fatigue becomes manifest. Jogging is a chore and frequently a depressing one. In much the same way, the student of Zen finds the meditation position at first impossible. Eventually, of course, it becomes quite natural—in fact, the preferred attitude.

Eventually, the jogger finds his nice slow pace, that comfortable level, settles into it, and relaxes. At that point, the jogger becomes content. There is no need to go farther. Good things are happening to his body. There is a perceptible difference in energy, in the waistline, in the response to tension and aggravation.

The jogger has found the way to accomplish the most in the least amount of time, then fills that quota day after day. Here at last is the way to dissipate stress, the method of handling a zero sum society where someone always wins and, therefore, others always have to lose. The jogger has discovered that the fittest do survive and has found a way to that fitness.

But if the jogger is goal oriented, so is the racer. The jogger has in mind correcting the physical effects of the sedentary life. The racer, on the other hand, is interested in remedying the psychological effects of that life: the boredom, the lack of self-esteem, the apathy, the depression, the loss of interest. Only later will they both see that the runner, without directly willing or seeking it, fills in the defects of his spiritual life.

Most people begin as joggers, then become racers, and finally grow to the status of runner. It seems to me that this is the normal progression, although others may go from being joggers to runners without ever entering a race.

WHY I RACE

I had been a racer in college and always thought of myself as a runner. Yet I recall in those four years at school only once running just for the fun of it—one day in the hills for enjoyment.

So when I began again almost three decades ago, I had no more hint about the truth of running than the other novice, the jogger. I began as a racer and only much later became a runner. Only then did I come to see running in perspective. I began much like the jogger.

"To jog," says *Webster's*, "is to run at a slow, leisurely, monotonous pace." I did just that on the ten-laps-to-the-mile track I laid out in my backyard. It was some time before I was willing to let anyone see me running the roads in my shorts and T-shirt. A runner in those days was a rare sight and an object of curiosity, if not ridicule.

In time, I increased my mileage and pace and took to the roads. I was still a jogger by the standards of the National Jogging Association—that is, my pace was slower than 7 minutes per mile. But by then I also was a racer. I had found a new world.

I had undertaken the activity because I needed a goal as a substitute for others that had failed. Joggers run for a different purpose. They may find jogging mindless and boring and time-consuming. But they are willing to do it for the sake of fitness. Jogging complements a full life, but they have other paths to fulfillment.

For me, it was life itself that was mindless and boring and time-consuming. I was racing to make it different. What I needed was something to satisfy ego, something that would set me apart, something that would justify me—even if it was as absurd as a person my age training for a mile race.

I pursued the 5-minute mile with the persistence of Ahab chasing the white whale. I ran race after race after race. Then, I got into longer and longer races. In time, I added the sub-3-hour marathon to my goals. All the while, I was learning more and more about myself and discovering again and again the satisfactions, the joys, the sense of a job well done that comes from the race.

Once experienced, the race became all. When I began racing, the family lost me. Every Sunday, I was on the highway in search of competition. One Sunday, I ran a 5000-meter race in

New York City and then traveled down to Philadelphia for a 9-mile race that evening. There were times, during the summer, when I ran as many as three races a week.

Racing was a revelation in many ways. I found I was capable of things I wouldn't have dreamed of attempting before. What's more, I found I was full of misconceptions about myself and others. With racing, I learned how to handle pain and give an improbable effort, and do it all alone. And in the end, I discovered that each of us racers had done the same. We were all brothers and sisters, and each of us commoners was a hero.

Why race? For all of the above reasons, I suppose, plus others: the need to be tested, perhaps; the need to take risks; and the chance to be number one.

BECOMING A RUNNER

Racing is the lovemaking of the runner. It is an excitement in the blood. There is the same agitation, the same stirring of the pulse, the same feeling in the chest, the same delightful apprehension that you feel when nearing the one you love.

But there is also an element of fear. If racing attracts, it also repels. As I try for my perfection, I am all too aware of my imperfections. When I race, I am the person the philosopher William James called the "twice-born." Such people see an element of real wrong in the world, especially in themselves. And they know this must be overcome by doing something heroic, that they themselves must be cleansed by suffering.

I accept that. I still seek the race, seek to be tested, ask to meet pain and to pass or fail. The difference now is that the race has become simply a race. I continue to race, and I never give less than my best. At the finish, I am on my hands and knees, gasping and thinking, "This is absurd." But I have put aside the winning and the losing, the getting of trophies and not getting trophies. I have had my fill of that. I have become a runner.

Jogging, they say, is competing against yourself. Racing is competing against others. Running is discovering that competing is only competing. It is essential and not essential. It is important and unimportant. Running is finally seeing everything in perspective. Running is discovering the wholeness, the unity that everyone seeks. Running is the fusion of body, mind, and soul in that beautiful relaxation that joggers and racers find so difficult to achieve.

Relaxation is the sign of the runner, not the racer or jogger. Somewhere along the way, I learned how to relax. I learned to relax not only my body but my mind and soul as well. I discovered that running is an art form and that I could be the running as the dancer is the dance. I found that running is play—and even more, a sort of spiritual discipline. It is a way of seeing reality, or perceiving the good and the true. Running gives me my special perspective.

"Each of us has a mission of truth," writes the Spanish philosopher Ortega y Gasset. "What my eye sees of reality is seen by no other eye. We are irreplaceable; we are necessary."

When I run, truly run, I am certain of that. It is all there. My body does what it does best. The mind like a kaleidoscope constantly rearranges the things it has stored into new and exciting patterns. And my soul utterly loses itself in the present.

The runner has a view of life that makes all the jogging and racing worthwhile.

RUNNING TO A NEW YOU

People take up running for a variety of reasons. They *adhere* to a running program, however, for one basic reason: to change themselves, physically or psychologically (or both). So say Arizona State University sociologists David Altheide and Erwin Puhl.

"Running is rooted in the biography of those who engage in it," they wrote. "The running experience is more rewarding and consonant with people's authentic selves than the roles they play, and is properly seen as the private conception of the self. Through becoming a runner one accomplishes a new type of being."

The study of nearly 800 runners, including 42 in-depth interviews, convinced these investigators that such transformations are the rule rather than the exception. The psychological profile has become almost as predictable as the physical and physiological one. Running has become an accepted method of taking charge of one's life and becoming one's personal best.

I know this to be true. I frequently address large groups of runners on the evening before a race. When I do, I tell the audience that I know every person in the room has a story to tell about what they were like before they began running and what they are like now, the "before" and "after" of every running life. Then I say, "But I don't want to hear it." The laughter that follows tells me that once more I've hit the mark.

Many people not only have stories; they have photos to go with them—graphic evidence of weight loss and other remarkable physical improvements brought about by running. Without these pictures, it would be almost impossible to visualize the person this lean, fit runner once was.

And while these pounds were being shed, while the physiological miracles were occurring with the heart and muscle and metabolism, psychological marvels were taking place as well. Just so, the world over, bodies, minds, and souls are constantly being born again, during miles on the road.

Many of these psychological changes so evident to me have been documented. Researchers have noted that well-conditioned people rate higher than the unconditioned in emotional stability, sensitivity, and diminished anxiety. Highly fit people have been found to be more imaginative, more adventurous, and more trustful.

William Morgan, Ed.D., sports psychologist at the University of Wisconsin, has described the "iceberg profile" present in elite runners. In a psychological test battery, these highly trained athletes score appreciably below the norm in negative traits such as tension, depression, fatigue, and confusion. They are, however, way above average in the one positive trait: vigor. Plotted on a graph, all the negative traits are below the midline, with the plot point for vigor rising high above the surface like the tip of the iceberg.

Running, as I see it, is one of the best "body therapies" (treatments based on the belief that the physical body is the tangible incarnation of the personality). The implication is that you must change your body to change your personality. Emotional and intellectual changes follow changes in the physical plane.

In running, this theory plainly works. A transformation of the psyche does follow the transformation of the body. The "before" and "after" that occurs in the physical and physiological realms is invariably accompanied by a "before" and "after" in the psychological life as well. Improvement in physique and physiology and psychology proceeds *pari passu*—they're inseparable.

One 39-year-old runner, a man interviewed by Altheide and Puhl, summed it up this way: "Running is the most important thing in my life. It's given me the freedom to be myself, to live a life I deemed not worth living. It has freed me from the hang-ups of my youth. It has matured and strengthened me. It is the most important thing I have ever done."

This runner has done what millions of other runners have done: They have accepted a moral imperative, the necessity of being a good animal, and have become a good person as well.

THE ROAD TO SELF-DISCOVERY

There are four elements to the running experience: competition, contemplation, conversation, companionship. All are equally available, but there have been periods in my life when one or two predominated. I had specific needs, and running became a way to satisfy them.

My running life began with competition. I returned to a sport in which I excelled during my youth. I sought to repeat those victories in races against my peers. I had entered middle age and was suffering those usual doubts of purpose, of self-image and self-esteem. I needed a means of self-renewal, even if only physically. My body became my self, the race a means of self-discovery.

To train for these races, I spent hours on the road. And there I found contemplation. I discovered how easy it was to escape from the body into a total encounter with my thoughts—thoughts I had never or rarely been conscious of before. Those training runs became my hour for exploring the meaning of my past, the treasures laid up in my subconscious mind.

I am by nature a loner. Being a runner comes naturally to me. Like Henry David Thoreau, I am never less lonely than when alone. The distance runner only appears to be lonely. People come upon me in all sorts of weather, far from home, looking like recluses who've wandered out-of-doors and forgotten where they live. Yet they actually enjoy their solitary state.

It has always been so for people whose work is done in their minds, for those who fish for ideas in their stream of consciousness. One must be alone to do this. New thought does not come from logic and reason. It comes from inspiration. "I am not sure," wrote British author and lecturer W. Macneile Dixon, "that I would entrust reason even with the arrangement of a bowl of flowers." Or with much else except the day-to-day ordering of the incidentals of existence.

In his book *Solitude: A Return to the Self,* Anthony Storr points this out. A degree of solitude, according to Storr, is essential for pursuits that call for original thought and the sustained use of the imagination. Storr cites many writers and thinkers who isolated themselves to achieve their creative work. In fact, English historian Edward Gibbon called solitude "The School of Genius."

I suspect that few, if any, of the solitary runners and walkers who pass by my study could be classified as geniuses. Yet each one of us has what Ralph Waldo Emerson called our individual genius, our special way of being in the world. And author Brenda Euland opens her book *So You Want to Write* with this line: "Everyone is talented and original and has something to say." I know of no better way to find my genius and discover what I have to say than running with no companion except the rhythm of my breathing.

And there's more to be found in this solitude: My hour on the road rehumanizes me (if there is such a word). It is the hour Swiss psychologist Carl Jung urged his patients to set aside each day for the active imagination—a period of reverie best achieved, if we are to believe the journals of thinkers, by walking or movement in which suppressed areas of the personality could creep to the surface. Jung believed in what he called "individuation," the development of the whole personality. This took place mainly in solitude.

My solitary run is also an hour when I can take a step back, get *off* the treadmill in a way, and examine my life. I am my own philosopher. Dixon comments on this as well: "The values of existence, our joys, our sorrows are not calculated for us by the philosophers, the theologians, and the moralists. In respect to those values we can make our own estimates and do very well with them. They are no better informed than we. You and I are here their equals and judge for ourselves. Aristotle, Spinoza, and the rest, let them for the moment keep their distance. No one, however sagacious or eminent, can figure out our personal existence."

And that is the crux of it. On my solitary run I am searching for the meaning within my experiences. In that hour devoid of distraction, where the world is on hold, I can focus on the troubles and joys of becoming myself and arrive at a sort of peace. I am the closest I will ever come to who I am, what I believe, and what I should do about it.

THE ULTIMATE RUNNER

One year when I was in Boston for the marathon, I saw an advertisement in the *Boston Globe:* "Runners Wanted!" The Dana Farber Cancer Institute was recruiting runners to participate in their research studies.

"We are engaged," the ad went on, "in our own difficult kind of marathon, a long road to discover solutions to complex problems about the cause and cure of cancer. . . . We need people with qualities you possess, dedication, discipline, energy, and the belief you change things for the better."

Those qualities come with the athletic experience. Whatever the sport, it develops not only the body but the mind and spirit as well. Sport is an essential element in education. The Greeks knew this centuries ago, and it's now becoming apparent to those who, long after graduation, have returned to the task of becoming athletes.

The athletic experience consists of three parts: the training, which the Greeks called *askesis;* the event, or *agon;* and the aftermath, which the Greeks termed *arete*, which can be variously translated as "excellence" or "vigor" or "virtue." The goal of Greek education was to create a citizen-soldier. This education, said Plato, was what develops virtue from childhood, what makes one able to rule the state or defend it.

The ultimate aim is self-mastery. If we are to dominate events, we must first dominate ourselves. Self-rule comes naturally to the athlete. Training, or *askesis*, brings with it the virtues of prudence and moderation. The lifestyle of athletes conforms to the laws of the body. "Breaking training" is physical sin. When I became a runner, I became my body and accepted its laws. This does not, of course, go unrewarded. Athletes perform at the peak of their powers. They have the energy the Dana Farber people seek.

Basketball player Bill Bradley, in speaking of his months of preseason in training, developed self-mastery: "I didn't buy the argument that I was going to lose because I wasn't working hard enough. I might lose because I wasn't *fast* enough; I might lose because I wasn't *tall* enough; but I wasn't going to lose because I wasn't *ready*."

But self-mastery goes beyond preparation. The race becomes the *agon*, where the self is developed. "The race to be run, the victory to be won, the defeat that one risked suffering," writes Michel Foucalt about the Greeks, "these are processes and events that took place between oneself and oneself. The adversaries the individual had to combat were not just with him and close by; they are part of him."

How well the runner knows that. At first, it appeared that I was fighting hills and terrain, heat and humidity, and the distance I had to race. But it was soon apparent that these were not my opponents. My opponent is me—the real me who would let this cup pass, the true self who is willing to settle for "a good try," and not the last desperate and painful and revealing plunge into the black hole of who I am.

The importance of this element of sport has not been lost on philosophers. After observing a football game, the philosopher George Santayana wrote, "There is then a great and continuous endeavor, a representation of all the primitive virtues and fundamental gifts of man." In the race, the runner searches for these virtues and values, the martial virtues now liberated from the attendant horrors of war. We have then, as Santayana states, "a drama in which all moral and emotional interests are involved. The whole soul is stirred by a spectacle that represents the basis for life."

Is this an exaggeration? Poet Robert Frost, attending a baseball all-star game, compared athletes to artists and rejoiced in their display of prowess, courage, knowledge, and justice. We see again and again the elevation of the whole person. Educators forced to reevaluate the athletic experience come to the same conclusions. A faculty committee at Dickinson College in Carlisle, Pennsylvania, in considering the role of sports in the students' lives, wrote: "The *agon* is not a matter of winning or losing. It is the willingness to compete. Let us not forget that the *agon* is freely accepted—it is a matter of committing the self to act and bear the consequences of action."

And there are other rewards seen by these educators: "To experience sport and analyze it critically is to be involved in an enterprise with dramatic and intense personal immediacy rarely, if ever, offered by more traditional studies." The report goes on: "Sport is an easily accessible laboratory of dedication, sacrifice, courage, mastery, order, cooperation, leadership, companionship, solitude, loyalty, and authority."

Therein lies the final part of the athletic experience— the transformation of the self brought about by these learning experiences. The deposition into the subconscious of the good news about the self—an entry into the world of William Blake, where we become "chariots of fire" and for which the best word is "exultation." We now are what we became in the race and ready for whatever the day brings.

What the day brings, as everyone learns sooner or later, is recurrent challenge. The *agon* is a daily experience. The Greek philosopher Epictetus told us that almost two centuries ago: "If anything laborious or pleasant, glorious or inglorious, be presented to you, remember now is the contest, now are the Olympic Games, and they cannot be deferred."

There will never be a day when we won't need energy, dedication, discipline, and the feeling that we can change things for the better. The people at the Dana Farber Cancer Institute know that. And we should, too.

2

How Your Body Works

Why weight is more important than age.

OUR LEGACY FROM THE ANCIENT GREEKS

When I began running in 1963, the fitness experts and the sports medicine specialists had yet to arrive on the scene. Dr. Kenneth Cooper's book on aerobics was still five years off. Becoming fit, therefore, was something I had to do on my own—my body became my instructor. It gave me the answers to those initial questions: How far? How fast? And how often? In a very short time, I learned the first and greatest commandment in fitness: Listen to your body.

Although I didn't know it at the time, I was rediscovering an ancient law, a tradition that went back to the Greeks. The Greeks explored their physical limits much the same as we do now. Their Olympic Games were based on the same philosophy as ours. Their attempts to go higher and faster and farther foreshadowed present-day competition. And they did all this using the body simultaneously as teacher and pupil.

In those days, people were expected to read their body like a book, learning what enabled them to perform well and what would interfere with performance. According to Tiberius, by the age of 20, an individual should take responsibility for his own health, knowing what was harmful or beneficial, and be able to take care of himself without medical aid.

Socrates was of the same mind. He felt that an intelligent man who was careful about his diet, exercise, and drinking habits should know better than a doctor what was good or bad for him. Centuries later, psychologist Abraham Maslow expressed the same idea, calling such people "self-actualizers." These people, wrote Maslow, become finely tuned to how best their body works and to those actions that harm them.

By the time we reach adulthood, we should be able to read the messages our body sends us. Technology is not only unnecessary; it is inadequate. The body has information that is technologically inaccessible. We are the sole recipients of this otherwise unavailable data. Why, then, should I need more than my own body to guide my program and record my improvement?

Back in 1963, that question was irrelevant. I had nothing to resort to other than my body. It had to give me all my answers. I didn't check with a physician before I began running. I didn't take a stress test. And I never checked my pulse. I simply went out and ran.

I quickly made my first and greatest discovery. Running is play. It is being a child again. I would go out on the roads and get lost in a child's world. I ran short and fast, I ran long and slow. I was having fun because my body was having fun. I was enjoying running because my body was enjoying running. And while this was happening, my body became better and better at running. Without consulting a book or an expert, I became fit. Even better, I became an athlete.

My experience has convinced me most of the testing and monitoring of fitness programs is unnecessary. We need little if any pretesting before getting into an activity. Nor do we need

28

to check our pulse or do all those annoying and occasionally alarming computations involving heart rate. The only things that should prompt us to see a doctor are things that would ordinarily send us to a doctor for treatment—things such as excess cholesterol, overweight, diabetes, or high blood pressure.

My body, over the years, has given me the correct answers to all my questions on running. I have had no need for other experts. But even if there were other avenues of information, there is one question only the body can answer. And it is the question that holds the answer to every successful lifelong fitness program: "Are you having fun?"

LIFE INSURANCE

Each of us is born with a 70-year warranty, but few of us read the instructions. We blindly go through life without consulting a manual for the operation of the human machine. The maintenance and preservation of our body doesn't concern us. We believe that longevity and freedom from malfunction have been built in by the Creator.

And they have. But we can live long and stay healthy only if we take care of our body as we would our automobiles. We have to follow certain rules to get maximum performance and maximum longevity out of what we were born with. We have to apply the biological wisdom gained over the centuries to our day-to-day living.

Make no mistake about it: Nature does not allow for error, and she is not reluctant to inflict capital punishment. Deviations from the correct regimen can certainly diminish one's daily well-being and eventually one's life span. True, aging is inexorable. And death is inevitable. But neither should occur before its appointed time.

Individual behavior determines individual health. It is up to us to avoid unnecessary illness and premature death. It is our own decision to be active or sedentary. To age fast or age slowly. To die at our time or before it.

But even if we are committed to following the rules, we may have to search to find them. Our disregard for the past puts us in the position of relearning truths that have been known for centuries. We should not ignore the conclusions of previous civilizations and cultures that have gone through the process of establishing rules for the optimum function of the human body.

What we need to know was already known by generations that have gone before us: Cro-Magnon man, the Greeks, the Romans, the Victorians, and, in contemporary life, people in Alameda County, California—a group researchers have found to be extraordinarily long lived, happy, and productive. Back in 1972, the average American thought all you had to do to assure health was eat a balanced diet, get a good night's sleep, and visit the doctor regularly—clearly an incomplete program for getting the most out of our bodies. But that year, we learned from these Californians rules that we can profit from following.

These rules, which have come to be known as The Alameda Seven, are as follows:

1. Exercise regularly.
2. Eat a good breakfast.
3. Don't eat between meals.
4. Maintain weight.
5. Don't smoke.
6. Drink moderately.
7. Get a good night's sleep.

These observances have stood the test of subsequent scientific investigation. They work. People who follow six of those rules live significantly longer than those who follow one or two. And not only do they live longer, they're less likely to be hospitalized, and they're more energetic and productive as well.

After all, our aim is not only a long life but one free of incapacitating disease. We want to get sick as little as possible, and if we do, we want to recover quickly. We would like to live a fully functioning life until the last possible moment. And The Alameda Seven will apparently ensure that as well. A study done in 1984 showed that those observing the rules had aged successfully—that is, they remained independent and healthy, free of debilitating disease.

How best to live long and live well? Following The Alameda Seven is a good start—and has good precedent. For past generations, lifestyle was their pharmacopoeia. They had no antibiotics, no cures for infectious disease. So the caveman had to be fit to survive.

Now we have grown soft, freed for the most part of the scourges of pneumonia and tuberculosis and other life-short-ening diseases. Our longevity may be increasing, but so are the diseases having to do with the way we live. We die of the afflu-ence and the sedentary life that prosperity has given to us. If we are indeed to prosper, we must look to the rules of the gen-erations that preceded us and that had to struggle for exist-ence—the people who read the warranty and followed it.

PREVENTION AND PERFORMANCE

Many Americans have done a 180-degree turnaround in the way they live. Millions have stopped smoking, started exercis-ing, and lost weight. More than half the population is set on trying to develop a fit, trim body that performs at its peak. On a spiritual plane, it appears Americans have looked to their physical selves for heightened self-expression and self-esteem.

I launched my own rejuvenation at the age of 45, when, even with a successful medical practice, I began to feel I was not living a full life. I was haunted by the feeling that the years were slipping by and that I had nothing to show for it.

I started to run and stayed with it simply because it was something I could *do,* even though I was born clumsy and had a crowded work schedule. Almost from the beginning, new and wonderful things happened. My body adapted well to the ac-tivity: I felt more relaxed. I dropped a few excess pounds. I slept better. And I found my day's run was becoming a kind of re-treat. Suddenly, I was more acutely aware of the sights and sounds, the touches and tastes, the pains and pleasures of my life. As I ran myself into better health, I was also running myself into my best ideas.

Many of the benefits of exercise fall between the physio-logical and the psychological. The runner realizes, for example, that the current approach to stopping smoking and drinking is backward. Exercise first, and the bad habits will take care of themselves. An exercising body doesn't want to smoke and drinks very moderately. The body that's exercised regularly usually maintains its correct weight, lowers its blood pressure, and reduces any diabetic tendencies.

Exercise has two faces: performance, and prevention. Performance focuses on today. Prevention looks to the future. Performance makes your body work better. Prevention permits it to do that work safely and for a longer time. Exercise that concentrates on performance is a science. Exercise physiology is the science of human performance. Athletes the world over follow training schedules with predictable results. Simply insert your individual statistics, settle on your particular goal, and there is a formula with a certified outcome.

With prevention, the response isn't so regular. Exercise will guarantee fitness, but it cannot guarantee health. Exercise sufficient for fitness may not rid an individual of some risk factors. If you exercise regularly but you're still overweight or your blood pressure is still high, you need to exercise more. If you *still* don't drop excess pounds or lower your blood pressure, you need to make further changes, mainly through your diet.

Fitness improves the quality of life by making life more enjoyable. Fitness gives us the elements necessary to lead a good life. We acquire the zest and vitality to face the day and its tasks with confidence and enthusiasm. We also produce the creative energy to solve problems easily and spontaneously. Fitness opens up the circuits in the amazing storage and retrieval system that is our brain. And it gives us another form of energy—the willpower that comes with discipline and the ascetic life.

Fitness is, simply, the ability to do work. It is movement and energy, not only muscular but also cognitive. Doctors have found that fitness fights disease on two fronts: It reduces life-threatening physical risk factors, and it reduces harmful psychological traits such as hostility, tension, and anxiety. What's more, fitness makes a person at home in the environment, no longer alien to it but filled with a new appreciation of the body and its contribution to the life of the mind and the life of the spirit.

Fitness also has a measurable effect on the quality of our life today, in the sense that when we are fit, we can, by definition, do more work. The day does not end at noon or at 5:00 P.M. The day becomes filled with physical, mental, and emotional activity. Because you are fit, you are able to do what must be done when you must do it. Running gives me a body that performs better at everything that I do. Because I'm fit, I can now accept the Olympic ideal—farther, faster, higher—as part of my day. Because I am fit, I am now an athlete.

As an athlete, the end of your work is the beginning of your day. Being fit allows for the full use of your body from sunup until bedtime. Many people say they can't find time to work out, but a fitness program actually produces more time. When you accept that, you can see the absurdity of saying fitness has nothing to do with the quantity of life.

Athletes are consumed with the idea of quantity. Everything they do is concerned with time and distance and measurable factors in performance. And so it is with any lifestyle activity: The quantity of life increases, and the day is filled with activity.

RULES TO RUN BY

The fitness formula is a matter of mode, duration, intensity, and frequency.

Mode. To build stamina, you should choose an exercise that involves the large muscles of your arms and legs. Walking, jogging, swimming, and cycling are the staple modes of exercise, but aerobics, cross-country skiing, rowing, backpacking, and rope skipping are equally good. Conventional weight lifting and bodybuilding are not considered stamina-building activities. Only by using very light weights and innumerable repetitions will you achieve fitness through weight lifting.

Duration. Whatever activity you choose, you should perform it continuously for at least 30 minutes, with a cumulative total of at least 2 hours a week. In tennis and other racket sports, it is best to have a friend hold a stopwatch on you to see how much of the time you are actually in motion. This 30 minutes eliminates any attention to miles or laps. There is no need to count anything except minutes. Personally, I prefer going 45 minutes or so instead of 30. My mind seems to open up more with the longer runs. A friend of mine (a walker) once told me, "The first 30 minutes is for my body. The second 30 minutes is for my soul."

Intensity. Most exercisers want to know how fast they should go or at what speed should the activity be performed. The answer is simple: Listen to your body. Exercise at a pace that your body says is comfortable, somewhere between easy and hard. Your body knows what it's doing, so start exercising comfortably, put everything on automatic pilot, and then forget what you are doing. Another method is the "talk test," the pace at which you can converse comfortably with a companion and exercise at the same time. These tricks can help you stay in the correct aerobic range until you learn to read your own body.

Frequency. The usual recommendation is to exercise every other day. The rest day gives the body a chance to recoup. It takes 48 hours for depleted muscle glycogen to be replaced, and other neuroendocrine (hormone-related) stresses probably take this long to adapt as well. Rest, as Olympic runner Noel Carroll has pointed out, is when the training effect takes place in the body. This is the time when the body adapts to the applied stress.

And what are the rewards?

At the end of a race, I no longer look, I see. I do not touch, I feel. I do not taste, I savor. The sunlight has become precious, the breeze a delight. I know the meaning of a handshake, the treasure in a smile. Being alive has become a spiritual and mystical experience.

Fitness can be the basis from which you learn the art of living, of bringing your body and mind and spirit into concert. Then, to paraphrase the Roman emperor Marcus Aurelius, you can rise in the morning and do the work of a human being. You'll be rid of the nagging fear that you are doing less than your best. British sculptor Henry Moore said, "The sculpture is within the stone." When you exercise, you start to discover the individual within yourself. You go through the concentration, patience, and joyful discipline of becoming that individual. It is struggle for the prize that is yourself.

HOW FIT ARE YOU?

One of the most accurate gauges of fitness is the distance a person can cover in 12 to 15 minutes. The accuracy of the 15-minute walk/run was established by researcher Bruno Balke in 1963. Balke studied 34 high school boys for 15-minute intervals, first on a treadmill, then on an oval track. The average maximum oxygen uptake on the treadmill was 43 milliliters per kilogram of body weight per minute of activity (ml/kg/min). On the track, the oxygen uptake was calculated at 44 ml/kg/min—an astounding correlation.

In 1968, Dr. Kenneth Cooper reported on his experience with 12-minute field performance as an estimate of individual fitness. Like Balke, Dr. Cooper found excellent agreement between the laboratory calculations of maximum oxygen uptake and those done on a quarter-mile track. Balke's figures were based on average speed measured in meters per minute. Dr. Cooper further simplified the mathematics by matching distance to oxygen consumption rather than to velocity.

The test is simple. All that's needed to test even large groups is a measured track, a stopwatch, and a whistle to indicate the end of the 12 minutes. Any individual interested in beginning a fitness program can go to a high school track and, by using this simple test, establish a baseline for personal reference.

A Quick and Easy Fitness Gauge

Based on 12-minute performance and maximal oxygen consumption.

Distance (mi.)	Maximum Oxygen Consumption (ml/kg/min)	Fitness Level
Less than 1	Less than 25	Very poor
1–1.25	25–33	Poor
1.25–1.5	33–42	Fair
1.5–1.75	42–51	Good
1.75 or more	51 or more	Excellent

WALK TALK

The interest in fitness has led to a reevaluation of walking. Physiologists are beginning to take a long, hard look at what walking can do and how its benefits can be measured. One year, three scientific studies on walking were presented at the annual meeting of the American College of Sports Medicine.

One report from the University of Massachusetts describes a fitness test based on the mile walk. Investigators asked 300 men and women (150 males, 150 females), aged 30 to 64, to complete a 1-mile walk on a quarter-mile track. They were given ratings ranging from poor to excellent on the basis of the fastest mile walked in two attempts. From this data, the researchers established categories for aerobic fitness, shown in the accompanying table.

Fitness Ratings for Timed Mile

Time (min.)		
Men	**Women**	**Fitness Rating**
Less than 10:12	Less than 11:40	Excellent
10:13–11:42	11:41–13:08	Good
11:43–13:13	13:09–14:36	High average
13:14–14:14	14:37–16:04	Low average
14:15–16:23	16:05–17:31	Fair
More than 16:24	More than 17:32	Poor

For the beginner, walking 1 mile as fast as possible is much more practical than the 12-minute walk/run test. Initially, jogging or running may be difficult, the pace therefore uneven, and the result unsatisfactory. On the other hand, walking 1 mile as fast as possible is something that, by definition, almost anyone can do. Compared to running, the pace is relatively even, and the effort feels satisfying.

Rating your performance in this way is an excellent method for establishing a baseline before initiating any sort of fitness program. Then it can be used to monitor your progress.

The one disagreement I have with this fitness test is the distinction that's made between male and female capabilities. Fitness is fitness, regardless of whether you are a man or a woman. While this chart shows how you would rank according to sex, I would ignore the women's category and advise everyone to aim for the higher levels achieved by males.

It's true that, on the average, men outperform women and have a higher maximum oxygen uptake. But this is a *group average*, not a individual measure. Joan Benoit Samuelson has a maximum oxygen uptake equal to that of international male competitors, a level far beyond what we thought was possible for females. So do other women runners. Nevertheless, whatever your time, don't be discouraged. Exercise will work miracles, if not in speed, then in endurance.

You should eventually be able to exercise for 30 minutes at a comfortable pace four times a week. Choose any activity that uses your legs—cycling, swimming, walking, jogging, aerobic dance, racquet sports, and so forth. Your speed should improve considerably in 12 weeks. After that, your endurance should improve.

STRIDE: DO WHAT COMES NATURALLY

Years back, after a 20-mile race in which I finished a half hour behind the winner, a runner friend with a scientific bent informed me that I had run the same number of strides per minute as the gold medalist. "The difference between being first and being in the back of the pack is the length of your stride," he told me.

This is true at times, not at others. In general, I think that stride length is much more important than stride frequency. But not always. My high school coach, who later coached the U.S. Olympic track team, emphasized stride frequency. "When you start your kick," he told me, "don't lengthen your stride, speed it up."

Watch Eammon Coghlan's arms when he makes his move in the mile. The faster he moves his arms, the faster his legs go. Lengthening the stride becomes counterproductive when a runner is running at top speed or sprinting to the finish.

But what about in distance races? Will simply increasing the distance covered with each stride improve performance? According to Peter Cavanaugh, Ph.D., an expert in such matters, it may not. Among the points Dr. Cavanaugh stresses are:

- Everyone has an optimal stride length at a given speed.
- You will probably settle on your optimal stride length subconsciously.
- Individuals differ substantially in their response to changes in stride length.

37

- Stride length should not arbitrarily be imposed on a runner.
- Never pattern your stride length after another runner.

Apparently, stride length is not something determined by your brain; rather, it's a function of various factors, including your endurance, strength, flexibility, and anatomy. The stride length reflects how good a runner you are. Any significant change would have to be accompanied by significant changes in your musculoskeletal system.

When it comes to attempts to alter your stride, then, you might say it's dangerous to fool with Mother Nature. There is a stride length that is most efficient for you at each speed. Taking strides shorter or longer than the optimum will involve increases in energy cost. Most runners have already found their optimum stride length simply by listening to their body. Just as they automatically lock in to their appropriate breathing cycle and training pace, they use their best (for them) stride length.

I think that as runners, we may have heard too many warnings about overstriding. In some of the runners Dr. Cavanaugh studied, understriding was twice as costly as overstriding. Yet one runner decreased his efficiency only 1 percent while shortening his stride over 6 inches. And the tallest runner had the shortest optimal stride length.

What it comes down to is that there is an optimum stride length for *me*. It wasn't my stride length that put me 1½ minutes per mile behind the winner of that 20-mile race. I was running my best. Lengthening my stride might well have put me farther back. If I ran at the winner's speed (however long I could do it), I might match his stride length.

Stride length varies with speed. And the ability to hold that speed longer (a 2:10:00 marathon is 26 consecutive sub-5-minute miles) is the real difference between victors and the vanquished.

Once again, it comes down to talent, training, nutrition, and perhaps, if only peripherally, running form. Some runners are 20 percent more economical than others. No one is quite sure whether this is due to running form or even, as some have suggested, a muscle enzyme.

It would appear that emphasis on stride length (particularly contrasting that of top marathoners to average runners) focuses on the result, not on the reason. Should I try to match Bill Rodgers's stride length in the Boston Marathon, for example, I would not last more than a half-mile.

The answer to the big questions in running is the same as the answer to the big questions in life. Do the best with what you've got. Your stride length is the sum of your present abilities. In order to increase it, you must first be a better runner.

PROPER BALANCE, PROPER BREATHING

When I run, my upper body sits atop my pelvis and legs like a jockey sitting on a horse. The jockey's job is to stay balanced; the power comes from the waist down.

I achieve balance by proper positioning of the chest and by minimizing side-to-side and up-and-down movement. The legendary runner Alfie Shrubb recommended a slight lean of what he called "the upper hamper." This forward inclination of the chest can be seen in a computerized study of Bill Rodgers's running form done by Gideon Ariel. And it seems to work for me.

There are those, to be sure, who advocate the straight upper body position. But in my experience, leaning forward slightly contributes to my forward movement and affords balance as well.

I have found that the way I carry my arms also helps my balance. The movement of the forearms doesn't matter as much as the position and movement of the elbows—they should move forward and backward, to keep inefficient side-to-side movement to a minimum.

It's also important to keep your upper body relaxed. My hands are a dead giveaway to my state of relaxation. When Harvard cross-country coach Shrubb had Bucky Fuller on his squad, Fuller told me that Shrubb would yell at him, "Fuller, stop running with your hands." When Fuller looked down, he could see his fists were clenched.

The other main job of the upper body, of course, is breathing. Proper breathing is essential to the efficient exchange of oxygen and carbon dioxide—it allows me to run at a high percentage of my maximum oxygen uptake. Incorrect breathing can decrease my performance, exaggerate my tendency to exercise-induced asthma, and lead to the much-dreaded side stitch. The most efficient way to breathe is not with the chest but with the abdomen, which uses the diaphragm (the muscle separating your chest and abdomen) as a bellows for the lungs. I take air in by expanding my abdomen, which lowers my diaphragm. I exhale by contracting my abdomen and elevating the diaphragm. This is the belly breathing we associate with yoga, and the technique is simple: breathe in, abdomen out; breathe out, abdomen in.

While this is how we normally breathe when we sleep, it's not usually how we breathe when we run. Frequently, I'm a mile into a race, and I notice I'm still breathing in reverse: When I inhale, my belly is going in instead out. And I'm trying to increase my air intake with my chest and shoulders.

Then I shift back to the prescribed method—either by breathing through pursed lips or by groaning with each exhalation. Either maneuver automatically engages the diaphragm, allowing a maximum inhalation followed by a somewhat shorter, forced exhalation.

Don't try to time your inhalation and exhalation exactly, though. Abdominal breathing should be natural, not studied. This natural effort is also best when coordinating your breathing with your stride—called "locomotor-respiratory coupling." It comes about instinctively. Neophytes in running sometimes try to coordinate their breathing with their footstrike. But this conscious effort is counterproductive. Veteran runners automatically adopt a 2-to-1 or 3-to-1 ratio; that is, two or three strides for each breathing cycle. The body knows best what this ratio should be. I find that in a race, I usually breathe once for every two times my right foot lands. At the end, when I sprint, the ratio is more likely to be one and a half strides per breath. But this is something that I observe, not dictate.

Although this is an individual matter and should be road tested, most runners have found they can go farther and faster obeying these few simple principles.

I mentally check my breathing and balance as part of my prerace warm-up: If I am to give this horse a good ride, I must be relaxed, balanced, and breathing correctly. Once I've established that, I turn my attention to the horse.

BIGGER AND BETTER

All distance runners are not created equal. Age, sex, and size create disparities, and the greatest handicap of all is size.

When it comes to distance running, David will beat Goliath every time. It's a sport where bigger is not better, a sport in which a little man can take on a big man and leave him in the dust.

If we use Boston Marathon winners as a criterion, the optimum height and weight for a distance runner is 5 feet 6 inches and 130 pounds—about 2 pounds of weight for every 1 inch of height. These measurements reflect the small size, the thin bones, and the stringy muscles of the prototype endurance athlete. And as size increases, performance decreases.

The question is, just how much of a handicap *is* this extra weight? Just how much time does each additional pound of weight or inch of height cost you in competition? This question piqued the interest of the late Joseph Law, founder of the Clydesdale Runners Association, a club dedicated to the cause of big runners.

The club promotes the concept of weight and age/weight awards. Its aim is to correct for the difference in abilities of lighter and heavier runners and to compensate for the increased demands that size makes on the runner.

Adjusting for nature's handicaps has always been part of the running scene. When I was a 45-year-old neophyte in a sport peopled largely by runners built like foxes, we had handicap races based on ability. The slowest runner started on "Go," and subsequent starts were commensurate with ability, until the best of all, the scratch man, brought up the rear.

This method of handicapping races eventually fell out of favor, chiefly due to inequitable time allowances, soon to be replaced by allowances for age and sex.

With the influx of older runners, it became apparent that ability declined with age, at a rate of about 5 percent per decade. It seemed only right to make allowances for runners competing against racers who were 10 or 20 or even 30 years younger.

As women entered running, it became equally clear that the average female runner was somewhat slower than the average male. So now nearly every race takes age and sex into consideration, with awards for both male and female runners in various age groups.

So far, so good. But this leveling of the race course makes no provision for runners who weigh considerably more than the optimum for distance running. Understand, these runners are not fat; they are what the Metropolitan Life height/weight charts term "large framed."

These big runners were Joe Law's constituency. He waged an almost single-handed war against this inequity. Just as previous research had determined the relationship of age to running achievement, Law began compiling statistics on the impact of size on performance in distance races. He took these statistics a step farther, collecting data that could be used to determine the overall male and female winners based on time, age, *and* weight.

One crucial finding, from Law's study of the Marine Corps Marathon, was that weight is a greater handicap than age. A runner weighing over 195 pounds will run approximately the same time, whether he's in his twenties or over 50. On the other hand, the average 50-year-old weighing less than 155 will outrun an average 30-year-old weighing 195.

Law came up with a chart of equivalent 10-K and marathon performances based on weight, consisting of what he considered realistic goals for light-framed runners. About 25 percent of runners weighing less than 155 pounds run 10 kilometers in 40 minutes, and about 15 percent can complete a marathon in 3 hours. By comparison, times for 25 percent of people weighing 195-plus are 48:18.0 in the 10-K and 3:58:00 for a marathon.

Only 1 out of 100 runners over 195 pounds will better 40 minutes in the 10-K. And only 1 out of 200 go under 3 hours in a marathon. This is roughly a 10-minute differential in the 10-K and a 30-minute differential in the marathon. Runners in the 175–194 class perform only slightly better—about 2 minutes faster in the 10-K and 15 minutes faster in the marathon.

When you weigh more than 175 pounds, the added weight costs over 1 minute per mile in both races. The same discrepancy in performance exists for female runners weighing more than 135 pounds.

My own experience confirms Law's studies. Up until my mid-sixties, I rarely saw a heavy runner of any age running in my vicinity. Now 70-plus, slowing down, and no longer competitive in the 60-and-over division, I am noticing bigger runners around me. This has made me keenly aware of the heavyweight's handicap. I believe meet directors should have weight awards in at least one and possibly two weight groups.

Given the magnitude of the weight handicap, it seems reasonable to have at least two weight classifications in a race. In boxing, the heavyweight classification begins at 175 pounds. So 175 could serve as one running category. The second could be the dreadnoughts or superheavyweights, beginning at 200 pounds.

In fact, several races now have weight or age/weight awards. They include: the Marine Corps Marathon, the Tulsa 15-K, the Honolulu Marathon, and the Huba Buba Classic. The Steamboat Classic in Peoria, Illinois, has an Anheuser-Busch Clydesdale Class with two weight groups: 190–219, and 220-plus.

This is all in the interest of fairness, and it seems a natural progression, in line with the tradition of running. First age groups, then male/female divisions, and now allowances for weight. Up until now, we've been able to make running a coed, multi-age sport. Now we should make it multi-weight as well.

All runners are created equal—we will make it so. Let's give our Goliath a chance.

CELEBRATING AGE AND SIZE

The Huba Buba Classic Age/Weight Division World Championship 5-Mile Road Race and Weekend Extravaganza would be a great event even if it weren't a world championship. What better way to start a weekend than a 5-mile race through the tree-lined streets of residential Lafayette, Louisiana? And what more satisfying postrace event than a party with a Cajun band, crawfish cakes, cayenne potatoes, and a beer truck with bottomless supplies of brew?

But the Huba Buba is more than a memorable race and party in Cajun country; it is a championship based on age, weight, and time. No matter how heavy or old you are, the Huba Buba gives you a shot at the gold medal and a place in the top ten. The faster runners—under 35 years old and less than 150 pounds—receive no handicaps; they must rely on talent alone. Everyone else has their time adjusted for the additional years and pounds.

The arithmetic is simple. A runner's time is divided by his or her weight. (Everyone under 150 pounds has the time divided by 150.) This gives the time in seconds per pound. That time is further reduced by 1 percent for each year over the age of 34. If the formula errs, it errs on the side of generosity: A 5 percent decline per decade is more in line with the way nature preserves our talents, at least until our mid-sixties. Up until I was 65, I ran quite close to what I did back when I started at the age of 45. Only now, at 70, have I experienced the decline factored into the formula used in the Huba Buba race.

I took that age advantage to the starting line at Lafayette. Around me were some of the biggest runners I have ever seen. Their size gave them a chance at the top ten spots just as my age did for me. We were not only running against the clock; we were running against a computer that would take all of our statistics and then place us in this field of 493 runners.

One thing we knew for certain. The runner who came in first would not be the winner and might not even be in the top ten. This is not the race for the young and the light. Here, only a very talented runner can beat an older and bigger runner. *And that's how it worked out!* The champion was Doty Foster, a 60-year-old who weighed 183 pounds and ran 34:10.0. His actual "seconds per pound" was 11.20, and his age-adjusted score was 8.20. Second place went to a 55-year-old who weighed 172 pounds. My 70 years on the planet brought me seventh place. The top ten runners weighed from 155 to 207 pounds and ranged from 34 to 70 years old.

The Huba Buba is a boon not only to the big runners but to the older ones as well. Of course, competing within your age group has its limitations. As I got older, I found fewer and fewer runners in my category. Every weekend, I compete with other runners over 60. Rarely are there more than a handful, and on some occasions, there is only one other runner besides myself. This makes winning a trophy a little embarrassing. When I tell friends that this is a hollow award, though, they say, "You beat all those people who didn't show up."

The Huba Buba gave me a chance to beat all those people who did show up. Doing my absolute best deep in the pack, I knew that I was actually going head-to-head with those a mile or more ahead of me. This once more was a race where every stride was important and maximum effort would be rewarded. The standards may be a little unbalanced, the advantages given for age and weight perhaps too liberal, but runners, I am sure, will like this concept. We want to have a race in which our own individual performance, with the necessary adjustments for size and age, is stacked up against the rest of the field.

3

Freedom from Injury (and Reinjury)

Running, per se, does not cause injuries. Here's what does.

TREATING RUNNERS RIGHT

Thirty years ago, when I became a runner, sports medicine was in the Stone Age. From there, it entered a classical period. And now it's entering a renaissance.

Three decades ago, orthopedic surgeons were *the* sports medicine specialists. They focused their attention on the damage that occurred when an irresistible force met an immovable object. Their sole interest was in what are euphemistically called "contact sports." The straight-talking Vince Lombardi said it best, though: "Dancing is a contact sport. Football is a *collision* sport."

The medical care necessitated by these collisions differs little from that required by other collision injuries, which haven't changed much since we emerged from the cave. Treatment may have improved, but it still requires very little thought. During this Neanderthal period, before the advent of running as a sport, orthopedic surgeons followed an established routine: Make the diagnosis, then do the appropriate operation.

Most orthopedic surgeons were former athletes, so this was a world where jocks treated jocks. However, the doctors' labors on the battlefields of their warlike sports left them completely unprepared for the hordes of runners who sought their advice in the early 1970s.

Saturday's heroes were soon outnumbered by the thousands—and eventually millions—of runners who dedicated their leisure time to doing quite unremarkable things for a remarkable number of times. Landing forcefully on one foot and then the other, and repeating this action thousands of times at a pretty good clip, generated a whole new kind of sports injury—the overuse syndrome. In order to cope with these new patients, sports medicine had to enlarge its scope.

To say that physicians were not prepared for this change in sports medicine practice is to put it mildly. They were surgeons, trained primarily in operating rooms. Now they were facing patients who didn't need an operation. What they needed was medical orthopedics. And medical orthopedics, as British physician James Cyriax pointed out at that time, was a vacuum that existed in the space between the family practitioner and the orthopedic surgeon.

That void was to be filled, but not by the orthopods. In my early running days, I consulted various advisors, none of whom had an M.D. behind their name. The orthopedic surgeons who were my friends had one piece of advice— "Stop running"— and that was unacceptable. So I learned how to handle my injuries with my own specialists: a podiatrist, a gymnastics coach, and an exercise physiologist. All provided information I had never been exposed to in medical school or, subsequently, in medical practice.

My podiatrist explained that a faulty foot causes most running injuries up to and including those involving the knee.

"With a knee injury," he told me, "ignore the knee and treat the foot." Running, a middle-class intellectual sport, had brought the intellect into sports medicine, and this new discipline was christened *biomechanics*. Other disciplines kept entering the field. Advances occurred on all fronts: balancing strength with flexibility; deep transverse friction massage; nutrition; cross-training; and—in the surgical area—arthroscopy. As physicians, we finally arrived at rational and generally effective measures to prevent and treat overuse syndrome.

As I think on these recent years, I see sports medicine in its Grecian phase and myself and other recreational athletes as the new Athenians. We were members of the elite. Sports medicine had been a specialty for special people.

This is changing. There is growing acceptance of the belief that everyone is an athlete, only some of us are in training and some are not. Regardless of age, sex, or state of health, we are all called to the athletic life. This life will demand a fitness beyond muscle, an attention to the person rather than to performance, and holistic medical care where the doctor (whatever the degree) becomes a teacher and a coach. This will be the renaissance that sports medicine will enjoy in years to come.

EXERCISE-INDUCED AILMENTS

Runners' pursuit of excellence has been accompanied by its own particular medical problems—the diseases of excellence, an entirely new area of medical practice. The miles on the road have resulted in a variety of heretofore unknown disorders that can best be called "exercise-induced diseases."

As you might expect, most of these disorders involve the musculoskeletal system. Few runners escape without some injury of the foot, knee, or other part of the leg. The great majority have experienced some transient but incapacitating complaints induced by upping the mileage or training more intensely. Very few are able to run pain-free year in and year out.

Over the past 20 years as medical columnist for *Runner's World*, I've received as many as 300 letters a month from runners with disabilities brought on by training. I have discovered that no body system is exempt from some sort of overuse syndrome. Letters on refractory shinsplints, Achilles tendinitis, and low back pain still come in every post. But I'm also getting more and more letters asking for help with diarrhea, headache, asthma, and heart palpitations, as well as a host of other problems.

The reason for this shift is obvious. Over the years, we've come up with a formula to deal with the foot, leg, and low back disorders. These injuries, we have discovered, are due to three factors: genes, training, and environment (which I call the "GTE formula").

Briefly put, the runner comes to the sport with some inherited structural weakness—most likely, a faulty foot, a short leg, or a lumbosacral anomaly. Training then adds postural stress by creating a strength/flexibility imbalance. The environment— that is, shoes, running surface, and terrain—brings the runner to the breaking point.

The physician, faced with an injured runner, needs only to apply this GTE formula and to tailor the treatment accordingly. Most musculoskeletal injuries will respond to devices to minimize the structural weaknesses, exercises to correct the postural ones, and attention to shoes, surface, and terrain to cope with the environment.

Most runners now have access to this type of competent orthopedic care. Sports medicine facilities are multiplying across the nation. The people who write to me about their bones and joints are those who've slipped through the cracks in this system. My response is to send them the name of someone in their vicinity who knows how to handle such problems.

Problems other than musculoskeletal disorders aren't handled nearly as efficiently, and runners who develop exercise-induced ailments receive little effective help. Frequently, they discover that their physicians aren't even aware such conditions occur and are usually unable to treat them.

I recall a phone call from a hematologist whose runner husband had been found to be anemic. "Could this be related to his running?" she asked. Despite the fact that she was a specialist in blood diseases, she hadn't even heard of runner's anemia.

To an extent, this ignorance is understandable, especially if the physician is not a runner or doesn't read a running magazine. Except for anecdotes from the runners themselves, little has been written in scientific literature about running-induced health problems. Doctors who treat runners are pioneers, with little to go on but their instincts, intuition, and general principles of medical practice.

My approach to such diseases has been to go back to fundamentals. I use the same game plan that works in musculoskeletal disease. I have found that the GTE formula can be used with all exercise-induced disorders. The analysis of runner's diarrhea or runner's headache or runner's stitch is no different from the analysis of runner's knee. I treat the cause, not the symptom. Here's how.

THE "NEW" SCIENCE OF BIOMECHANICS

Soon after I started running and began having injuries, I made an important discovery: *Running does not cause injuries.* Some people run a lifetime without injury. Every one of my injuries had its roots in a structural weakness I was born with, a postural weakness I developed through training, or other stresses due to shoes, surface, and terrain. Once the problem was corrected, I was assured of pain-free running. Runner after runner has found this to be true. In time, it became accepted dogma among runners.

Unfortunately, the biomechanical approach was a creed unsupported by scientific proof. *We* knew attention to biomechanics worked, but we had not yet gotten around to proving it. At that time, no studies had been done showing the biomechanical approach—attention to human engineering—is more effective than anti-inflammatory drugs, cortisone shots, and electric therapy devices.

Sometimes, paying attention to human engineering includes the use of orthotics, specially made shoe inserts that correct faulty foot structure. Orthopedic physicians among my colleagues have chided me about my obsession with attributing every injury to events occurring at footstrike. One time at the hospital lunch table, when I was discussing the treatment of a patient with a brain tumor, an orthopedic surgeon asked me, "George, have you tried orthotics?" And whenever I broached the subject of using orthotics, or suggested that the whole spec-

trum of foot and lower leg injuries was due to faulty biomechanics, they looked at me as if I were a "dropout" from ortho-
dox medicine. "Prove it," they said.

But I'm not a scientist, I'm a practitioner. I rely on faith,
logic, and experience to arrive at my "proof." I had proved this
theory to myself in hundreds of ways. I had testimony after
testimony from runners. But scientific proof is another matter. A protocol that will satisfy entrenched skeptics is hard to
come by.

So the years slid by. My theory was accepted by the runners. Podiatrists who dealt in biomechanics of the foot became
the sports physicians for those of us out on the roads. But there
was still no acceptable study proving the value of what they
were doing.

Now there is. And not one but two such studies exist. The
first comes from Timothy Noakes, M.D., and his colleagues in
Cape Town, South Africa; the second, from Douglas Clement,
M.D., and his associates in Vancouver, British Columbia,
Canada.

The Cape Town team reported on 196 running injuries
treated solely by correction of biomechanical abnormalities.
Within eight weeks after the start of treatment, nearly 77 percent
of the runners were training completely pain-free. Only 13 percent of the runners were not helped at all. Most of these had not
adhered to the prescribed regimen or had iliotibial band syndrome, an injury with cause or causes that are still conjectural.

The most significant structural weaknesses were foot abnormalities and disparities in leg length. Practitioners detect
foot abnormalities by observing the runner as he or she stands
and runs and by examining wear patterns on the runner's
shoes. Wear at the midfoot and forefoot indicate either pronation (the foot rolls inward) or supination (the foot rolls out-
ward). Wear at the heel is a sign of a discrepancy in leg length,
measured while the runner is standing.

The Cape Town team found the following treatments to be
the most effective:

- Prescribing appropriate running shoes.
- Prescribing in-shoe orthotics (corrective devices) for
  more treatment-resistant injuries.

- Inserting heel lifts or other corrective footwear devices for leg length discrepancies.
- Devising a built-in midsole wedge for runners not helped by orthotics.
- Scheduling deep massage for all chronic muscle injuries.

Unlike the Cape Town team, the Vancouver researchers focused on one specific running injury—Achilles tendinitis. Their program differed only slightly from the one in South Africa, and their findings were almost identical. They attribute their success to the following:

- Muscle retraining (that is, strength and flexibility exercises for the calf muscle).
- Control of overpronation (a tendency in 95 of the 109 patients studied).
- Heel lifts (in both shoes where there was no leg length discrepancy).
- Well-designed running shoes, preferably with a snug heel counter, a flexible sole that gives under the metatarsal heads (between the instep and the toes), and a heel wedge of 12 to 15 millimeters (with 7 to 15 millimeters additional lift during the toe-off phase).

These two groups of researchers arrived at the same basic conclusions: Biomechanical factors play an important part in running injuries. The Cape Town group concluded that physicians who treat runners need to know three things: which running shoes are appropriate for different running injuries, how to detect subtle structural abnormalities in the legs, and when to prescribe in-shoe orthotics.

The Vancouver team is just as positive: "We believe that virtually all cases of Achilles tendon injury appear to result from structural or dynamic disturbances in normal lower leg mechanics."

So there you have it. *Your running injury is not due to running.* It has a specific cause, an error that must be corrected. If you cannot find that cause and detect that error, seek help from someone who has studied the biomechanical approach to injuries and knows how to apply it.

BEST SHOE FOR YOU

Novice runners frequently ask me to name the best running shoe. Their concern is well founded. Selecting a running shoe is the most important decision a runner can make. Injury-free running depends upon wearing the right shoe.

Exactly what constitutes "the best shoe," however, varies from runner to runner, depending on individual difference in gait, foot, and body type. The best shoe for me might be the worst for the person questioning me. I've had a runner praise a style of shoe to the sky and, only a day later, met one who blamed the very same shoe for all sorts of trouble.

The problem is not in the shoes. Running footwear is getting better and better. "The major shoe companies," says sports podiatrist Joe Ellis, D.P.M., "are producing the best shoes they've ever made." These shoes are high-tech marvels. "A change to the correct shoe," says Dr. Ellis, "will clear up at least 25 percent of injuries."

How, then, to choose this correct shoe? The key is to learn how much the foot pronates, or rolls inward, as it progresses from heel strike to standing position and then to toe-off. About 50 percent of runners pronate too much. The rest are about evenly split between those who pronate within a normal range and those who don't pronate enough.

To measure pronation, Dr. Ellis suggests the "wet test." Wet the bottom of your foot and step on a flat surface. If your footstep leaves a print of your entire foot, arch and all, you have a flat, "mushy" foot that overpronates. If your footprint shows just your heel, the ball of your foot, and a thin line on the outside, you have a rigid foot with a high arch that underpronates. If the print shows about half the arch, you probably have a normal foot.

The mushy, overpronating foot requires stability and control. The high-impact, underpronating foot requires shock absorption. No shoe can deliver both. The more stability provided, the less shock absorption, and the more cushioning, the less control you have. No wonder, then, that a shoe may be perfect for one runner and a disaster for another.

My shoe needs are pretty obvious: I flunked the wet test. I overpronate. My arch appears well defined but flattens out when I stand on it. I also have shortened calf muscles. When I run, I need help from my shoes: a firm, snug heel counter, a firm midsole, and shoe flexibility, especially in the arch.

Over time, I found that I needed additional help. My shoes provided a fair amount of control, but it wasn't sufficient: I was still overpronating. And the heel was not high enough to compensate for my shortened calf muscle. I now use a rigid orthotic to prevent overpronation. I also use a heel lift.

My running friend with a rigid foot gets increased shock absorption with a soft orthotic made of cork and rubber. When an orthotic is used, there must be a good match between the foot, the shoe, and the orthotic. I have known runners to blame the orthotic when the fault was in the shoe, or the shoe when the fault was the orthotic.

I am fortunate that I weigh only 140 pounds and have a narrow foot and a running style that generates relatively soft impact. Runners who weigh 170 pounds or more, or have wide feet, or have a high-impact footstrike have trouble selecting or modifying their shoes.

Rest assured, though: Somewhere out there, there *is* a shoe that's right for you. It may not, however, incorporate all the features necessary for your needs. You may require an orthotic or heel lift or even modifications of the shoe itself. That will take care of 25 percent of the injuries. Attention to the biomechanics will take care of most of the other problems. Dr. Noakes has reported that over 77 percent of injured runners in his clinic responded to treatment directed at correcting biomechanics.

One axiom all runners should learn is a paraphrase of the message of the oracle at Delphi: Know thy foot.

One quite popular shoe nowadays is the cross-training shoe supposedly made for the multi-sport athlete. This shoe is an aberration. The only thing it fits is the wearer's image. It doesn't do anything well. It is not only inflexible, it lacks stability and shock absorption. The fact that it is usually worn with laces untied says it all. This is a fashion shoe. It is not made for a serious runner.

WHAT IS AN ORTHOTIC?

An orthotic is a specially made shoe insert designed to increase the mechanical efficiency of the foot. It allows your foot to adapt to a hard, flat surface. An orthotic compensates for any structural or postural instability in the foot, thereby relieving abnormal stresses on the foot, particularly in distance running.

How does an orthotic differ from an arch support you can buy at the drugstore?

The arch support does just that—it helps the arch support your full weight. In many instances, this may be all the runner needs. The orthotic, on the other hand, maintains the foot in the normal position through the entire footstrike, from heel contact through midstance to toe-off.

Why is this overall control of footstrike necessary? Because errors in footstrike cause most overuse injuries, contributing to injuries in the foot, leg, knee, and lower back. Depending on the individual foot, the origin of injury may arise in the rearfoot, midfoot, or a combination.

Does every runner need an orthotic?

No, not if the runner is running pain-free. Anything you put in your shoe to make you better can make things worse if it's unnecessary. Orthotics are tricky, and so are feet. If things are going well, don't rock the boat.

By the way: You're more likely to need an orthotic if you have a history of repeated overuse injuries. This almost always indicates a problem foot that needs help. Delayed pain is also a sign of a basic biomechanical difficulty. Dr. Richard Schuster has pointed out that distance runners who are helped by orthotics frequently experience pain only after covering a certain number of miles in their daily run or at a specific level of weekly mileage.

Well, then, does every injured runner need an orthotic?

I think there are a number of things an injured runner can do before trying orthotics. A podiatrist who immediately prescribes an orthotic is much like the physician who always treats the same problem with the anti-inflammatory drug Indocin or Butazolidin. He hasn't taken the time to evaluate the runner and the injury.

Over the years, I referred a number of injured runners to one excellent sports podiatrist, and only about 10 percent ended up wearing orthotics. Another fine sports podiatrist has told me that he prescribes orthotics for only one out of six injured runners. In general, I would say that about 60 percent of injuries are due to training errors and can be helped by relatively simple changes in shoes, surface, weekly mileage, running form, and exercise.

How do you know if you need an orthotic if you're injured?

First, review your training habits. Have you done something different lately? Have you changed shoes, for instance, or increased mileage, or started running on a hard surface, or added a lot of hill- and speedwork? Be flexible enough to make adjustments in these factors: Reduce your mileage. Wear a shoe you know agrees with you. Exercise regularly. Stretch, then stretch, and then stretch some more. Finally, add an over-the-counter arch support.

Then, if all this fails, see an experienced sports podiatrist, preferably one who is a runner himself, and let him decide whether you need an orthotic.

Some runners have told me they spent hundreds of dollars for orthotics and are still in trouble. Why is that?

Orthotics do fail. Sometimes it's the podiatrist's fault, sometimes it's the runner's. There may be a limit to the mileage a highly arched foot can handle running on a hard concrete surface, orthotic or no. In general, the reasons an orthotic fails are as follows:

- The "neutral position" of the foot is difficult to find and mold, leading to either under- or overcorrection of the problem. When overcorrected, the initial complaint is frequently cured, but the runner develops a new pain, usually on the outside of the foot, leg, or knee.
- No correction is made for abnormalities in the leg, thigh, or hip. The foot is the only place the lower extremity can adapt to these biomechanical errors. Therefore, the orthotic must be designed in such a way to compensate for any misalignments higher up. For this reason, an orthotic may help where the foot is actually normal, but the rest of the leg is not.

- The runner's leg muscles are too tight to handle the orthotic. The leg is a foot-to-hip continuum. Short thigh muscles, inflexible calf muscles, and tight hamstring muscles put additional stress on the foot and arch. Unless these muscles are stretched to full range of normal motion, the orthotic can't do the job.
- The runner is wearing the wrong shoes. In a surprising number of cases, orthotics don't work until the runner changes to a particular type of shoe. The best shoe may be a standard running shoe with some modification—the side flanges removed, or a new crepe sole added. But tennis shoes, basketball sneakers, or Army boots might also work. Only an experienced sports podiatrist would know for sure.
- The orthotic may need further correction, so that you and the orthotic work as a unit.
- You may need a heel lift to compensate for a leg that's shorter than the other.

As for me, I can't do without orthotics. I was once introduced at a sports medicine clinic as a runner who wore his orthotics to bed. I said, "Of course I do. There's always the chance I'll have to get up and go to the bathroom."

Of course, all the orthotics in the world won't protect you from injuries if you don't stretch. Here's why.

THE MAGIC SIX, PLUS TWO

When you run, three things happen to your muscles. Two are bad. The Prime Movers—the calf, hamstring, and low back muscles—become tight and inflexible. The Antagonists—the shin, quadricep, gluteal, and abdominal muscles—become relatively weak. This creates a strength/flexibility imbalance that must be corrected.

I once suggested to runners that they perform a series of six stretching exercises—the Magic Six, I called them—to correct and prevent this imbalance. This routine, I now know, had two flaws. One exercise, the Backover, was dangerous if done incorrectly. More important, however, I didn't realize that flexibility of the spine meant flexibility in both directions, backward as well as forward.

The following is an amended version, which I call the Magic Six, Plus Two. It changes the Backover to the Knee Clasp and includes two extension exercises for the low back. (Remember, stretch slowly and only to the point of tension.)

Wall Push-Up. This stretches the calf muscles. Stand about 3 feet from the wall. Lean in, with the legs straight and knees locked, feet flat and pointed straight ahead. Counting "one elephant, two elephants . . . ," hold for 10 "elephants." Relax. Then repeat. Do morning and night.

Hamstring Stretch. Straighten one leg, and place it, with knee locked, first on a footstool. Keep the other leg straight with knee locked. Bring your head toward the knee of the extended leg. Hold for a count of 10 "elephants." Relax. Repeat for 1 minute. Do morning and night, graduating to a toilet seat, then a chair, and finally a table as you improve.

Knee Clasp. Lie on the floor. Bring both knees up to your chest. Put your arms around your shins and pull your knees toward the chest. Hold for 10 "elephants." Relax. Repeat for 1 minute. Do morning and night.

Chest Push-Up. Lie on floor. Keep your lower abdomen flat on the floor. With your hands flat on the floor under your shoulders, push up the chest with your arms. Hold for 10 "elephants." Relax. Repeat for 1 minute. Do morning and night.

Backward Stretch. Stand straight, and place the palms of your hands against the small of your back. Tighten your buttocks and bend backwards. Hold for a count of 10 "elephants." Relax. Repeat for 1 minute. Do this stretch whenever you come to a standing position.

Shin Splinter. This is a strengthening exercise. Sit on a table, with your legs hanging over the side. Hang a 3- to 5-pound weight over your toes. Flex your foot at the ankle. Hold for a count of 6 "elephants." Relax. Repeat for 1 minute with each leg.

Leg Extension. This is a second strengthening exercise, for your quads. Assume the same position with the weights as for the Shin Splinter. This time, straighten the leg, locking the knee. Hold for a count of 6 "elephants." Relax. Repeat for 1 minute with each leg.

Bent Leg Sit-Up. Another strengthening exercise, this must be done correctly. Do *not* hold or lock the feet into position. The sit-up must not be a thrust but quite gradual, moving one vertebra at a time. Lie on the floor with your knees bent. Tighten your buttocks. Come to a position 30 degrees from the floor. Lie back. Repeat for a count of 20 or until you can't do anymore. Do once daily.

If you stretch conscientiously and still have problems, it may be time for some further detective work.

4

Freedom from Illness

Runners may be fit, but they're not invulnerable.

LIVING WITH DANGER

One night, a police car cruised the streets of our small town, its loudspeaker blaring "Don't drink the water until tomorrow morning." We obeyed. We weren't sure what the danger was, but we obeyed. No one in town drank the water that night. We believed that the water was hazardous to our health.

The next day, it was business as usual. We were up to our customary hazardous behavior. Some of us smoking. Some overeating, others drinking too much. Most of us forgetting to buckle our seat belt. We also have our share of citizens who take other health risks, people who don't know their critical numbers: cholesterol, blood pressure, and percentage of body fat. And there are those with high blood pressure and diabetes and heart disease who rely on drugs when diet and exercise might control their problems.

Why is it that we didn't drink the water, yet we ignore the risks in our everyday life? One reason was the immediacy of the threat. A risk is defined as the probability of something bad happening within a stated time. A nocturnal warning by a public authority suggests the high probability of something bad happening in a very short period of time.

Most other risks are long-term. They threaten our life span. And until people get on in years or develop some life-threatening illness, they rarely think about how long they're going to live.

Untoward reactions to present behavior seem to most of us to be far down the road. We become inured to threats. The more the authorities scream and scold, the less relevant they seem to our present life and to living each day to the fullest.

The truth is, we've grown blasé about risks. Hardly a day goes by without the media alerting me to yet another hazard in my daily activities. It seems that danger exists everywhere— in a plane, on my porch, asleep in my bed. There is no escape. There is always the possibility of something bad happening to me.

Such threats are effective, if at all, only in the short run. If nothing harmful occurs today or tomorrow or the next day, we are inclined to resume our regular routine. The consequences no longer frighten us. Unless we can see an immediate benefit, we're not likely to comply.

When it comes to assessing risk, probability is a key factor. Most of the risks we read about stress possibility. Anything is possible. In the morning, I set out for what I assume will be a risk-free walk on the boardwalk. But is it? I might be bitten by a dog, shot by a deranged person, or struck by a cyclist. I might fall and break my hip, get hit by lightning, or have a heart attack.

Obviously, none of these is probable enough to deter me from taking a walk. I'm no statistician, but I know the likelihood of some of these things happening is about equal to my chances of winning the lottery. Some well-publicized threats, like the Alar scare and the contamination of Perrier water a few years ago, were so minimal as to be virtually nonexistent. The authorities cried wolf at what amounted to no more than a housefly.

If we are to heed the epidemiologists when they sound the alarm about risks taken in our day-to-day life, I think the outcome of our behavior should be translated into simple terms. One way is to quantify risk into loss of days of potential life. These figures can be very illuminating. Many of the things we are warned about have very low risk. Another method of understanding risk is to equate it with some of our usual activities. Having a chest X ray, for instance, is about as risky as flying 1,000 miles on a commercial airline. Comparing relative risk puts the risk in proper perspective.

Quantifying risks allows us to make better judgments. For instance, a large group of people drinking Perrier with that infinitesimal amount of benzene for the rest of their lives might at worst have a loss of a few minutes of life. In comparison, a person who smokes two packs of cigarettes a day potentially loses 2,200 days (about six years) from his or her life.

Even still, I think people would be much more responsive to risks that diminish their days than to those that diminish their lives. We have habits that rob us of precious minutes and hours of what Emerson called "an everstanding miracle," the new day we are presented with every morning.

"We lead lives inferior to ourselves," writes American philosopher William James. That is the greatest risk—the danger of not having lived at all; of not fulfilling the promise of our birth. To live to the fullest, as Emerson says, "we must first be a good animal."

And how to do that? Follow nature's rules. They have not changed over the centuries. Finding out how your body works best, and following those instructions, remains the surest way of having something good happening in your life.

ONE MORE STEP AWAY
FROM HEART DISEASE

An important distinction should be made between coronary *artery* disease and coronary *heart* disease. Coronary artery disease is a narrowing of the coronary arteries due to cholesterol deposits on the walls of these vessels. Coronary heart disease is the damage that occurs when a clot forms in one of these narrowed arteries.

When coronary arteries narrow, the victim occasionally feels angina, or chest pain. This discomfort occurs when demands on the heart muscle temporarily exceed the blood supply coursing through the narrowed artery. When and if a clot totally blocks the artery, causing a heart attack and damage to the heart muscle, you have coronary heart disease.

A heart attack, therefore, is the result of two processes: excessive cholesterol in the blood, plus an increased tendency for the blood to clot. Any program to protect both the heart and its arteries must take these two factors into account. It is not sufficient to concentrate on lowering cholesterol levels while ignoring elevation of the clotting factors in the blood.

A study of a sizable group of middle-aged men in Wales has emphasized the role of clotting factors in heart attacks. In a population of 4,500 men, blood fibrinogen levels and blood viscosity (both indicators of the tendency to form clots) seemed to serve as substitutes for the generally accepted standard risk factors for heart disease (that is, cholesterol, smoking, blood pressure, and obesity). In fact, fibrinogen is now part of the coronary risk factor profile used in the highly regarded Framingham Heart Study.

Fortunately, several treatments are available to discourage dangerous blood clotting—an important strategy if cholesterol levels are persistently high.

One of the better anticlotting therapies is exercise. I have been impressed by the number of runners who develop coronary artery disease but do not sustain heart attacks. In many instances, these runners come from families that tend to develop premature coronary disease and have elevated cholesterol (which may be either "built in" or caused by bad diet). These runners usually develop chest pain while they are exerting themselves but rarely sustain heart damage. Many medical studies have shown that exercisers enjoy a certain degree of protection from heart attacks and sudden death.

What other measures can be taken by a person at risk because of abnormal clotting? The most effective drug tested thus far has been aspirin.

The aspirin research compared the effect of half a standard aspirin tablet a day versus a placebo in a large group of physicians. The study was stopped after 18 months, because the proof of aspirin's ability to lower the heart attack rate was overwhelming.

People with normal total cholesterol but low HDL (high-density lipoprotein)—the beneficial type of cholesterol—may be at particular risk for clotting. In the absence of a history of peptic ulcer or a hiatal hernia, aspirin may be of some benefit. Otherwise, other therapy should be used.

Other surveys have shown that eating fish twice a week or drinking two glasses of alcohol a day can cut the risk of heart attack in half. The report on the benefits of fish consumption came from a coronary disease project in the Netherlands and has since been confirmed by a few other studies. The relative freedom of Eskimos from heart disease is also thought to be due to their fish intake.

The benefits of alcohol have been extolled through the centuries. Recent reports confirm the good things the ancients had to say about drinking. A Kaiser-Permanente research team reviewed the medical records of 100,000 people and found that two-drinks-a-day people were half as likely to be admitted to a hospital for coronary heart disease as were total abstainers. Researchers in Hawaii and at Framingham have made much the same findings.

Smoking cigarettes or eating a meal high in saturated fat increases the tendency of the blood to clot. So a low-fat diet and abstention from smoking become imperative when evidence indicates that cholesterol has narrowed the coronary arteries.

A person with progressive obstruction of the coronary vessels should be on two complementary regimens—one to slow or reverse the buildup of cholesterol in the arteries, the other to protect against clots that will convert coronary artery disease to coronary heart disease. Exercise, because of its dual action as both a cholesterol-lowering and fibrinolytic agent, should be an essential part of this new lifestyle. Its effect on cholesterol and blood lipids is well documented. And even when risk factors persist, exercise, as shown by the well-publicized Harvard alumni study, reduces your chances of dying from coronary heart disease.

ON-THE-JOB TRAINING

Are you one of those people who think that getting fit must be strenuous and exhausting? Are you intimidated by the slogan "No pain, no gain"? Are you bewildered by exercise charts and target heart rates? Are you looking for an easy, pleasant, effective way to get fit?

Look no more. You know someone on just such a program, someone who visits your house on a regular basis: your letter carrier. Delivering mail is a perfect example of a low-key fitness program that is easy *and* pleasant *and* effective. It requires no special formulas, no scientific monitoring, no pulse taking, and it is never accompanied by pain or suffering.

You will never find any fit person more low-key than the mail carrier. Letter carriers do not go rushing about and making their presence known. They do not stand around huffing and puffing, waiting for approval. You are not likely to see a sweating mailman showing off his biceps.

No, mail carriers blend into the landscape, moving, as it were, with the slow rhythm of the day. So inconspicuous are postal carriers that English author G. K. Chesterton made one the murderer in a Father Brown story; none of the characters even remembered seeing him.

But mailmen are indeed fit. A Pittsburgh University study of 35 male postal carriers showed that they had cholesterol levels that put them at low risk for coronary artery disease. These men walked an averaged of 25 miles a week. This sustained, low-intensity exercise also prompted significant rises in HDL cholesterol.

What, then, about the recommended target heart rate of 70 percent of your age-predicted maximum? Most tests of aerobic exercise assume that to be effective, exercise must stay above this intensity level. Anything less, they imply, is a waste of time. But my guess is that postal carriers rarely achieve 70 percent of their maximum heart rate. Only a menacing Doberman or German Shepherd would spur our neighborhood couriers to the level of effort made by people enrolled in fitness classes. And although I don't spend hours a day observing mailmen, I have yet to see one taking his pulse to be sure his exercise is at an effective level.

The mailmen are perfect examples of the "slow, steady exercise" Sir William Osler prescribed for coronary artery disease a century ago. Without fanfare, postal carriers do their 25 miles a week. They use up the 2,000 calories or more that long-lived Harvard alumni have become known for.

Exercise is a necessity. What is not necessary is constant checking on one's pulse. There is no need to reach for your carotid artery (in the neck) or radial artery (on the inside of the wrist, at the base of the thumb), no benefit in making those mental calculations to see if you are at your target rate.

Observe the postal carriers. Their walk is not a high-intensity effort. Yet it's not a saunter, either. They are not out for a leisurely stroll. There is work to be done. Their walks have a purpose, which they accomplish at a comfortable, efficient pace.

The Pittsburgh University study supports the view that this is just the kind of sustained, low-intensity exercise we need to stay fit—in this case, fit to walk 25 miles a week. *And* it makes you healthy—in this case, triggering favorable changes in cholesterol.

As with Aesop's instructive fable about the tortoise and the hare, "slow" and "steady" are the watchwords. Slow and steady not only win races, they deliver the mail, and they do away with fat and cholesterol.

One more thing: If you would exercise like your letter carrier, neither rain nor snow, nor heat, nor gloom of night, must stay you from the completion of your appointed rounds.

HEALTHIER-THAN-THOU?

Runners frequently develop a biological arrogance. Their attitude may not be holier-than-thou, but it certainly is healthier-than-thou. They view themselves as a paragon of health.

But this is not necessarily the case. Without a doubt, runners are exemplars of fitness. They are endurance marvels, trained to travel incredible distances at an outlandish speed. But this does not always translate into good health.

Two recent reports suggest that the average runner probably does not adhere to a completely healthy lifestyle. One study comes from the former German Democratic Republic

(GDR), whose athletes set an outstanding record across the board in the Olympic Games. Despite this impressive showing, a World Health Organization study reported that the general population of the GDR ranks fairly high among countries surveyed when it comes to deaths from heart disease and strokes. Like their countrymen, the East German athletes ate too much fat, too little carbohydrates, and too little protein. "It becomes clear," stated the German researchers, "that traditions and secular dietary trends do work in similar directions for both the population and the athletes."

I think it is reasonable to assume that athletes in our country are also eating the diet of the general population—and in so doing, repeating the nutritional mistakes of their German counterparts.

Runners cannot assume that the diet and lifestyle they pursue while setting personal bests will automatically translate to a life span equal to that of the "wonderful one horse shay, that lasted 100 years and a day." Runners can break all sorts of rules and still win. The winner of a local race may have a blood cholesterol of 300, or smoke a pack a day, or drink heavily on weekends.

Long-term health, however, is a different story. Cholesterol and alcohol and even smoking may not increase your 10-K time, but they certainly increase your chances of unnecessary illness and premature death. Many runners apparently run these risks and deviate from accepted health practices in other ways. A poll of 966 habitual runners in South Carolina found that only half of them practiced five or more of The Alameda Seven—exercising regularly, eating breakfast, not snacking, maintaining desirable weight, not smoking, drinking moderately, and sleeping 7 to 8 hours per night—the acknowledged hallmarks of good health.

Except for maintaining ideal weight and high levels of physical activity, runners in South Carolina tend to ape their nonathletic countrymen. It is true, however, that this study failed to give credit to smokers who quit, counting only those who never smoked at all. Had they counted quitters, runners would have scored well in this category—42 percent were ex-smokers, while only 3 percent were current smokers.

So if you count ex-smokers, almost half of the South Carolina runners followed six of The Alameda Seven. That means they stand a good chance of living up to ten years longer than people who had adhered to only one or two of the recommended practices. Nevertheless, there's still room for improvement. One-third of these alleged role models weighed more than a desirable weight; 20 percent called themselves runners but did not run often enough to qualify as regular exercisers; and depending on the criteria used, 30 percent drank too much.

The results of this study suggest that many runners weigh too much, drink more than they should, don't get enough sleep, and seldom or never eat breakfast. It's odd that runners who will do almost anything to take a few seconds off their time in a race won't take precautions to ensure more years to their lives.

EXERCISE IS NOT ENOUGH

It has taken us a long time to realize that fitness and health are not synonymous. A person may be fit and not be healthy. Almost every week I hear or read about a very fit person who has had a heart attack.

On the day I was to address the Connecticut Academy of Family Practice on this subject, just such an episode occurred. As my wife was leaving our beach house, a man came off the boardwalk wheeling his bicycle. Ashen-faced, he told my wife he was having severe pain in his chest. While waiting for the ambulance, he told her he had been biking 10 miles a day for the past two years. Later, when I called the hospital, the coronary unit physician confirmed that the man had suffered a heart attack.

"Why did this happen?" I implored in my address to the academy. "How is it that a man that fit could develop serious and potentially fatal heart disease?" Then I proceeded to show how fitness and health care are indeed quite different.

Dr. Kenneth Cooper introduced us to fitness in 1968. In 1989, he wrote *Controlling Cholesterol*, and the advertisement in the *New York Times* read: "The man who made you fit is now going to make you healthy"—again, implying that fitness and health are not one and the same.

Fitness is the ability to do work. Health is the prevention of unnecessary disease and premature death. Fitness is physiology. Health is metabolism. Fitness is a physical rehabilitation. Health is a metabolic rehabilitation.

When we exercise to get fit, we are improving muscle function. Even the most out-of-shape individual can have excellent lungs and a quite adequate heart but a terrible body. The muscles, the motor of the body, may be weak and inefficient. In unfit individuals, this motor requires a great amount of oxygen and blood to do very little work.

Fitness makes the muscles more efficient. The motor now does more with less. It gets more miles per gallon of blood. This is accomplished through changes at the cellular level. Lung power doesn't change, and with a training program devoid of speed and hills, heart function, too, changes very little.

Fitness, therefore, is no more than any other form of physical therapy, the training of muscle. Our goal, however, is not speed or strength or flexibility but stamina. When used to describe what we attain through an aerobic exercise program, the term *cardiopulmonary fitness* is a misnomer. In advising runners on training methods, exercise physiologist Jack Daniels, Ph.D., points out that long, steady, slow distance running is used to develop basic muscle cell adaptation. Only through those agonizing, high-intensity interval quarter-miles (or their equivalent) do we improve our maximum oxygen uptake and increase heart function.

In any case, training, even with all these variations, may not make us healthy. Our health depends to a major extent on our ability to metabolize fat. The main coronary risk factors—high cholesterol, excess poundage, high blood pressure, and diabetes—are all related to difficulties in metabolizing fat. None of these factors diminishes fitness. Someone with a cholesterol level of 350 milligrams could win this week's local road race. Someone who exercises daily could still have high blood pressure or abnormal glucose tolerance, and may even be overweight.

Fat is the enemy of health, and exercise still remains our most potent weapon. But first comes a diet to prevent access of fat into the body. Then we must use exercise to burn up the excess. To prevent coronary disease, runners must pay attention to *all* the coronary risk factors. Being fit is certainly a good start. Alone, it confers a certain amount of protection against coronary disease (at least, statistically speaking). That is, even if he or she is overweight or smokes or runs other risk factors, the exerciser is less likely to have a heart attack than a sedentary individual.

But exercise is not a panacea. While health can probably not exist without exercise, investing an hour a day in exercise cannot automatically buy you health.

When a man dies, he dies of his entire life. Health is not a matter of strength or speed or flexibility or even fantastic feats of endurance. Those functions have to do with our muscles. Health is achieving a metabolic state that keeps the arteries to our vital organs open and free from disease.

Fortunately, the intensity of exercise needed to burn up fat is that same "comfortable" conversational pace that will make us fit. The difference in a fitness program and a health-promotion program is that the latter requires attention to coronary risk factors as well.

Everyone should know their cholesterol level and whether it needs treatment. They should be aware of whether their family's health status puts them at risk for heart disease. Ideally, that includes blood pressure, clotting tendency, waist/hip ratio, diabetes, and the rest. Exercise alone can go a long way toward correcting many of these abnormal findings, but it may not be enough. The giants in medicine who prescribed exercise for coronary artery disease also advised a low-fat diet, naps or other forms of stress management, and adequate sleep.

I ended my talk with the Connecticut physicians by saying, "We cannot assume that exercise alone will make a person healthy.

"We begin with exercise, then make the diet/exercise connection, and end as we always do by treating the whole patient. An incident like this indicates a break somewhere along the chain. Fitness will give you great legs but not necessarily great coronary arteries. We need them both."

PRITIKIN'S LEGACY TO EXERCISE

When Jim Fixx died, I was on the phone constantly for the following two weeks. When Nathan Pritikin died, I received one phone call. Fixx was recognized as a pioneer in the running movement, a prime mover in America's interest in exercise. Along with Dr. Ken Cooper, the aerobics innovator, and Frank Shorter, gold medal winner in the 1972 Olympics, Fixx was credited with getting this country out on the roads.

Yet around the same time, equally persuasive voices were calling for changes in our diet. Nutrition dominated their philosophy just as exercise was the all-consuming interest of those counseling jogging and cycling and swimming. The two camps championed two different lifestyles. "You are what you eat," said the diet adherents. "You can be born again through running," claimed advocates of athletic training. The exercise people gave only lip service to diet. And there was only passing mention of exercise in the diet books.

Nathan Pritikin was the pioneer who reconciled these two points of view. He made the diet/exercise connection. He was the first to alert the public to the equal importance of both factors in the good life. His therapeutic program was based on the intimate and obligatory relationship between the type of food we eat, the exercise we get, and the state of our health.

The diet/exercise link isn't a new concept in medicine. Hippocrates recommended exercise and diet to his patients. The great Sir William Osler prescribed diet and steady, quiet exercise. So did my professor Dr. William Dock. Dr. Dock also practiced what he taught. He followed a low-fat diet while continuing with his hiking and gardening and bird watching.

Back in the 1950s, the legendary Paul Dudley White, M.D., a cyclist until well into his eighties, gave James Michener the same advice. After Michener suffered a heart attack, Dr. White told him to never again drink whole milk or eat an egg and to go light on cheese. "Exercise to the limit of your endurance," said Dr. White, "but also take a nap every day."

Nevertheless, the public remained uninformed until Nathan Pritikin put these recommendations into a best-selling book, *The Pritikin Program for Diet and Exercise*, in 1979. Here were the rules of Hippocrates and Osler, of Dock and White, but now in the popular press. Degenerative disease could be prevented or retarded, perhaps even reversed, by a combination of diet and exercise. High blood pressure and coronary artery disease—America's greatest health problems (aside from the effects of cigarette smoking)—could be brought under control by attention to diet and sufficient exercise. If you wish to live longer, said Pritikin, follow my diet and run or walk (or both) up to 10 miles a day.

Pritikin set up residential programs to put his principles into practice. A patient of mine who attended his first Longevity Center told me what took place. "I walked 6 miles a day and ate cereal."

The diet consists of more than cereal, of course—but not by much: lots of complex carbohydrates, 10 percent fat, and just enough protein by Pritikin's standards. Significantly, calories were not restricted. You ate as much as your appetite allowed.

Looking back, we can now see the relevance of the Pritikin commandments. Nevertheless, many nutritionists thought it possible to eliminate obesity, high blood pressure, high cholesterol, and abnormal glucose tolerance without exercise. Without moving anything but your eating utensils, you could join the low-risk group and enjoy relative immunity to coronary artery disease.

Each side was half right. Without attention to diet, an intensive exercise program will sometimes achieve that low-risk profile. Far less often, dietary measures alone will be satisfactory.

What Pritikin did was combine sufficient exercise with a diet emphasizing low sodium levels, high fiber intake, and complex carbohydrates. While aimed at controlling blood lipids, this diet also helps you lose stubborn pounds, control diabetes, and lower blood pressure.

But just how much exercise is needed? And how stringent must the diet be? Those questions remain unanswered. Nevertheless, it is clear Pritikin put us on the right track. The diet/exercise connection tells us what nature's laws are and how to obey them.

VOICES OF DISSENT

Not everyone sees the current interest in health and fitness as an entirely good thing. *New York Times* columnist Russell Baker describes how he feels about being given responsibility for his own mortality. "I realize that if I die now, it will be my fault. My friends will be saying, 'Tough buns, sweetheart. If you had exercised regularly, watched your cholesterol, and eaten a high-fiber diet, we wouldn't have to stand listening to your death rattle.' "

Baker is not the only one who feels that our preoccupation with health and fitness has been carried too far. Other critics point out that death may be deferred for a few months or years but not forever. There are important elements in living the good life that can be lost in our obsession with coronary risk factors and so forth. Naysayers concede the necessity for attention to lifestyle, but only to help us in the pursuit of happiness. No need at all, says Baker, for this "staggering quantity of mind-stunning blather we hear nowadays about diet, muscularity, and sound innards."

Newsweek columnist George Will is another observer who sees an overemphasis on diet and exercise. "Some people," he writes, "have an unhealthy interest in health." Will, himself a proponent of fitness, cites the more reasonable approach of Dr. Cooper, the aerobics pioneer. Dr. Cooper has stated that jogging more than 15 miles a week is unnecessary. His dietary recommendations on cholesterol are right down the middle of the fairway—not too stringent, but not too liberal, either. There's no doubt that Dr. Cooper has a balanced view of fitness and health.

What Will quarrels with is carrying the case for good health to extremes. The pursuit of health, according to Will, has become a dawn-to-dusk regimen, with plenty of bedside reading. Health books have replaced philosophy as a guide to the good life. Baker has also pursued this theme. "A fleshly Puritanism," Baker called the health movement, "which frowned on any deviation from it and saw the ultimate good in the healthy, fit body."

Add to the list of opponents the *Boston Globe*'s Mark Muro, who writes, "The American fetish for fitness has taken all the fun out of exercise. It's now a joyless quest for immortality." And even worse, it has led to "the creation of a religion of running, a philosophy of fitness that left its adherents bereft of the deeper conciliation of a true philosophy that reconciles them to their true selves."

The *Christian Science Monitor*, which promotes its own version of that "true philosophy," weighed in with another attack, this time on dietary advice. In protesting what the editors considered a spate of nitpicking comments on all sorts of presumably dangerous foods, the *Monitor* quoted a New Testament recommendation that we not concern ourselves about what we eat.

But enough of such statements. The general theme of the opposition, as you can see, is that fitness adherents are trying to reduce the complexities of existence to simple regimens of physical well-being. For myself, a lifelong guinea pig in the human experiment, I see no better beginning to the solution of the complexities of existence than these very simple regimens.

Like any field, fitness has its share of kooks, fanatics, and incompetents. The fitness field is peopled with its share of "experts" who have neither credentials nor credibility. They, and the people who follow their advice, have gone too far. Do's and don'ts proliferate daily. Everything we eat or do is subjected to scrutiny. Some days, I wonder if *anything* I do is without risk. And I am constantly being offered alternative methods of feeding and training my body that have no scientific basis.

I support, therefore, any call for moderation. This was the Greek ideal. It means adhering to a schedule that makes for the best possible you. Moderation fine-tunes the body, mind, and spirit. It is the philosophy behind the development of the self. The appropriate regimen is, however, something each person has to develop for himself or herself.

Finally, I dispute any implication that exercisers and especially my breed, the runners, are a joyless lot. William James made a comment that seems apropos in this instance. "The human trait that make angels cry," James wrote, "is our tendency to criticize another person's way of being happy."

I have made my own judgment on my lifestyle. And I have made it through my own experience. I have taken the truth presented by experts, for and against and in between, and then tested it against my own truth (as have, I hope, all those critics who would have me lead their lives instead of mine).

5

Eating for Peak Performance

How diet can help achieve a personal best.

EAT TO WIN—AND TO LIVE

Because I am a runner, I follow two diets—one for performance, one for disease prevention; one for a successful race, one for a successful life; one for my muscles, one for my arteries.

There is a difference between eating to win and eating to live. Races are lost by not eating enough. Lives are lost by eating too much. It is excess—too many calories, too much saturated fat—that ages arteries. Should I eat a daily breakfast of ham and eggs and whole milk and end the day with quantities of ice cream, my racing times wouldn't increase, but my cholesterol certainly would.

Health and longevity depend on eating only what is nec-essary to sustain life. Since time began, groups of people who eat subsistence-level diets have proved that less is better. The diet that comes with the affluent life is the killer. When we study long-lived people, we find that they eat only when hungry and no more than is needed.

For running, however, "more" is the watchword, not "less." The diet that lessens performance does so because it is defi-cient. My running suffers when I don't eat enough—not enough calories, not enough carbohydrates, not enough water, not enough of the nutrients intimately related to maximum mus-cular function.

The essentials of a training diet are simple. Sufficient water is a prime consideration. Most people, including myself, are in a chronically dehydrated state. For a runner, dehydration is especially serious, because adequate water is needed to main-tain blood volume. Blood volume is *also* critical in maximum performance and in resistance to heat syndromes (see chap-ter 6).

The second requirement is sufficient carbohydrates. The racing body runs on glucose, and this energy source must be replenished every day. Carbohydrate-loading should not be limited to prerace preparation; it should be part of the daily diet.

When extra pounds are a problem, I go on a reducing diet. It's low in fat but not in calories. And I tend to eat *more* car-bohydrates, not less. Too many women runners who diet regu-larly limit both calories and carbohydrates. This is a mistake and leads to muscle fatigue and stress fractures.

High-mileage runners sometimes find it almost impossible to meet their caloric needs without high-carbohydrate bever-ages. This is partly due to the loss of appetite that follows pro-longed, all-out effort. But on my minimal training schedule, I've never encountered that problem.

A study of a group of Irish runners suggests that I would be wise to also supplement my dietary supplies of other nu-trients: iron, folic acid, vitamin B_6 (pyridoxine). There is con-siderable evidence that most women runners and many men runners have iron deficiency. In fact, some physicians have sug-gested that every woman runner take an iron supplement. Iron does more than contribute to hemoglobin: It's essential to muscle function.

Folic acid, too, is related to muscle performance. Folic acid deficiency has also been found in patients with depression and hence may be a factor in the periods of staleness that I have experienced over the years.

Vitamin B_6 is important because it is a necessary cofactor for numerous enzymes and is especially prominent in the metabolism of glucose, the prime source of energy for training and racing.

These reports, of course, are not conclusive. I have, however, taken them to heart and have made some adjustment in my diet to correct any deficiencies. There are several breakfast cereals that provide the Recommended Daily Allowance (RDA) of these nutrients. I include these cereals in a breakfast that features the whites of eggs but not their yolks—a concession to my eat-to-live diet.

I suspect that my racing diet should also have sufficient trace metals, plus an adequate supply of magnesium and potassium. So I occasionally go on a one-a-day vitamin/mineral preparation.

I recognize that food is important only insofar as it provides the optimal internal environment for doing my best. The role of diet is not to improve my performance. It is to guarantee that I will perform at the level corresponding to my talent and training.

I cannot expect to run a personal best simply because I am on a good diet, but I *can* expect a subpar race if I am on a poor one.

RUN TO PERFORM, DIET TO PREVENT

I was conducting a runner's clinic the week before the Cincinnati Heart Association Half-Marathon. A man in the front row stood up and said, "Three years ago, I had a heart attack while I was running in a marathon." Such events cause physicians to have second thoughts about prescribing exercise for their patients— *and*, in the general public, raise doubts about the merits of exercise.

"When I got to the hospital," the man continued, "they discovered that my cholesterol was 325!" There was the crux of it. Despite the mileage he had put in preparing for the marathon, despite his ability to go the distance, his cholesterol was at a level associated with a *fourfold* increase in risk of coronary disease.

"So I became a vegetarian," he said. "Now my cholesterol is 98 and I'm running better than ever." Adding a low-fat diet to his running regimen was now increasing protection against clogging of his coronary arteries.

This man's story puts the whole subject of exercise in perspective. There are things exercise will do—things exercise is *guaranteed* to do.

Then there are also things exercise can do—but, as in this instance, only if additional measures are taken.

When Roger Bannister set out to break 4 minutes in the mile, he programmed his exercise to accomplish it. The runner who said he'd had a heart attack had done the same thing to train for the marathon.

Athletes the world over use training schedules with predictable results. Exercise physiology is the science of human performance. Insert your individual statistics, settle on your particular goal, and there is a formula with a certified outcome.

In exercise physiology, each individual responds in like fashion to the exercise program. The response may vary to a degree, but not markedly so. Individuals in a three-month fitness program show remarkable similarities in improvement in physical work capacity.

But in prevention, this regularity in response is not always the case. Exercise guarantees fitness; it does not guarantee health.

When exercise is used for prevention, its deficiencies sometimes become apparent. Mileage sufficient for fitness may not rid an individual of one or several risk factors. A stubborn weight problem or controlled high blood pressure suggests that more exercise is needed. And you may have to change your diet, too. In other words, 2 hours of exercise a week may be enough to make you fit, but it may not be enough to make you healthy.

When someone develops a heart problem despite regular

exercise, it's usually due to high blood cholesterol levels. All other risk factors are obvious. You know if you smoke, are overweight, or (perhaps) have an elevated blood pressure. But you probably don't know your cholesterol count. So you might have no idea that exercise is failing to give you the necessary protection.

Exercise used as a preventive measure *should* be enough to stop a person from smoking and get him back to the 12 percent body fat of his youth. But it isn't always. The marathoner in Cincinnati had exercised aplenty, but he still had not lowered his cholesterol to an acceptable level. His post–heart attack diet did the rest. If you already exercise, learning about diet and nutrition may be the key to your health in the future.

LESSONS IN LABELS

When I visited a nationally known health and fitness resort, one of the directors was disappointed. Evidently, I wouldn't be able to meet a group of chief executive officers that was spending a week learning how to live a healthy lifestyle.

"They're at the supermarket learning how to read labels," she explained. Apparently it's not enough to learn the general principles of dietary intake. To survive in the 1990s, we must be able to shop for food intelligently.

Health has many enemies, but in the United States, one of our major foes is the food we eat. From a health standpoint, the ordinary American diet is atrocious. It prompted the *British Medical Journal* to state that "obesity is endemic in the United States." Our diet and sedentary lifestyle not only have left Americans very overweight but have caused our death rate from heart disease to be one of the highest in the Western world.

In response to public demand for lower-fat products, supermarkets and restaurants have declared war on fat. While you can still buy plenty of products with unacceptably high levels of fat—dairy products, cold cuts, baked goods, and so forth—low-fat food is easier to ferret out than it has been in the past.

Hunting for fat wasn't a concern when I grew up. Few people ate out. Almost all food was prepared in the kitchen. Even baked goods were homemade. So we knew exactly what was present in the items brought to the table and how much, even though we knew very little about fat and its consequences.

Now that fat is the enemy, we have forfeited our high ground. We eat at fast-food restaurants, and while home, we eat food that was prepared elsewhere. We have only a hazy knowledge of the ingredients in our baked goods, lunch meats, snack foods, and the items we slip into the microwave oven. Our meals go from the grocery shelves onto the dining room table without a security check for dangerous ingredients.

Boot camp for this life-and-death struggle must include training for shopping at a supermarket. The first rule for the neophyte is to circle the outside aisles of the store. Along the periphery are essential foods like fruits and vegetables. This same circular route will give access to dairy products. Choose only the nonfat items—mozzarella, cottage cheese, yogurt, skim milk, and so forth. Milk products usually list fat by percentage of weight, not percentage of calories. Foods listed as 1 or 2 percent may sound innocuous, but in reality they provide a considerable number of calories from fat.

The outer aisles also supply acceptable low-fat sources of protein: poultry, fish, and lean meat. Know, too, that eggs are a first-rate source of protein, but seriously consider discarding the yolks—they are densely packed with cholesterol.

When you venture into the central aisles, be careful. This is trench warfare. The manufacturers have any number of subterfuges to induce you to buy products well over the limit in fat. Foods listed as 95 percent fat-free may have a majority of their calories in fat. "Low fat" guarantees no more than that item contains less fat than the industry standard. "Lite" can refer to taste rather than to calories of fat.

Labeling a food "cholesterol-free" is another frequent ploy. It's the amount of *saturated fat* in the diet that is decisive, not cholesterol. A cholesterol-free food may have considerable saturated fat. Another clue to unwanted amounts of saturated fat is the term "partially hydrogenated." When unsaturated fats are partially hydrogenated, their chemical nature changes, and they become *saturated* fats.

Label reading is the essential survival skill of a trained shopper. Label reading is akin to deciphering coded messages. Beyond the various misdirections mentioned above, one has to be able to interpret the limited information provided by the manufacturer. Each gram of fat you consume creates 9 calories of energy stored in the body. By comparison, a gram of carbohydrate or protein results in 4 calories. Look at it this way: If a gram of fat were a poker chip, it would supply twice as much available energy as a gram of carbohydrate or protein.

This excess energy intake is what has led to rampant overweight and heart disease. If we eat fat, we have to exercise to burn it up. This war will be won by reducing intake of fat— and then exercising off the excess.

Once you turn your back on fat, you needn't feel deprived either. You'll be turning *toward* carbohydrates.

CARBOS: FOR THE ATHLETE IN ALL OF US

"Aside from talent and training," says exercise physiologist David Costill, Ph.D., "no factor plays a bigger role in exercise performance than does nutrition." This is not news. As far back as the 1920s, scientists observed that eating a higher-than-usual amount of carbohydrates enhanced endurance and delayed the onset of fatigue by stockpiling glycogen (sugar) stores in the muscles and liver.

Acting on this evidence, distance runners for some years have been carbo-loading to improve their performances. Nevertheless, many athletes still go into an event with suboptimal sugar stores in their muscles and liver. They have not mastered the techniques necessary for storing maximal amounts of glycogen in their muscles.

According to Dr. Costill, the proper regimen is quite simple. A runner runs his or her best race when well trained, well rested, and well fed. Highly trained runners can stockpile twice as much glycogen as newcomers to the sport. They can also replace depleted glycogen stores faster after a long training bout.

Even runners who religiously carbo-load for a race sometimes neglect posttraining glycogen replacement. Yet even a run of 1 hour can reduce muscle glycogen considerably. And if glycogen isn't replaced, three training runs in a week can cause complete depletion of muscle glycogen stores.

Not only are runners unaware of this effect, but they don't realize that a normal diet is usually not sufficient to replace glycogen used in training. Over time, the runner will develop fatigue and perform poorly. Carbo-loading, therefore, isn't something to be reserved for the night before a race, but should be done on a regular basis to maintain the body's glycogen reserves. And for carbo-loading to work, the runner must be well rested. For several days before a race, taper activity and reduce the intensity and duration of training to minimize the daily demands on muscle stores. Then, with the race at hand, comes the final step: arranging carbohydrate intake before and during the race. This is to insure adequate supplies of liver glycogen and blood sugar, which is something preliminary carbo-loading doesn't accomplish. Liver glycogen can get reduced significantly inside of 24 hours, even while at rest.

You should, therefore, eat a high-carbohydrate meal 2 to 4 hours before the event. This also avoids an episode of hypoglycemia, or low blood sugar, which may occur if sugar is taken 30 to 90 minutes before the race. Additional sugar can, however, be taken just before the gun. These feedings assure adequate liver glycogen and blood glucose levels for the strenuous effort to come.

Further insurance comes from taking in sugar at regular intervals during the run. Replacement drinks with 8 to 10 percent sugar, or even higher, are well tolerated and absorbed when consumed frequently, in small amounts. In the beginning of a race, muscle glycogen is the main source of energy. Later, sugar derived from the liver and replacement drinks becomes a significant factor.

Only lately has it been recognized that muscle glycogen influences power output in short races of 1 hour or less as well as in distance events—something few runners realize.

In attempting to refill their glycogen stores, many athletes confuse meal volume with content and consider themselves well fed. Dietitian Jacqueline Benning surveyed the dietary habits of the U.S. National and U.S. Olympic swimming teams and found that like typical Americans, these athletes consumed more fat than carbohydrates in their diets.

Such diets are not only bad for Olympians, they're bad for all of us. The direct relationship of carbohydrates to performance is important to the athlete in each one of us. Whether you are a worker (an "industrial athlete"), a housewife (a "domestic athlete"), or someone battling a chronic disease (a "patient athlete"), your daily work output depends upon being well trained, well rested, and well fed—and that requires a high-carbohydrate, low-fat diet.

BOOST THE BLOOD SUGAR

Dr. Timothy Noakes of Cape Town, South Africa, has called low blood sugar in marathon runners "the forgotten disease." First brought to medical attention in 1924 by Samuel Levine, M.D., in his study of runners in the Boston Marathon, hypoglycemia has been virtually ignored ever since. It seems that investigators of endurance performance rarely visit the scenes where such performance is put to the test. So no one has connected incidents of exhaustion and collapse among long-distance racers to blood sugar problems.

Nevertheless, physicians on patrol duty at the Boston Marathon have suspected that they were seeing instances of low blood sugar. "Some runners respond to fluids," one doctor told me. "Others seem to need sugar." Back in 1961, the legendary Sir Adolphe Abrahams, M.D., expressed the same belief. "When exhausting exercise is undertaken in circumstances conducive to heatstroke," said Dr. Abrahams, "it is impossible to separate the symptoms from those caused by accompanying hypoglycemia."

A classic case of blood sugar–related collapse occurred at one Comrades Marathon. A number of runners who completed the 56-mile run in near-collapse were taken to the aid tent, and their blood sugar levels were tested. One marathoner in particular, a runner-up, finished in a terrible state. A test tape showed a blood sugar reading of less than 40 milligrams per milliliter, a situation usually associated with coma. Within a few minutes of receiving intravenous glucose, the runner became quite coherent, cheerful, and eager to get up and go.

Dr. Noakes believes that distance runners should learn more about this old but now rediscovered marathon malady. The primary aim should be to store a maximum amount of sugar in the muscles as glycogen. Most runners already do this by carbohydrate-loading. What most runners do not do, however, is increase storage of sugar in the liver to be used as fuel, nor do they maintain their blood sugar by taking carbohydrates during the run.

One very important consideration is the early pace. Running too fast too soon uses up precious stores of carbohydrates. It is much as though you took off down the turnpike with a full tank of gas doing 80 miles per hour, while a friend did the same at 50 miles per hour. He would get a lot farther on a full tank than you would.

Dr. Noakes lists four major carbohydrate errors committed by distance runners—mistakes that lead to hitting the wall, finishing the race in collapse, or not finishing at all.

An early pace that's too fast. The prudent thing is to take your average minutes per mile, then add 30 seconds to 1 minute for the first 7 to 10 miles. At most, this will cost you 10 minutes at the finish. At best, it will ensure that you finish with a full head of steam, still running on a partially filled tank of sugar.

No carbohydrate-loading. Unless it's done right, carbo-loading tactics can trigger stomach and intestinal upsets. The trick is to eat only carbos that you like, and then only when you are hungry. Food eaten when you are not hungry seems to reassemble in your stomach and remain there until race time. Learning what's best for you is essential to running your best marathon, and probably most distances over 5 kilometers, too.

No prerace breakfast. As I've stated, liver glycogen is rapidly depleted and must be renewed daily. If you skip breakfast, that means your last big meal was up to 16 hours before the race. A good-sized, carbohydrate-centered breakfast can be a big help.

Not drinking carbohydrates on the run. Exercise physiologists tell us that sugar taken during the run is not utilized by the muscles. Maybe so. But it *will* keep blood sugar high enough to help maintain coordination, comprehension, and even consciousness.

BEYOND CARBOS: BALANCE WITH SUPPLEMENTS

For years, the first commandment in nutrition has been "Eat a well-balanced diet." In this respect, I'm a sinner, or I suspect I am. When night falls and supper is over, I am no more satisfied with the examination of my dietary conscience than I am with my spiritual one.

The righteous road being so difficult, I quiet that small voice of rectitude not with changes in my diet but with extra vitamins and a mineral or two. I hope thereby to escape the punishment that my nutritional misdemeanors will mete out to me.

But vitamin/mineral supplements can be no less haphazard than the diet that I should be taking. An unbalanced vitamin/mineral intake can cause as many problems as an unbalanced diet. Susan Smith, clinical nutrition manager at Long Island College Hospital in Brooklyn, New York, gives the following advice for those of us who suspect we need additional vitamins.

Choose a balanced multivitamin. Taking excessive levels of one nutrient can disrupt the body's balance and alter requirements of other nutrients. In any case, if you're deficient in one nutrient, chances are several other deficiencies exist, too.

Select supplements that provide approximately 100 percent of the RDA. You need no more than 100 percent of any vitamin. On the other hand, much smaller amounts are of little value.

Synthetic vitamins are as good as those from "natural" sources. In fact, some synthetic vitamin preparations are *more* effective than their natural counterparts.

These very basic recommendations undoubtedly are not the last word in nutrition. These guidelines do, however, represent the current thinking of the nutrition establishment and make good sense. The best choice is a balanced diet. The second best is an unbalanced diet with a balanced vitamin/mineral supplement. I recommend it for other sinners who wish to join the nutritional elect.

Aside from adding a few minerals to your diet with supplements, you might want to subtract one—sodium.

SHAKE THE SALT HABIT

My first assignment as a columnist was to cover the 1968 Olympics in Mexico City. One particular aspect of the Games that interested me was how to prepare for high-altitude competition. I discussed this problem with Dr. Sodi-Pollares, a Mexican M.D. and cardiologist whose work I had come to know through his Polarizing Solution, a concoction of distilled water, sugar, insulin, and potassium given intravenously to patients with heart attacks.

Theoretically, this formula would help heart muscle, damaged or not, to use sugar for energy, and at the same time, it would help draw potassium into the muscle cell while driving sodium out. The ultimate effect would be to improve heart function and reduce a tendency toward irregular heart rhythms.

I had used this solution for all my patients with acute heart attacks, with great success. Before our local hospital had a coronary care unit, patients of mine who received the polarizing solution along with an anti-arrhythmic drug stood virtually the same chance for survival as patients treated years later in a high-tech coronary care facility.

It therefore came as no surprise to me when Dr. Sodi-Pollares said an athlete would perform better at Mexico City, and indeed at any altitude, on a high-carbohydrate, high-potassium, low-salt diet.

It makes sense. We are genetically programmed to lose potassium and retain salt. Given the amount of salt we consume daily, it seems odd that nature planned it that way. But in nature, there is very little available salt. Our progenitors, the cave dwellers, had a great deal of potassium available to them in fruit, game, and vegetables, but very little available salt. Even now, there are Amazon tribes that have no salt whatsoever in their diets. We tend to forget that in the past, salt was scarce enough to be used as money.

Our diets, therefore, need to have very little salt in order to satisfy our daily requirements. On the other hand, muscles need considerable potassium to operate at their peak. When our potassium stores are depleted (as, for instance, when diuretics are taken), fatigue, heart rhythm disturbances, and even dangerous dips in blood sugar can result.

After my conversation with Dr. Sodi-Pollares, I decided to test his high-carb, high-potassium, low-salt diet myself. I increased my fruit and vegetable consumption and added soups and bouillon made with unsalted meat stock to my daily menu. I also avoided salty foods and stopped salting food at the table. Two things happened: I lost weight, and my running times improved. In a matter of months I set a world record in the indoor mile for my age group.

Despite this satisfying result, I could not abide a prolonged period of time without salt. It has always been my custom to salt my food before I taste it, and to add some more after I do. It was only a matter of time until I would succumb once more to this addiction. One day, I came downstairs for breakfast and smelled bacon frying. That was the end of my low-salt, high-potassium diet.

My story is obviously not a scientific report, but one runner's experience with one cardiologist's theory—hardly enough to satisfy even the gullible. Despite the fact that people with heart failure and high blood pressure do well on such a low-salt regimen, we have little evidence of its effect on athletic performance.

One could argue that what best serves the body in adversity is what should be done when it is in health. The diet that helps us when we are sick is the one to adhere to when we are at out best. But in this, as in most things, the real truth lies in what works for you. The case for a high-potassium, low-salt diet rests on individual experience.

It is likely that all we need to know we either know or have forgotten. Nature has written the rules, if we would read them. They have been the same since the Stone Age—what we eat and how we train determines our athletic performance. A low-salt, high-potassium intake could well be the key to doing your personal best.

ELIMINATE THE TROUBLEMAKERS

It's quite likely that many minor deviations from feeling vibrant and healthy are due to foods and what is put into them. When we are just not up to par physically, mentally, emotionally, or socially, it may indeed be due to something we ate.

I have a friend who has a violent reaction when she eats any kind of fish. Within an hour, she has a severe headache, feels deathly ill, and begins to vomit and have diarrhea. Another woman I know cannot eat crab meat. On rare occasions when she has inadvertently had crab, her face has swollen to the point where she's almost unrecognizable.

"Restaurant syndromes" like these range from difficulty breathing to hivelike rashes, flushing, and palpitations, and they occur in a significant percentage of the general population. Anyone who suffers any kind of food sensitivity runs a risk of an abnormal response to something they are about to eat.

The following are the primary causes of adverse reactions to food.

Food allergens. While peanuts, eggs, fish, nuts, and milk are the most common food allergy triggers, almost any food can be a problem. Usually, people who are allergic to foods have suffered some other kind of allergy in the past. Probably about 20 percent or more of our population is at risk for this type of food reaction.

Preservatives. Of all the food preservatives used, sulfites are probably the most troublesome. The usual symptoms include flushing, shortness of breath, and light-headedness. Various forms of sulfite are frequently used in restaurant salads, pickles, cheese mixtures, and fruit juices.

Flavor enhancers. Monosodium glutamate (MSG) is a flavor enhancer found in many foods, most notably in Chinese food. It causes a variety of symptoms, ranging from headache to heart palpitations. About one out of five people is sensitive to small amounts of MSG, but almost everyone will react if the dose is large enough.

Color additives. Tartrazine, or yellow dye no. 5, is the most common color additive found in food and drugs. Many people who are allergic to aspirin are also sensitive to tartrazine. Symptoms include hives and shortness of breath.

Amines. Tyramine and related substances that occur naturally in foods such as cheese, red wine, and chocolate can cause headache and high blood pressure.

Sugar substitutes. Aspartame (NutraSweet, Equal) has proven to be a problem for many people. Also, sorbitol (usually found in low-calorie candies and mints) frequently causes diarrhea in susceptible people.

In discussing these various restaurant syndromes, Guy Settipance, M.D., a Providence, Rhode Island, allergist, points out the difficulty in confirming the exact cause of the reaction. In most instances, it is food intolerance, not a food allergy. Hence allergy tests are usually of limited help. An oral challenge, where neither the patient nor the physician is aware of what is in the test capsule, may be needed.

Just such a study was done on 43 children at the Pediatric Allergy Clinic of St. Mary's Hospital in London. All had complaints of urticaria (hives); other symptoms included stuffy nose, wheezing, and facial swelling. All improved on an additive-free diet. Then they were challenged with a variety of additives, including tartrazine, sunset yellow, amaranth dye, sodium benzoate, and MSG. Twenty-four children reacted to the additives, 18 did not. The 18 were able to resume a normal diet without symptoms.

All of which suggests that food intolerance is an enormous factor in our everyday enjoyment of health. And food allergens detectable by skin and immunoglobulin tests represent a minority of the foods and additives that can cause problems. The restaurant syndromes should be looked on as extreme manifestations of intolerance to what we eat.

Nondietary factors often influence food reactions. Fatigue, stress, loss of sleep, or severe effort may be enough to overload the body's defense mechanisms and trigger symptoms. I know this occurs in runners who experience food-induced symptoms after a very competitive race. At other times, the same food may cause no problems.

It's becoming increasingly clear that food intolerance causes many exercise-induced symptoms. If the food can be identified and removed from the diet, the exercise-induced symptoms usually disappear. Examples come to mind that demonstrate how effective this *modus operandi* can be:

- A runner with a history of headaches began to experience head pain 4 hours after his run. The headache cleared when he stopped drinking coffee immediately after his training session.

- A runner with a known soybean allergy had violent cramps after every marathon. He was carbohydrate-loading with pizza that contained soy as a meat extender.
- A runner with heart palpitation unresponsive to medication obtained complete relief when she eliminated milk and dairy products.
- A runner with a family history of colitis and intractable diarrhea from running was relieved of symptoms by going on a gluten-free diet.
- A runner/cyclist/tennis player developed an itch after running, but not after her other activities. The itch disappeared when she eliminated eggs from her diet.

This is, in any case, the most satisfactory approach. When faced with exercise-induced symptoms, you have four alternatives: (1) ignore them; (2) give up running; (3) find a drug that will stop them (this means taking something every time you run, not to mention the unpleasant side effects), or (4) find out what's triggering your symptoms.

Diagnosing allergy-related symptoms isn't easy. Current allergy tests are inaccurate and expensive. Further, there are many nonallergic pathways by which foods cause trouble. Allergy tests at their best only scratch the surface. The best single way to cope with this problem is to follow an elimination diet, along with careful trial and error, to determine what might be causing the problem.

On an elimination diet, you start out by limiting yourself to just a few "safe" foods for a few days. Then you add one food at a time, one day at a time, to test your reaction. In my view, the best diet to start with is the B.R.A.T. diet (bananas, rice, applesauce, and tea), frequently used by pediatricians for hyperactive children and others with suspected allergies. Start with this simple diet, and keep running for three to five days at the pace or mileage that usually causes symptoms. If running no longer produces the symptoms, the next step is to add foods, one at a time, until the symptoms reappear. Begin with fruits and vegetables, and leave the most likely offenders—milk, eggs, and coffee—until last.

More often than not, if food intolerance is triggering your symptoms, the offender will be something you eat every day or something that is part of your prerace routine. You may be able to refine your search for the culprit still further, however. If you have a special fondness for certain foods, such as chocolate, nuts, peanut butter, or dairy products, they should immediately be suspect. Stop all such items immediately. When your symptoms are under control, you can test these items one by one. Perhaps you can eat some, but not all, of these known troublemakers.

Most runners have the notion that eating certain foods will help them run better. They would be better occupied with detecting foods that interfere with performance, often in subtle ways. Dr. Timothy Noakes told me of a runner who was able to double his mileage when he stopped eating chocolate.

A sedentary person might not notice subtle signs of food intolerance. Running, however, imposes an enormous strain on the body's homeostatic mechanisms. For runners, the equation is simple: Prolonged or intense exercise plus food intolerance results in symptoms. I know of any number of runners whose running-induced symptoms subsided when they found and eliminated an offending food.

WHY RUNNERS AREN'T FAT

The overweight person is faced with three choices: (1) be fat; (2) be hungry; (3) exercise. The first choice is unacceptable to many: Most people would rather be lean and trim. By middle age, more than 50 percent of Americans are overweight and hate it. They have doubled their risk of heart disease, tripled their chance of having gallstones, and quadrupled their incidence of diabetes.

The second choice—dieting—is ineffective. Nevertheless, despite the 20-to-1 odds against permanent success, one out of every four adults in the United States is dieting to lose weight. These people have accepted an alternative to being fat: being hungry. In order to maintain weight loss, they have to eat less and less. They must resign themselves to an unceasing craving for food. They are engaged in a never-ending battle against lard.

It is a war they can never win. With dieting, the initial weight lost is due to water loss, then muscle, then fat. Losing muscle results in lowering the metabolism and, therefore, in a need for fewer and fewer calories. Eventually, the diet that caused weight loss no longer works. The fat returns, so 95 percent of all dieters return to their original weight. What's more, they have less muscle, less energy, and more fat than they started out with.

Fortunately, the third alternative *does* work. Exercise is the rational, scientific, and successful way to lose weight. I know one group of exercisers intimately: runners. My medical colleagues who treat the sedentary overweight have been studying the defeated. I have found it much more instructive to study the winners. It is a rare runner who is overweight or, even more important, overfat.

Contrast the dismal sequence of weight lost and weight regained in dieters against what occurs in runners. Runners lose weight, sometimes in enormous amounts. But they also replace fat with muscle. Consequently, their metabolism speeds up rather than slows down as in dieters. A runner burns as many as 500 extra calories a day. As the weight drops, the runner can eat *more*, not less. A new body weight is established based on the weekly mileage.

Exercise affords other important metabolic benefits. The blood lipid profile approaches the ideal: Total cholesterol and triglycerides go down, high-density lipoproteins (HDLs) go up, glucose tolerance improves, insulin levels decrease, blood pressure drops—all reducing the threat to your heart health.

These physical and physiological consequences of running, and indeed of any aerobic exercise program, make exercise the only rational and scientific choice for overweight people. But there are other benefits as well—benefits that make it easier to keep weight under control: the mental and emotional benefits conferred on people who use their body with intensity. Runners tell of the positive influence on mental health and creative processes. They speak of the self-esteem and self-confidence they develop out on the roads.

I tell you all this, and you may remain unmotivated to try exercise to handle your weight problem. Perhaps this fact may help you decide: Runners can eat anything they want. Runners look on food as their friend. Dieters look on food as the enemy.

While dieters are engaged in hand-to-hand combat with food, runners are on a high—eating to their heart's content.

While dieters fast, runners load. While dieters count calories, runners can't get enough.

ARE YOU OVERFAT?

When you step on your bathroom scale, the weight registered is the sum of two body components: lean body weight plus fat. Lean body weight—bones, skin, muscle, vital organs—is an asset. Within limits, the more, the better. But excess fat is a hazard to your health.

What you need to know is not whether you are overweight but whether you are over*fat,* for it's an abundance of fat that puts us at risk for unnecessary illness and premature death. A high percentage of body fat ranks right up there with high cholesterol and hypertension in increasing our tendency toward coronary disease.

But your bathroom scale gives no indication of body fat. Nor will your family physician. Doctors have been trained to assess weight based on "ideal weight charts" using height, age, and body frame. These benchmarks can be misleading, however. Going by the chart alone, a very muscular person with little fat—someone like Arnold Schwarzenegger, for example—may be told he's too heavy, based on height and weight alone. Yet someone else with an acceptable weight for his height may carry a higher-than-acceptable percentage of that weight in the form of fat.

There are accurate ways to measure body fat, but most are expensive, cumbersome, or difficult to perform. So they haven't made their way into a doctor's office. I once purchased skinfold calipers to use in my medical practice but never became adept at taking measurements. I finally put them back in the box and never used them again.

Fortunately, there are tests for body fat percentage that you can actually do yourself with no more than your bathroom scale and a tape measure. They were devised by physiologist Jack Wilmore, Ph.D., a long-time researcher in the study of body composition. These methods are based on common observation: In men, excess fat tends to accumulate at the waist. In women, it tends to collect in the hips.

Using this knowledge, Dr. Wilmore developed two methods of determining body fat percentage—one for women, the other for men. Both tests require only two simple measurements—height and hip measurement in women, weight and waist measurement in men.

If you are a man, note your weight in pounds. Then measure the girth of your waist (at the belly button) in inches. Make sure the tape measure is perfectly horizontal. If you are a woman, determine your height and hip measurement in inches; the hips should be measured at their widest point. Using your two measurements, refer to the following chart, reprinted from Dr. Wilmore's book *Sensible Fitness*, to estimate your body fat.

Draw a line between your two values. It will intersect a line listing your approximate fat reading. According to Dr. Wilmore, men should measure between 12 and 17 percent body fat, and women, between 19 and 24 percent. Doctors consider anything above the upper readings for each sex obese, to some degree.

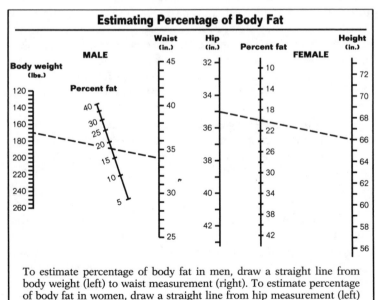

Estimating Percentage of Body Fat

To estimate percentage of body fat in men, draw a straight line from body weight (left) to waist measurement (right). To estimate percentage of body fat in women, draw a straight line from hip measurement (left) to height (right).

Men who run typically have 10 percent body fat, and world-class male runners usually drop below 6 percent. Women runners average 5 to 10 percent higher than men with similar training. Extremely low levels of fat can cause problems in women. For example, women who drop below 18 percent may stop menstruating or develop other difficulties.

Your body fat percentage is a most important statistic, and these simple tests determine it quickly. They are not precise enough to satisfy scientific research. But they are sufficient to let you know if you need to do something about your fat.

HAVE A CUP OF COFFEE

There are a couple of more nutritional points to consider before you have the full picture. Whenever I hold a running clinic, the question of caffeine is bound to come up. "Is there any benefit from taking coffee before a race?" someone will ask. My answer has always been "It gets *me* to the line."

I have never been a scientist about caffeine. I have ignored the evidence, pro *and* con. Drinking coffee or some other drink containing caffeine has always been the way I jump-start *my* engine in the morning. Life does not get under way until my first cup of morning coffee.

On race day, my standard operating procedure consists of coffee on arising, followed by a diet cola on the drive to the race. Runners have been described as people with energy, dedication, and discipline. I like to think I share in those qualities— but not before my cup of coffee. Coffee takes me out of my drowsy, half-awakened state and transforms me into someone eager to get on with the heroic quest.

Coffee lovers are familiar with these early-morning effects. Even before the cup is in hand, hearing the coffee perking and smelling its aroma impel me to rise and face this new day. Once I've drunk that first cup, the world is ready to be conquered, and I am equal to the task.

These psychological effects of caffeine cannot be denied. It does away with what the psychologists call "task aversion." I am no longer thinking of reasons not to run the race. I am willing and *wanting* to join my friends at the starting line of this agony-to-be.

Exercise physiologists, however, look beyond these familiar effects. They are interested in caffeine's effect on performance. Will caffeine lower a runner's time in a road race? This is also the question that concerns runners who would not otherwise drink anything containing caffeine before a race. Those of us who do depend on caffeine suspect it also helps our time, but we don't care whether it does or not.

Some years ago, Dr. David Costill reported experiments suggesting that caffeine made more fat available for energy in running. If so, this would conserve valuable muscle glycogen, needed during the later stages of long-distance runs.

Initially, this notion caused quite a stir. Dr. Costill stated that this was a research experiment and not a recommendation to use caffeine. The upshot of the controversy was a loss of interest in further study of the effects of caffeine on endurance performance. Then, at an American College of Sports Medicine meeting, two reports (one from Sweden, the other from Canada) revived interest in the possible benefits of caffeine for distance runners and cyclists. The cyclist study was done at the prestigious Karolinska Institute in Stockholm. Eight cyclists were given 9 milligrams of caffeine per kilogram of body weight (mg/kg)—about the amount contained in 20 ounces of coffee—1 hour before one time trial, and an inactive look-alike 1 hour before the other. They exercised to exhaustion at 78 percent of their VO_2 max (maximum oxygen uptake), which is about marathon pace for a runner.

Muscle glycogen was measured during the time trials. The caffeine group used less glycogen during the first 15 minutes and also had more glycogen left at the point of exhaustion. The investigators concluded that the caffeine spares muscle glycogen during the first 15 minutes. Thus, a greater amount of glycogen is available in later stages.

The running study came out of the University of Guelph in Ontario. Seven elite runners exercised to exhaustion at 85 percent of their VO_2 max, both on the treadmill and on an exercise bike. Consuming 9 mg/kg of caffeine 1 hour prior to running increased their endurance time to 71 minutes, compared to 49 minutes with the inactive substance. The investigators also noticed that caffeine increased adrenaline output. Mild elevations occurred prior to a run, but major changes took place during exercise.

These reports should be viewed in context with the considerable research being done on carbohydrate-loading before and during races. Many of those studies have shown improved performance and increased time to exhaustion by supplementing the body's sugar stores. Some experiments suggest, however, that once muscle glycogen is used during a race, no replacement drink will replenish those muscle stores.

It now appears that caffeine may be the final ingredient in assuring maximal performance. The distance runner, for a variety of reasons, needs to carbohydrate-load before a race. But he or she *also* needs to take in a certain amount of carbohydrate at regular intervals during the race. And most likely, the runner has to add at least one more item to that program before the races begins—caffeine.

My body knew that all along.

DRINK ALCOHOL IN MODERATION

During my talks (and earlier in this book), I frequently refer to The Alameda Seven, a summary of the lifestyle practices of a large group of happy, healthy, long-lived, and productive people in Alameda County, California. One of these seven rules is: Drink moderately.

Quite often, someone in the audience questions this advice. Am I suggesting that moderation is better than abstinence? Am I urging nondrinkers (including the questioner) to start drinking?

Heavens no! But close to 90 percent of Americans already drink. Hence this admonition of moderation. The experts, who may not be in agreement as to what constitutes the upper limit of safe drinking, are in accord on the safety of two drinks a day.

There is also fairly convincing evidence that moderate drinkers have an advantage over total abstainers with regard to coronary artery disease. Surveys of large groups of people reveal that two-drinks-a-day people have significantly fewer heart attacks than those who do not drink at all.

But on the whole, it's better not to start drinking at all. Those who never take that first drink will not be exposed to the hazards that face every new drinker.

First is the very real possibility of going beyond moderation and becoming a problem drinker. Almost half the men who drink have alcohol-induced problems at some point, even if temporarily, and at least 10 percent go on to become alcoholics.

Alcohol intake can vary from sharing a toast at the holidays to being totally down and out and in need of treatment, from taking a sip of sherry at Christmas to drinking a fifth of whiskey—or more—a day.

The danger to the moderate drinker is that two drinks will be the floor rather than the ceiling. I lived through that very real possibility. A neighbor of mine, who was in Alcoholics Anonymous, once told me "George, you are one drink away from being an alcoholic." I'm not sure about that, but I was probably one drink away from being a problem drinker.

I was saved, I suspect, by running. My first year as a runner, my alcohol intake plummeted. I averaged little more than a beer a month. Other factors aided in my escape from this danger—one being the severity of my hangovers. With the way I felt the morning after, I couldn't even *conceive* of taking a drink in the immediate future. I was further protected by the discipline of my profession. As a doctor, I was on duty every other night and every other weekend for my entire professional life, so I was afforded few opportunities to destroy myself.

For whatever reason, I never reached the point where alcohol meant more to me than the problems it created.

6

Adapting to Your Surroundings

Why terrain, heat, and traffic serve as a training ground for champions.

THOUGHTS ON THE SEA

The late Ruth Orkin, a photographer who lived on Central Park West, captured film images of the year as it appeared through her window on the 14th floor: the park at sunrise. The park at dusk. The city at night. The seasons as they appear in the Sheep Meadow. She called her photo essay "A World through My Window."

I see a world through my window on the third floor of the seashore guest house in New Jersey that we've made our home. I live at the ocean's edge, and the ocean, instead of Central Park, reflects the world. Here, the wind is more important than the season. The cycles of the moon are more of a factor than the equinoxes. And the sky is a participant in every picture my window presents.

I have become an expert on the sea. When I look at a seascape, I am a different person from when I look at any other art. No longer deferential, I am sure when I see success or failure. It is, I suspect, a most difficult subject to paint. And in some respects, I doubt that a painter can succeed. Unlike a landscape, the sea is always in motion. A painter freezes this action and, in effect, removes the very essence of what we see.

I recall once seeing an attempt to cope with this mobility in a film shown at the Whitney Museum of Art. It was a continuous videotape of the surf, just one wave after another breaking on the shore. Someone had discarded traditional art in an effort to show that the sea can only be represented by ceaseless energetic motion.

It is this energy that I see every day, but in different guises. At times, the power of the sea is awesome—during the height of a northeaster, for example, or a typhoon I once weathered on a destroyer off the coast of Japan. When I attempt to enter the surf the day after such a storm, I never feel less in command of my existence.

Perhaps those memories prompt me to look at the calm and peaceful expanse I see today and still see the power that is present. For now, the ocean is a sleeping giant. Tomorrow it may well give me another glimpse of the disinterested and enduring forces of nature.

The sea is seldom the same. Each morning when I awake, I look at an ocean that is different from the day before and the days before that. Wind and tides and cloud influence the water before me. Color and texture and surf vary with the breeze and the sun and the time of day. The ocean has moods much like my own. Sometimes happy, sometimes depressed. Sometimes placid, sometimes upset. And because it shares half my horizon, it shares in my moods as well.

When the day is beautiful, the ocean is beautiful. But when the day is overcast, the ocean offers no solace. The sky becomes gray, the ocean grays below it. The wind shifts offshore, and the day turns cold and the ocean uninviting.

Living by the sea is like living with a person. The sea is not a single self. It has many selves. One day it is a lake, the surf a mere ripple. The next day it is a raging being, waves breaking a hundred yards out and the water threatening to take away beach and boardwalk.

This morning, I run south on the boardwalk, with the sun off to my left and slightly in front of me. The sea is an impressionist painting, with innumerable dots of light flashing off the water. I am gazing at a world that seems to be in the process of creation—not the stark reality of the ocean but the beauty it contains.

I reach the bridge that would take me to the next town and turn for home. Now I am running with my back to the sun. I now see the ocean in the north light. Gone is the impressionist painting. I am looking at an etching. Every feature clear and sharp. The waves no longer dappled dots of light, but focused patterns of energy. Every detail in place. The blue waves building to a crest emphasize the sudden whiteness when they break. In the space of minutes, I have gone from the contemplation of beauty to the recognition of the ceaseless activity going on within and about us. Merely by changing direction, I find in the same ocean, in the same surf, two different messages, two different images, two different relationships with the world around me.

What is true of the ocean is true of all of nature. Runners who are looking for new courses merely have to turn around and run their course in reverse. They will be surprised at how different familiar surroundings now look. We usually depend upon the seasons to do that. Spring and fall, winter and summer open our eyes to different aspects of life around us. They help us cope with the ebb and flow of our interest and energies. They are therapy for boredom and a remedy for self-doubt.

My ocean does this for me daily. Its ever-changing face makes me feel as if I am seeing it, and perhaps life, for the first time. And all the while it is waiting for me. Then, still breathless from my finishing sprint, I plunge in and find a peace and refreshment for my body to match what I have found in my mind.

MAKING A MOUNTAIN OUT OF A SANDPILE

It's early morning at the shore, and I am running on the soft, yielding, uneven sand of the beach. I began this run as I do most every day, heading south on the boardwalk to the Belmar bridge: I ran at a "thinking" pace, my body enjoying the warmth of the morning sun, my mind occupied with the thoughts flowing through my head. All very pleasant, indeed, until I turned for home.

Then it was off the boardwalk onto the beach, and this mile of running in the sand. The lovely setting of beach and ocean and sky in which I run always had one deficiency—no hills. But I now realize that sand can be a substitute for hills. Simply by descending from the boardwalk, I can encounter a "hill" as long and as high as I please.

The sand on our beach is excellent for resistance training. Farther south along the coast, past Atlantic City, the beaches are as hard and flat as the streets. Miles spent on them are no different from miles on the roads. But here the sand is soft and yielding. Running on our sand is like trying to climb out of a pit. It becomes what all resistance training should be—an uphill struggle.

When people learn we live on the ocean, they quite often ask me whether I run on the beach. My usual answer has been "Only to have my picture taken." Beach running is a photo opportunity few editors can resist. But in the real world, training on the beach has hazards that cause injuries. The slant near the water stresses the uppermost foot. The soft sand can overload the calf and the Achilles complex. And the heavy going can become downright unpleasant. The most feared event in our area is an annual 4-mile beach run which seems like twice that and has been described as an experience rather than a race.

Almost all the runners who pass our house run on the boardwalk. A few run on the ocean road, apparently finding the level asphalt more to their liking. Only quite rarely do I see a person running on the sand. For myself, I have come to realize that beach running is a valuable addition to my training, and now when people ask me do I run on the beach, I answer, "Of course."

And I do. First I run south on the boardwalk for an easy 20 minutes, then turn back and start slogging through the sand. I call it "slogging" because beach running is slow going and not very graceful. The harder I push, the more ground I lose. I am like one of my patients with a leaky heart valve. Each time the heart pumps out the blood, a significant amount flows back. The heart has to do more work per beat. And the sand makes me do the same.

Within seconds, my perceived exertion goes from comfortable to hard—and continues to escalate. Within minutes, I am reexperiencing the discontent and fatigue of the annual beach race. My quads are burning, my breath coming in gasps. The pier that marks the end of my run isn't getting any closer. This mile or so on the beach is as difficult as the worst hill I have ever faced.

The runner's nightmare is a coach's delight. The great Percy Cerutty trained the equally great Herb Elliott by having him run sand dunes until he was about to drop. Marty Liquori has said that running on the beach is the reason he was able to break the 4-minute mile as a senior in high school. The beach, it appears, can be the breeding ground of champions.

What the beach is breeding mostly is the burn in my quadriceps, the muscles forming the front of the thigh. I learned about the burn from an exceptional hill runner. He told me he increased his speed going up a hill until he felt the burn; and then held it there. He believed that the burn represented a buildup of lactic acid; and he had to teach his body how to deal with it.

Bikers are also familiar with the burn. It occurs when riding in too high a gear. Veteran bikers maintain a constant tempo, then raise or lower the gear to maintain the effort. I've had a friend ride up next to me and say, "George, lower your gear and it will be easier for you." And I reply, "I don't want it to be easy. This is my hill work."

Even at its best, hill running is torture. One reaches the crest wobbly legged and hungering for air. The beach is no different. I can, of course, walk if I care to. But even in training, there is victory or defeat. So I push on. When I finally reach the pier, I feel as if I couldn't take another step. I have to bend over, my hands on my knees, gasping for air.

Afterward, I have the good feeling that follows great effort. A run that began at a pace so automatic it freed my mind for thinking turned into one in which my body was purged of past sins and prepared for tasks to come. In a short 40 minutes, I have experienced two completely different rewards of running. I've gone from effortless ease to dogged acceptance of pain and exhaustion. One is aesthetic; the other ascetic. Running as art, running as discipline. This was a run not only for speed, endurance, and strength but for body, mind, and spirit as well. My boardwalk and beach make me more than a runner; they make me whole as well.

RUNNING AWAY FROM CARS

Now that I have access to the boardwalk for my daily runs, I no longer worry about the runner's worst enemy, short of heat and heart disease—the automobile. For us runners, who have learned to deal intelligently with summer weather and narrow coronary arteries, running in traffic is the most dangerous thing we do.

On the few occasions when I run the roads, I do so like a fighter pilot—with my head up and my eyes moving. I know when the odds are against me, and I try to equalize them. I never run at night. I never run on the right side, with traffic. I seldom run two abreast. Statistics show those are the actions that have serious consequences.

These statistics make sense to anyone who has logged considerable miles on the roads. Running with my back to traffic makes the real danger—cars coming from the rear—invisible to me. I lose control of my own safety. Lower visibility at night significantly decreases reaction time for both me and the driver. Running alongside another runner puts me farther out in the traffic stream and more likely to be hit.

Even when I follow these precautions to a tee, I remain wary of two types of drivers: the old, and the young. "In the extremes of life," my physician father used to say, "you see the extremes of tuberculosis." Well, in the extremes of life, you also see the extremes of driving. The old drive too slow, the young drive too fast. The old are too rigid. The young are too reckless.

Older motorists tend to hold course. Most drivers will veer away somewhat when they see me running toward them. But not the elderly. Even if there is no shoulder, nowhere for the runner to go to get out of the way, the older driver is not likely to deviate an inch. If the approaching car is going relatively slowly and the driver's head can barely be seen above the steering wheel, I go on red alert. I am prepared to bail out if necessary, knowing I'll get no latitude from whomever is behind the wheel.

Young drivers are a much more serious threat. They tend to be impatient and in a hurry. They are also living out fantasies in unnecessarily powerful cars. Their specialty is passing other cars at high speed. Should they do this coming toward me, although the noise and velocity can be alarming, they pose no threat. It is when they come from behind that my life is in danger. Now they are in the passing lane—my lane—with me unaware of their presence. My survival depends on luck. They are usually upon me before they are aware of my presence. I have had several alarming incidents of this nature and have no desire to repeat them.

How best to avoid these potentially fatal encounters? Avoid two-lane roads where passing requires sudden, high-speed maneuvers. In such situations, I now know that the absence of cars up ahead means the monster cars behind me are likely to gun their fuel-injected overhead cams and pass anything in their way. In other words, when there's nothing up ahead, I look out for something coming from behind.

One other dangerous situation occurs when running against traffic. Drivers making a right turn into traffic look to the left, but very seldom do they look right. Unfortunately, the right is where I'm coming from, and I am, for that moment, invisible. Unless I know this and act accordingly, I am likely to be hit by a driver who will be as surprised as I am.

The best rule for safe running is to run defensively. It is not that runners must view everyone driving a car as the enemy. But hard-earned experience has taught me that people are largely unaware of the destructive potential of the machines they drive. Out on the roads, I am unwilling to trust any driver to keep me alive and well. That's my job.

105

HEAT CAN KILL

Despite all we have learned in recent years about heatstroke, runners continue to die from the destruction it wreaks on the human body. These deaths are due to two factors: first, the failure to take the necessary precautions to avoid heatstroke; and second, incorrect management when it occurs.

Precautions against heatstroke are the responsibility of the runner. The protocol to prepare for heat stress, especially encountered in competition, is well established. It includes training in hot weather, carbo-loading, hydrating with fluids, and running at an appropriate pace. During the race, water should be taken at regular intervals as well as splashed or sprayed over the body.

When I run, I wear a painter's cap in which I place a bag of ice cubes, and I continually soak the cap with water. I never pass a water station without stopping to drink two full glasses and pour one over my head. Wherever there is a hose, I run through the spray, and I carry a cup in the hope that I can fill it with water. And I purposely run 15 to 30 seconds per mile slower than my usual time.

These practices have become so common among runners that the number of heat injuries sustained in races declines each year. Nevertheless, there are always some runners who push too hard, don't take time to stop for water, or cut corners in other ways. These are mainly highly motivated recreational runners or newcomers to the sport, not veterans. And they are the ones who collapse with heatstroke. Typical symptoms include dry skin, dizziness, headache, thirst, nausea, muscular cramps, and elevated body temperature.

Heatstroke can be a catastrophe, but it need not be. Despite the seriousness of the situation—it's potentially fatal—correct medical care can and will save the day. And by correct care, I mean the type provided by disaster teams at two of the biggest races in the world run in high heat stress conditions—the Sydney City-to-Surf Race in Australia and the Atlanta Peachtree Run in Georgia, held in July.

While we continue to see random reports of people succumbing to heatstroke, the Sydney medical team has supervised 200,000 runners without a death from heatstroke. In a nine-year period, only two patients were even hospitalized.

There is good reason for this—immediate treatment. Dr. Rowland Richards thinks his Sydney group has arrived at the correct way to treat heatstroke and the correct place to do it: *at the race site.* Getting a heatstroke victim to a hospital wastes precious time, risking delay in diagnosis and treatment. John R. Sutton, M.D., professor of medicine at McMaster University in Hamilton, Ontario, Canada, agrees: "Hospitalization may be the very worst approach, especially with subjects whose vital organs are cooking at 107° to 109°F."

That, in a nutshell, is the problem. Fatal heat injury is the result of prolonged exposure to high temperatures. The Sydney physicians are able to reduce initial core body temperatures, taken rectally, of 107° to 109°F down to 100°F in as little as 50 minutes, on the average. This is achieved by applying instant cold packs over the neck, armpits, and groin, along with rapid intravenous rehydration, in every runner with a core temperature of over 100°F. If low blood sugar is suspected, 50 cc's of 50 percent glucose is given intravenously. "Failure to follow this routine," says Dr. Richards, "could result in serious consequences, including death."

Fortunately, in the one instance in which a heatstroke victim was not given this therapy (a misdirected ambulance was 40 minutes late, *then* took him to the hospital), the runner did survive.

The Atlanta medical team works on much the same principle. Again, the emphasis is on cooling. Joe Wilson, M.D., the physician in charge, stresses the urgency of bringing down the temperature as quickly as possible. Often this is all that need be done. Within 30 minutes, patients are usually alert, no longer nauseated, and able to take fluids. If not, intravenous fluids are started. And as in Sydney, no runner has ever died from heatstroke at the Atlanta race.

After reading Dr. Richards and talking with Dr. Wilson, I realized that preventive measures are important, but nowhere near as important as adhering to a tried-and-true protocol aimed at rapidly reducing core body temperature. A heatstroke is a heatstroke. A runner can do everything right and still push himself or herself into a heatstroke as severe as one incurred by an untrained, unacclimatized beginner. At that point, the runner's life may depend on on-the-spot treatment by an experienced disaster team.

"What is required," says Dr. Sutton, "is an immediate diagnosis, followed by rapid cooling at the site of race. Every moment's delay may worsen the outcome. It is no longer acceptable to have some amateur 'ad hoc' arrangement."

The facts bear that statement out. When we have amateurs running in hot-weather races, we should not have amateurs treating them.

Even the presence of the best professional on-site disaster team should not keep you from doing your homework, however.

(OVER)DRESSING FOR THE HEAT

It's a beautiful early spring day—the sun already high in a cloudless sky, the temperature an unseasonably mild 65°F. I'm out for my daily run wearing sweatpants, a turtleneck with a T-shirt over it, gloves, and a ski hat.

A runner passes by and calls out, "You're overdressed, Doc." Of course I am. If I were in a race today, I would wear nothing but shorts. But I'm not racing. I'm preparing to race. I'm training my body to handle the heat that is coming on the heels of this lovely day.

Overdressing is the simplest way to simulate the heat stress that is present in a hot-weather race. Two weeks of this sort of training and I'll be ready, no matter how high the temperature on race day. My body will learn what it must do to preserve homeostasis and maintain performance.

The distance runner operates best when the outside temperature is 45°F and skies are overcast. Under those conditions, body heat dissipates as quickly as it's produced. However, with each degree above 45°F, the body uses energy getting rid of excess heat stress. The runner does this mainly through sweat, with help from convection if it's breezy and the wind is head-on. But if the wind is blowing at 8 miles per hour and coming from behind, the runner is a cocoon of heat, which adds to the load.

Training in heat is the first requisite in avoidance of heat syndromes. Next I must take steps to prevent dehydration and thereby to maintain my blood volume. When blood volume drops below a critical level, I begin to succumb. My temperature regulation fails. Heat exhaustion or heatstroke may occur.

In monitoring my body to prevent either heatstroke or heat exhaustion, I need to know two things before and after I run: my weight, and my rectal temperature. The difference in weight before and after the run will tell me how much I usually sweat on a hot day. The temperature tells me if I have made the necessary adjustments in preparatory training and replacement of perspiration.

You lose about 1 pound for every pint of fluid lost through sweat. So if I drop 2 pounds during a run, that means I've sweat out 1 quart of fluid. I can make up for that loss by replacing that amount, taking about 10 ounces at the start and 10 ounces every 20 minutes.

If the rectal temperature remains high despite training and fluid replacement, I must adjust in my pace. I shouldn't aim to set PRs in hot weather anyway. A considerable part of the cardiac output is diverted to the skin to dissipate heat—thereby lessening performance.

Today is the first day of a summer of running. If I want to race well when I'll be wearing very little, I must train wearing too much.

QUENCH YOUR THIRST—AND THEN SOME

Summer is here, and the water fountain is back in operation on the back porch of our beach house. On these hot, humid days, runners are regular visitors to this little oasis. They interrupt their miles on the boardwalk to refresh themselves with the clear, cool water, then move on.

The water fountain was my wife's idea. She believes that no one drinks enough water. And she's right. Half of what is the matter with us now, and most of the terrible things that will happen to us in the future, are due to not drinking enough water. We don't follow the time-honored prescription of eight glasses a day to flush out our systems. And runners are prime offenders. They lose more fluid than they take in. For the runner, water loss is continuous and inexorable. We breathe out water, we sweat out water, we lose it through our kidneys. While we carry enough fat to run on for almost a week, and have enough air available to go indefinitely, we can lose water at a rate that can incapacitate us in as little as an hour or two.

As a matter of fact, the average person (and certainly the average runner) is usually in a mildly dehydrated state. We cannot rely on thirst to tell us when to drink. "Listen to your body" is a rule that works in almost every instance—except with thirst. Thirst is a sensation that lags behind the body's needs. Thirst is an unreliable reporter. So fluid balance is an area where common sense takes precedence over body wisdom.

I first learned this when I was an intern. I did my own laboratory tests and soon found that most patients' urine had a high specific gravity, a sign that the body is concentrating urine to conserve water. Most patients, I discovered, drank a little less water than they needed. Later, I saw a report that even patients with kidney stones, who were specifically instructed to drink more water than their bodies told them to, also had urine with high specific gravity. If this is so, what about the runners going by our beach house? Usually, they are dripping with sweat, their T-shirts sopping wet. Some look as if they just stepped out of a shower. If they began their run with a fluid deficit, they are certainly risking dehydration problems further on.

Most of the boardwalk runners do forget to take fluids before they start. By the time they reach our house, they're like Samuel Coleridge's Ancient Mariner—"Water, water everywhere, nor any drop to drink." They are ready to appreciate the refreshment one gets from clear, cool water.

Obviously, runners should consume enough or even an excess of fluid before beginning a run. The most accurate way to determine this is to check the specific gravity of the urine. In my medical practice, I used a urinometer, which is no more than a glass tube that holds the urine and a glass measuring device you float in it. There is also a test tape made by the Ames company that can be dipped into the urine and then read directly. The goal is a specific gravity reading of less than 1.010.

Having sufficient fluid aboard makes everything easier. The runners who use our fountain have come to know they feel better if they drink water about every 30 minutes. Otherwise, their performance suffers. When dehydration occurs, body temperature rises, greater demands are made on the heart to dissipate heat, and the runner faces the possibility of heat exhaustion or heatstroke.

So pay special attention to fluid intake. Drink enough before the run. And rest assured, water brings relief without bloating. Also, taking time out from a race to stop for a drink will save time later. The runner who stops for water will run faster and longer than those who are in too great a hurry to make a pit stop.

I make my own pit stops at the water cooler—the first just before I start, ten solid gulps; the second when I return with the sweat dripping off me. With the second fill-up, the water has a special quality. It reminds me of another water source in my youth. In my teens, I played golf in the summer on a course that had a spring on the 13th hole. I remember it was a par three, the tee high on a hill, and we hit out over some woods to the green below. In the woods on the path to the green was a spring with a constant stream of water. By the time we reached the spring, we were hot and sweaty and dusty and tired. We would take turns with the ladle, savoring the cool, satisfying taste. Stopping at that spring was always the highlight of our round. At the time, I couldn't think of a drink that could compare to it.

But now I've found something almost the equal of that golf course spring—our beach house water fountain after a long run on a hot summer day.

REPLACING THE SWEAT DEBT

To spell out three salient points about running distance races in hot weather:

1. Distance runners usually do not take enough water before and during a race to cover their losses.
2. Women runners respond differently than men to hot weather and high humidity. They sweat less, and their faces get red.
3. The harder the race, and the more fluid I lose, the more likely I am to have cramps and/or diarrhea.

A report from the University of Limburg, in the Netherlands, lends support to all these observations. The Dutch researchers studied 114 novice runners who trained for one year to compete at the 25-kilometer distance and then in the marathon. They found that runners do not take enough fluid, that women do indeed sweat less than men, and that gastrointestinal symptoms increase with the level of fluid deficit.

Sweating volume was determined by measuring weight loss, which averaged 5.4 pounds in men and 3.3 pounds in women, amounting to an average loss of body weight of 3.4 percent in men and 2.6 percent in women. It appears that both male and female runners did not take enough fluid to maintain fluid balance. In many instances, their losses were enough to diminish performance and put them in danger of heatstroke.

The amount of water weight these runners lost averaged almost 90 ounces of fluid for men and 45 ounces for women—roughly anywhere from 1½ to 3 *quarts* of liquid. To make up for the deficit, the runners should make nine water stops, with men drinking 10 ounces of water at each stop and women drinking 5 ounces. Women should then douse themselves with another cup of water to make up for their relative lack of sweat.

At first glance, the women would seem less vulnerable to the heat because of their smaller fluid deficit. But actually, less sweating makes them perhaps *more* liable to heat complications, because they're less able to dissipate heat. Studies by Dr. Oded Bar-Or at McMaster Hospital in Hamilton, Ontario, Canada, have shown that women's sweating rates do not double at puberty as men's do. Hence they have only half the sweating rate of the men running the same marathon. Other research indicates that women require a higher core body temperature to initiate sweating. So wetting themselves down frequently helps women runners cope with this physiological distinction. We know that in extreme instances of people incapable of sweating (a condition called anhidrosis, in medical terms), continuously wetting the runner down will maintain body temperature at reasonable limits. Women runners don't have to go to such an extreme, but the principle holds.

The Dutch investigators also discovered, as have I, a relationship between the amount of fluid lost and the incidence of gastrointestinal distress. The higher the fluid loss, the higher the likelihood of gastrointestinal complaints. Almost 80 percent of runners who lost more than 4 percent body weight through dehydration had gastrointestinal symptoms. Why that happens is a matter of speculation. Perhaps it's due to an excess of a substance known as prostaglandins in the intestinal tract. We do know that anti-prostaglandin drugs like ibuprofen are extremely helpful in relieving postrace cramps and diarrhea. But if it *is* the prostaglandins, what causes this excess? No one knows.

We do know that in many instances, runners have loose bowels due to intolerance of a particular food—milk, eggs, wheat, and so forth. However, when 80 percent of a specific segment of runners (in this case, those losing 4 percent body weight) develop symptoms, they must be violating some general rule of the body. Whatever the mechanism, however, drinking enough fluid apparently can prevent it.

WEATHER WATCHER

It was early morning at a TV station in Oklahoma City. I was waiting to be a guest on the sort of program that begins the day in most large American cities: general news, local news, sports, the weather, and a couple of guests promoting local events.

The weatherman was showing me how he prepared his segment of the show. The weather has become high-tech in presentation as well as in prediction. He had two computers that he used to set up his charts and graphs, the satellite photos, and the jet stream indicators. And then, with just a few minutes to air time, he stood up and started for the door. Then he turned back to me and explained, "I'm following the first rule of reporting the weather: Look outside."

"Look outside" is the meteorologist's version of the classic Greek axiom "Look inside." When I report on another sort of weather—my internal climate—I look inside. If I don't, I may make the mistake of assuming that the external data of my existence reflect what's going on inside of me. A satellite photo of my professional life shows that all is well. My domestic radar picks up no rain that will fall on my parade. And my social barometer is rising and assuring me of another perfect day in a perfect life.

We all know people whose lives appear to be like that—nothing but fair weather at home and at the office, not even a cloud to mar their day-to-day activities. If you compare their lives to days, a weatherman might rate them among the "year's ten best."

But their lives may not really be as sunny as they seem. In *Adaptation to Life*, George Vaillant admits that judging who is successful in life is quite difficult and certainly controversial. Perhaps only God knows. But next to him would be ourselves. And as with weathermen, the first rule is to look inside.

What I must scrutinize is not what I have or what people think of me, but who I am. True, there is a self determined by possessions and public opinion, and the inner self may reflect that success. But it need not. Only people quite close to me could know at what cost to my personality this success has been achieved. No one, not even myself, might be aware of the inner turbulence that accompanied this having and getting. Inside, the barometer is falling, the small craft warnings are up, and nasty weather is filling my subconscious—while all the external information is telling me I am living a long, happy season in the sun.

My own observations of the weather are immediate and personal. When I awake in the morning, I immediately can see what kind of a day it is—and a look at the weather vane on the house next door tells what kind of a day it will be. If the wind is from the west and the sun is shining, I know it will be one of those very special days at the shore.

Unfortunately, I don't also look inside of me to see my personal weather. Without a thought to my internal climate, I rise to start another day. I am too busy living my external life to spend time on my inner one. If I was asked if I am happy, I would probably answer, like any Irishman, with a question: "Now why would you think I wasn't?" Why, indeed. If you inspected my life using only facts and figures, you might well be reassured that I am indeed happy.

But that may very well not be the case. Only looking very deep inside—so deep I have difficulty reaching down, so deep the thought that emerges is, in Ortega y Gasset's expression, covered with seaweed—only there in that darkness can I tell whether my sun is shining and my wind is from the west.

7

Training to Run Longer, Faster

*How to be your own coach—
from one who knows.*

COUNT MINUTES, NOT MILES

A few years ago, in a column complaining of having to run races measured in kilometers, I wrote, "We think in miles. We train in miles. We should race in miles." Now that I'm seventysomething, I would like to amend that statement: "I think in minutes. I train in minutes. I race in minutes."

In recommending an attitude that ignores distance, I'm following rules set forth by exercise physiologists. They've always told us that the formula for achieving fitness is a matter of frequency, time, and intensity. The seminal work on fitness resulting from jogging, cycling, and walking, done by Michael Pollack, Ph.D., and his colleagues, makes no reference to distance whatsoever. Likewise, most fitness programs described

115

in scientific journals, as well as those in the popular press, are based on some formula of frequency, intensity, and time. You won't find any mention of mileage.

Since entering my eighth decade, I can apply this concept to my running. I now realize that running has never been a matter of distance. It has always been a product of intensity over time. The results produced by this equation range from comfort to pain and even agony. The distance I cover while this equation is played out is immaterial.

This wisdom evolved as my ability decreased with age. Expending the same effort (about 95 percent of max) for the same length of time, I cover about one-third less ground than I did ten years ago. A 10-K has become a very long race. In my early sixties, I would finish in 40 minutes. Now after 40 minutes I still have a mile and a half to go.

In the past, I considered the 5-mile run the optimal race. Now my 5-mile time is longer than I used to average for a 10-K. So I am inclined to favor the 25 minutes it takes me to run 5 kilometers.

Minutes also become important in hot-weather races. Meet directors usually put the first water stop at 3 miles. That's okay for the front-runners, but for me and my friends, who arrive at that point 25 to 30 minutes after the start, this is a long time. So I'm careful to drink as much fluid as possible just before the starting gun sounds. When I reach the water station, I drink twice as much as I would have in previous years, because now it takes me longer to finish the race.

But race directors don't control my training, *I* do. And I define my training in terms of time. When people see me out on the boardwalk, they often ask how far I am running. I usually answer, "45 minutes," or on some days, "An hour." My body knows time and intensity. It is not aware of distance.

I run these minutes at a comfortable pace, which allows me to spend most of my time in deep thought. But after running for an hour, my body begins to protest. I stop thinking, and I wish I were home.

When I was younger, I ran my hour at a thinking pace as well, but I covered a lot more ground. Then I knew how many miles a week I ran, but now I don't. I'm putting in the same number of minutes, however, as I have always done. My training formula hasn't changed.

The same phenomenon has occurred in my interval training. Two age groups ago, I did my repeat quarter-miles virtually flat out in 70 seconds. Now I go virtually flat out for 70 seconds and stop wherever I am. I am holding to the same time and intensity formula as before.

Injury prevention follows the same formula as fitness. The books tell us that the frequency of injuries rises rapidly when mileage reaches 40 miles per week. But injuries result from repeated impact at footstrike, and almost all runners, whatever their age or ability, take 5,000 strides on each foot per hour. So the critical factor in injuries is time, and injuries begin at 4 hours of training per week, not 40 miles.

Measuring runs in miles instead of minutes is a big mistake. Using time and intensity as guidelines will make the necessary adjustments as performance decreases with age. As I grow older, I find the running experience has not changed. The secret is to focus on logging in the same amount of time rather than the same number of miles.

WHY PUSH IT?

This past year, I spoke at a running clinic where I followed a panel of elite runners (three men and three women) who had outlined their individual training programs. The common denominator was weekly mileage. Every one of them averaged well over 100 miles per week.

When the runners stepped down and I took over the microphone, I said, "Forget everything these people told you. They're not like us. They're animals." Such training programs do not make champions, they discover them. They identify the "motor geniuses" (as miler Roger Bannister called them) who can handle great distances.

I had seen that happen in my college days. Coaches who turned out championship squads using repeated, long training sessions usually were actually just excellent recruiters. The talented athletes survived their training methods. The rest of their teams ended up sick or injured.

I never succumbed to the lures of high mileage. I was a member of two intercollegiate championship cross-country teams, yet I don't recall doing more than 5 miles in any given practice. When I returned to running in the 1960s, I found that the veterans I met trained 5 miles a day and ran a race every week. And that's been my practice ever since. Except for races, I remember running more than 10 miles only once or twice.

We forget that Roger Bannister broke the 4-minute-mile barrier on 5 hours of training a week. Bannister later wrote that an additional 10 seconds of improvement would require *four times* as much training.

Research by exercise physiologist Dr. David Costill confirms Bannister's theory. Dr. Costill found that the greatest percentage of improvement occurs with 25 miles a week. Close to maximum improvement takes place with 50 miles a week. Beyond this—training as much as 200 to 225 miles per week—resulted in no further increase in maximum oxygen uptake or the ability of the heart to pump blood. In fact, training beyond 50 miles a week *reduces* a runner's anaerobic strength (that is, non-oxygen-using effort), which affects speed and the "push" at the finish.

I discovered these truths on my own. First I found I could run a respectable marathon on 30 miles of training per week. By observing my colleagues, I also figured out that if I doubled my weekly mileage, I could probably improve my marathon time by 5 minutes. But in return, I would risk the staleness, illness, and injury that comes with excessive mileage.

I also had to deal with my body. It likes to run 45 minutes to 1 hour and not much more. When I ran a 10-mile loop, I always spent the last 15 to 20 minutes wishing it were over. By then, the optimum time for creativity, thinking, and problem solving had passed. My body wanted to be home. (And so did I!)

I refer to this productive time for thinking as the "third wind." A "second wind" occurs about 6 to 10 minutes into the run, which physiologist Walter Cannon described as "an almost miraculous refreshment and renewal of vigor." Then, about 35 minutes out, there is this third wind, and with it comes a rush of ideas, memories, and experiences associated with whatever topic I have chosen to think about.

I've never run a mile I didn't like. Every mile I run is productive, either for my body or for my mind. Every minute spent on the roads is a reward in itself. I follow my own schedule. I run because I *want* to, not because some expert tells me I have to. When I read about some of these high-mileage programs, I ask myself two questions: "What would I gain?" and "What is the cost?"

Any gain from high mileage follows the law of diminishing returns. The more miles I put in, the less I have to gain. The cost, on the other hand, has the opposite tendency. The more miles I log, the more illness and injuries are likely. Even worse, I run the possibility of staleness and burnout—frightening possibilities, since I am determined to run as long as I live.

Yet runners maintain the notion that the more they run, the better they will get. Some years back, I got a call from a woman runner who had sustained numerous injuries and periods of staleness and overtraining. "Am I fated never to be able to run over 70 miles a week?" she wailed. She wouldn't listen to my answer that her body would do best on a lot less.

Bill Bowerman, thought by many to be the greatest American coach, has made his views on the subject known: "The idea that the harder you work, the better you're going to be is garbage." Perhaps that's why those many unneeded miles on the road are called "junk miles," of little value to the body or the brain.

A SIMPLE FOUR-PART
SPEED TRAINING FORMULA

From time to time, great thinkers have pointed out that although things can be made simple, they cannot be made easy. So it is with French verbs, war strategy, and life itself. The same maxim can be applied to running. Running cannot be made easy, but it can be made simple.

I've simplified my running program, reduced it to notes on a few 3-by-5 index cards. My training schedule is based on one fundamental fact. My body has four speeds: my flat-out mile, my pace in a 10-K race, my average mile in a marathon, and my training rate. They differ by approximately 1 minute each—

that is, I average 5:30 in the mile, 6:30 in a 10-K, and 7:30 in a marathon, and I customarily train at an 8:30 pace.

I use this four-speed concept to plan my training and predict my race times. About three times a year, I strive for a peak performance. The rest of the time, I'm on a maintenance schedule, which is streamlined to 20 to 25 miles a week of slow distance running and a race every weekend. This is a sufficient amount of high- and low-intensity work to keep me at a level I consider acceptable by personal standards.

When I wish to peak—to compete in Boston, for instance—I increase my high-intensity training using intervals based on my best mile time. I do 220s, 440s, and 880s at the pace I should be able to hold for the mile. These workouts are the only way to improve my cruising speed. Then I add a little more distance to increase my endurance. The end product is better performance at all distances, from the mile to the marathon.

Improvement in all four speeds comes from those two types of training—high-intensity training to increase speed, and low-intensity training to increase endurance. The gains in speed are joined with the gains in endurance. Training for me is either fast (to develop speed) or slow (to achieve the stamina needed to hold that speed). There is nothing in between.

It's important to see the intimate connection between performance in the mile, the 10-K, and the marathon. Exercise physiologists have devised elaborate charts showing the relationships between times in each of these events. If you know what you can do in one, you can estimate your potential in the others.

Estimating time and speed is particularly important to first-time marathoners and to those marathoners who continually hit the wall and wonder why. Knowing your 10-K time can give you a realistic marathon goal. The physiologists' charts are much more precise, of course, than simply adding 1 minute per mile. Nevertheless, I find my method to be a good rule of thumb.

Olympic gold medal winner Frank Shorter has said that the best way to train for a marathon is to train for the 10-K race. I would take that advice still further and say that the best way to train for a 10-K is to train for the mile. The reason? The faster my cruising speed in the mile, the faster it will be in the longer races. As I become a better miler, I become better in both the 10-K and the marathon.

Of course, this assumes you're also running adequate long, slow distance—a minimum of 30 miles a week, in my estimation. Doubling that would probably give me maximum performance. However, injury would then become a factor. Staleness seems to relate more to unrelenting intensity than to distance. Witness those runners who have covered 30 to 40 miles daily in coast-to-coast runs. Peter Karpovich, Ph.D., the great exercise physiologist, had individuals working on stationary bicycles at low intensity for as long as they could. Every time they rode, they tried to break their previous day's record. The subjects tolerated the program well. Usually, severe exertion on one day was followed by a drop in performance the next, and it sometimes took a couple of days to recover. Despite such a strenuous schedule, though, the subjects showed no symptoms of staleness.

I use races as my high-intensity training. I run my 20 to 25 miles per week at my slow, comfortable, "thinking" pace. Then every weekend, I enter a race and push myself to the limit. This is excellent maintenance. Studies show you can cut your frequency by two-thirds, and your mileage by two-thirds, and maintain conditioning as long as you maintain intensity. I could cut my mileage to 10 miles a week and maintain performance, *if* I did those 10 miles at top effort.

Racing every weekend has assured me of a constant level of performance. However, unless I do speedwork and increase my mileage, I'm locked in to my present times. My present program guarantees me an injury-free performance with no threat of staleness.

THINK QUALITY, NOT QUANTITY

My program goes back almost 30 years, to my start in road racing. I took my cue from observing the old-timers in the game. Train 5 miles a day, five days a week, take a day off, and then race. Over the years, I modified this regimen, taking more and more days off, putting in one training day on the track doing interval quarters, but still racing every weekend.

At times, I've been astounded by how little training I need once I reach a peak. On occasion, I've limited my entire running program to one race a week, with no training in between. I followed such a schedule for as long as a month with no noticeable change in my racing times. I know of other runners who, for one reason or another, had to reduce their running to one race a week and had the same experience. One of my most formidable age group competitors ran only on weekends, 20 miles on Saturday and a race on Sunday. I rarely beat him.

It now appears that other runners have also discovered that "less is more." The Bare Minimum Track Club in Columbia, South Carolina, has followed a program much like mine with considerable success. Members have done measurably better in both the 10-K and the marathon despite reducing their mileage to about 30 miles per week.

The Bare Minimum program centers on a long group run on weekends and a track workout every Wednesday night. Members claim that some of their success stems from other features of their program. "Bare Minimers" have learned to "reel out" other runners, widening their lead gradually rather than surging ahead, especially in the beginning of a race. They can also be distinguished from other competitors by a "brook trout" expression on their face—totally relaxed, mouth agape— a look that accompanies top performance achieved with minimum effort.

Research, however, would credit the success of the Bare Minimum program (and mine) to our high-intensity training. A report in the *Journal of Applied Physiology* on the relative importance of duration, frequency, and intensity in aerobic power and short-term and long-term endurance emphasized the paramount role of intensity. In this study, runners began by training 40 minutes a day, six days a week, running as fast as they could. Then in three separate trials, they reduced either frequency or duration or intensity. When intensity was maintained, reducing frequency by one-third (running four days a week instead of six) or duration by one-third (28 minutes instead of 40) had no effect. Further decreasing frequency by two-thirds (two days a week) and duration by two-thirds (15 minutes instead of 40) had only minor effects over a 15-week period.

However, running less intensely while maintaining both frequency and duration caused significant decreases in oxygen uptake, heart function, and long- and short-term endurance (all measures of physical capacity). What's more, these drop-offs occurred rather rapidly—within five weeks of changing the training program. The conclusions: Frequency has little effect on running ability, and duration is important only when reduced by two-thirds.

All this suggests that runners can cut their running programs significantly and still run as well (or even *better*) than usual. First take off three days a week. On the remaining four days, run for a total of 3 hours. This may include a short distance race, a workout of interval quarters, and a couple of longish runs—45 minutes to 1 hour at an easy pace.

This is not to say that frequency and duration are unimportant. But it points out that high-intensity training— namely, interval training and races—is the key to getting the most out of one's ability with a minimum amount of time.

There are hazards, of course, to such programs. While high mileage can lead to injury, high intensity may lead to staleness. My difficulties have rarely been due to overtraining. More often, they've been due to over*racing.* So from time to time— and especially after setting a PR—I find it helpful to back off from interval workouts and to substitute leisurely runs to allow my body to recoup.

There is a time, as the French farmers say, "when the land must sleep."

THE BODY KNOWS BEST

Frank Shorter tells a story about training with one of those wrist devices that records the pulse. He was running at his usual pace, only to discover that his pulse was well below the rate prescribed for his level of training. Ignoring the proven accuracy of his body—he had once run on demand within a second of his anaerobic threshold—Shorter increased his speed until his pulse conformed to the theoretically prescribed rate. But it took him *two days* to recover from the workout.

My mail suggests that many runners have similar experiences with target heart rates. Most, however, tend to err on the high side, reaching levels considerably higher than their predicted age-adjusted maximum heart rate (220 minus age). They are comfortable at heart rates considerably in excess of the prescribed 70 percent of maximum used for training.

Nevertheless, the target pulse rate has become one of the immutable tenets of the running and fitness movement, part of the dogma of fitness. People deeply involved in their exercise program tend to be preoccupied with their target pulse rate. Beginners in running, walking, aerobic dance, and other activities are invariably taught to monitor their heart rate right from the start. If Rodin were alive today and were to do a statue representing the man of the 1990s, he would have his hand on his carotid pulse, not on his chin.

Taking a target pulse rate is not only misleading, it's unnecessary. When I started running over 20 years ago, I took no screening tests. I never took my pulse. I simply suited up, went for an hour's run, then toweled off and resumed my work. I listened to my body and did what it told me to do. Now fitness is high technology. We have all sorts of sophisticated equipment to make us fit—and ways to monitor the pulse while we do it. We are admonished to exercise at a certain percentage of our age-adjusted maximum heart rate to achieve results.

These formulas are based on statistics that have normal, built-in variations. For instance, the predicted maximum pulse rate (MPR) allows for a variation of plus or minus 19 beats per minute. When you work at 70 percent of the MPR (the level that supposedly ensures fitness), there is another deviation of plus or minus 17 beats.

"It should not be at all surprising," writes Edward Winslow, M.D., of Northwestern Medical School, "that some normal, healthy subjects are quite comfortable exercising at heart rates up to 36 beats higher than we recommend utilizing this 'rule of thumb.'" Exercise physiologist Bob Holly, who directs the adult fitness and rehabilitation center at the University of California, Davis, agrees: "A person's heartbeat may be 30 beats higher or lower than predicted."

So, then, it's best to go back to the first rule in managing physical activity: Listen to your body. The body has information that is technologically inaccessible, data that your pulse rate will not reveal. When we bypass the body, we ignore a basic form of knowledge, our physical intelligence.

Don't let your brain get in the way when you exercise. Rely on your body's own rating of perceived exertion (RPE), also known as the Borg scale, developed by Swedish physiologist G. A. V. Borg a few years ago. The Borg scale of perceived exertion is fast replacing target heart rate monitoring as the preferred way to gauge exercise intensity.

When using the Borg scale, keep in mind that perceived exertion is a gestalt that takes into consideration everything about the external and internal milieu—the time of day, the

---

Rate of Perceived Exertion

Here's a simple scale to help gauge exercise intensity, based on a widely used rating scale devised by exercise physiologist G. A. V. Borg. Rate your effort on a scale of 6 to 19, based on how you feel physically. If you exercise at a "comfortable" intensity or slightly higher, chances are you'll be within your target heart rate zone. To approximate your heart rate during exercise, just add a "0" to the number in the column (left) that reflects *your* perceived exertion level (right).

Rating	Perception of Effort
6	
7	Very, very light
8	
9	Very light
10	
11	Fairly light
12	COMFORTABLE
13	Somewhat hard
14	
15	Hard
16	
17	Very hard
18	
19	Very, very hard

last time you ate, the level of emotional stress, heat, humidity, terrain, and a variety of other factors—and comes up with a simple answer. This pace is comfortable, another is not.

The body does not speak English, but it tells us exactly how much we are doing. "This is comfortable," it says, and it will brook no argument. There is no better way to find out what's comfortable for *you* at any given time, in any given running situation.

EXPLORING THE COMFORT ZONE

I was running along the ocean road when a young man came alongside me and asked, "How fast are you going?" It was apparent that he expected an answer in minutes per mile. It was the question of a novice. I gave him the answer of a veteran: "Comfortable."

My pace is not a matter of the distance I can cover or how fast I can go. I measure my intensity with my body, not with a stopwatch or mile markers. I dial my body to "comfortable," not knowing or caring how many minutes it takes me to run a mile.

In the beginning, I was like the runner who now questioned me. I wanted to know exactly how far I had run so I could calculate my speed. I would count laps on a track, or even retrace my route in a car so I could be quite sure.

At times, this scorekeeping was frustrating. I would lose count of the laps—I used my fingers and got mixed up going from one hand to the other—and not know whether it was 20 or 21 or some such number. So I gave up and concentrated on running at a comfortable pace.

So when this particular runner caught up to me, I honestly didn't know whether I was running 8-minute miles or 10-minute miles. Nor did I care. I had put my body on automatic pilot and had taken off into my head. This was my thinking pace, one I can hold indefinitely. Some days, my thinking pace is faster than others, but it's *always* comfortable.

I hoped the runner would linger to chat, but he sped on, and I let him. Trying to stay with him would have been hard going for me. Rarely does my training require that level of effort. Training is for thinking or talking, for contemplation or conversation. Neither can be accomplished if I step up the pace.

There is no place in my daily runs for pain or shortness of breath, no room for pushing to the limits. Those tortures come every weekend—they're part of every race. My weekday runs, however, are time-outs from all stress, physical and mental. They become retreats inside myself or opportunities for a revealing talk with a friend.

On another occasion, after I finished an out-and-back run on the boardwalk with another runner, he said to me, "That was the shortest hour I've had in some time." We had run at a pace that was congenial to communicating our thoughts to each other. We were in the world on the other side of sweat. There, competence and self-esteem make me feel at my absolute best, and thoughts and feelings ordinarily too private to utter leap spontaneously from my lips. Once, when I ran an hour with my daughter, we had the longest and best talk in memory.

How fast must I go to enjoy these unexpected gifts from running? Do they only occur at a certain speed, at so many miles per hour? No. All I need do is run at a comfortable level: fast enough to open up the sweat glands. Fast enough to dispel my worries about the world. Fast enough to enjoy the workings of my body. And slow enough to let me observe the world around me. Slow enough to escape into the world within.

By a comfortable pace, I don't mean just *physically* comfortable. Comfort is related to my mental and emotional state as well. Comfort has to do with my entire person. When I am comfortable, I am finally at peace with myself. I am an animal happy in its own habitat. I have said "yes" to myself and to life.

EXERCISING OF OPPOSITES

It was reveille on the campus of a boys' prep school in northwestern Connecticut. The 300 runners attending a week-long running camp were beginning to stir. Two of us were already out on the cinder track, up on the playing fields. I was jogging leisurely in the outer lane while Pete Squires, the camp director, churned out 80-second quarters in the inner lane.

Squires, who had an outstanding season a few years earlier, was training hard for a comeback. Bill Dellinger, a former Olympic medalist now coaching in Oregon, was noting Squires's times for him and encouraging at each lap. I was plodding along at half Squires's speed. He kept passing me every other lap. I was running slower, at the speed the great Alfie Shrubb had once recommended for long-distance runs—one at which you could fall asleep. I was lost in a reverie.

Meanwhile, Squires was powering his way around the track, his muscular calves prominent as he went by. He was, I am sure, monitoring everything going on in his body—form, breathing, pace, footing. He couldn't for a moment absent himself from the continuous, stride-after-stride performance of his task. For Squires was playing with the edge of maximum effort. He was training at the anaerobic threshold, where work is being done without sufficient oxygen and lactic acid begins to build up in the muscle.

I was running in a completely different physiological environment. I was propelled by oxygen, using fat for energy, and running at a pace that was probably only 50 percent of my maximum capacity, a gait where all those metabolic functions used in the anaerobic work are on hold.

So it went, Squires passing me again and again while I occasionally passed Dellinger standing with the watch. Finally, Dellinger called out to me, "How far are you running, Doc?"

"An hour," I answered.

When I am doing aerobic work, I simply put in my 60 minutes and get all the benefits. No need, then, to log miles and add them up at the end of the week or month. I add the hours instead.

So there we were, putting in time. Each working at a different level of intensity. Each having a different running experience. He concerned with his body; I concerned with my mind. He out to rewrite the record book, me out to rewrite the book of life.

I came back to reality to see a middle-aged man jogging beside me.

"May I run with you?" he asked.

"Of course," I said. Then, looking at my watch, I remarked, "I have 10 minutes to go."

The man was a research chemist. We started to talk about anesthesia I had been given for some minor surgery. Then, quite suddenly, the hour was up. Time for me to quit.

He commented, "At that pace, you forget you're running." It's true. When you train at a speed just slightly faster than walking, the running becomes automatic.

Don't misunderstand me. There are days when I'm doing just what Squires was doing then: weekends, when I reach that anaerobic threshold and cross it. Saturdays, when pain fills my consciousness—when I use everything I ever learned to maintain my pace and keep the pain to an acceptable level. But this morning run is the base of that racing performance—and the reward. Paradoxically, the slower I run, the faster the time goes. The 10 minutes that flew by in conversation with the chemist is a sample of the hour that flies by in conversation with myself.

Squires had finished his miles. I had finished my minutes. Dellinger had put away his watch. The camp was now alive with activity, the lovely campus filled with runners converging on the track.

Later that day, a 50-year-old sprinter who happened to be a very successful dentist told us that this was not a running camp, it was a survival camp. We, all of us, were runners for life, and we were being taught how we could do that. Squires and I, each in our own way, were taking those lessons to heart.

SPECIFIC IS TERRIFIC

An axiom in physiology says that exercise is specific—that is, when a person trains for one sport, there is little carryover to another sport. When I began to compete in triathlons, I found that each event requires training of its own. Undoubtedly, each activity helps me to preserve overall fitness. But swimming does not improve my cycling, nor does cycling help my swimming, and neither are of benefit to my running.

To improve in any one of these three disciplines, I have to practice. The particular muscles used in each event have to be trained in distinct functions: speed, power, and endurance. In order to be sure that I am indeed conditioning the same muscles, it's essential that my form remain the same, whether I'm running, swimming, or cycling.

This comes naturally in cycling and swimming. Whether I bicycle fast or slowly, my form is the same, my tempo is the same; what varies is effort. I am always cycling in my racing style, even when doing endurance practices. In cycling, I alter only one thing—the gear ratio. Whether I'm striving for speed, power, or endurance, identical muscles are being used.

It's the same with swimming. "We swimmers are always working on technique," a national masters champion once told me. "Whatever the distance, we try to simulate the same mechanics." Whether I swim for speed or endurance, I'm preoccupied with perfecting my form. I have no meditative swims where I forget about my breathing and arm entry, or about my hand action and staying high in the water. As bad as I am at swimming, each stroke I take follows the pattern I've been taught.

This, however, is something that many runners (including myself) have yet to learn about running. When I am out on my long, slow endurance runs, I forget all about racing style. I stop using my big toe to push off. I don't maximize my forward thrust and lift my knees. In short, I don't use my racing form as I do in cycling and swimming.

Clearly, better runners *do* follow racing form. Once, in Cincinnati, I saw a runner jogging slowly toward me and recognized instantly from his running style that it was Billy Rodgers. Whether Rodgers is running a mile or a marathon or jogging around the Charles River in Boston, he has the same form. He trains the same muscles all the time.

This is a lesson we lesser practitioners of the art should keep in mind: Training form should not differ from racing form. And racing form should be the way we run in a short race, say the 220 or 440. In order for running long, slow distances to help us run long, fast distances, we should be using the identical muscles we use for speed while training for endurance.

We know that we need speedwork to develop speed. And we have learned that the same running style must be maintained throughout a race. We have not taken the next logical step—to use the same racing form and the same racing muscles when we do our distance training. Speed, power, and endurance each require different programs.

And finally, exercise is specific to the muscles you use in the specific event. If I change my running form, I may be practicing the same sport and presumably developing a specific function, but it may well be for muscles I will not use in the race.

I'm guilty of this myself. When I do my intervals, I am definitely in the speed mode. But on 10-mile runs, I am a plodder, running heel to toe. I am not training the muscles I will use in a weekend 10-K.

When I see our local running champion Harry Nolan out on his 10-mile training runs, he uses much the same form I see him use while winning our Monday night 5000-meter races at nearby Lake Takanassee. The same biomechanics come into play. Only the effort is reduced.

It makes me wonder what my previous long, slow training had been worth. I had been shuffling along, using muscles that were of little use except to keep me shuffling along. No wonder an old adage says that "long, slow distance trains you to do long, slow distance."

Should you accept my reasoning and care to put this theory into practice, there is one caveat. Racing technique is highly stressful to the Achilles tendon and attached calf muscle. So the transition to total use of racing form in training should be made gradually, preferably on a forgiving surface, like a dirt path.

REST AND RECOVERY

There are two philosophies about interval training. Some runners go for frequent repetitions with short rest periods. They believe the time between the runs should be kept to a minimum. Others subscribe to a different program: high-intensity activity punctuated by longer rest periods.

It's been my custom to do my 220 or 440 meters, wait 2 minutes, and then do another repeat. This routine made me set very modest goals. If I were to do ten repeats of 440s or 20 repeats of 220s, I had to run a good deal slower than if I made a flat-out effort.

But I have friends who subscribe to a completely different type of interval training. They think high intensity means just that. Therefore they lower the repetitions, increase the speed, and increase the rest period. Their repeat 220s and 440s are done close to peak effort. The recovery takes considerable time, so there is a prolonged rest period between these efforts.

With proper rest, intervals involving high-intensity training can be done all day. A report on Russian rowers outlined just such a program. Crews went for 8 hours doing quality repeat sprints when given sufficient recovery time.

What this amounts to is allowing blood lactate levels, which rise with intense effort, to return to acceptable limits. Research on this "return to baseline" has provided some guidelines on the amount of time needed for recovery. One such report came from a British group using a portable lactate analyzer to determine when an individual runner had sufficiently recovered to do another repetition. The investigators studied an international sprinter over 19 weeks of training. They collected blood samples at 1-minute intervals after a 255-yard sprint. The lactate level peaked at 4 minutes, then fell to 7 mmols (a high but acceptable level) in 8 minutes.

Eight minutes was thus established as the interval between the sprinter's four repeats of the 255-yard sprint. He was then followed over the course of his training, and his blood lactate levels peaked progressively earlier and lower.

In doing 440s, the time required for blood lactate to return to near baseline levels would be somewhat longer. One experiment measured maximal exercise for three separate 6-minute bouts with a 10-minute recovery between loads. It took blood lactate 15 to 20 minutes to return to the 7 mmol level and 40 minutes to return to the resting level. Recovery was speeded by continuing light effort.

Apparently, if you want to do high-intensity interval training, you must do fewer reps and greatly increase the time between them. Rest time is an individual matter, but as a rule, resting for 8 minutes between 220s (and 16 minutes between 440s) should suffice.

One last bit of advice: Whether you opt for high repeats and a short rest period or intense effort with prolonged rest, it seems best to walk or jog slowly during the wait. This speeds removal of lactate from the blood.

WHEN YOU'RE RUN-DOWN, REST

The road to staleness is paved in several stages. Overtraining follows a typical pattern. Acute fatigue is the first symptom. If the athlete rests, recovery is rapid. However, continuing to train despite fatigue leads to exhaustion, with a loss of enthusiasm, lethargy, poor concentration, and sleep problems. Unless training is suspended, exhaustion may persist for weeks or even months.

Usually, staleness follows a protracted period of high-intensity training. It can also follow a series of races run one after the other. For many athletes, the first sign of staleness is some sort of respiratory infection. I have raced myself into colds on a regular basis.

In *The Lore of Running,* Dr. Timothy Noakes tells of several nationally ranked runners who experienced typical symptoms of training-induced staleness. One runner complained of lethargy and ill humor, coupled with a loss of enthusiasm for running in general and for competition in particular. He was also sleeping poorly at night, his morning pulse had increased by ten beats per minute, and he had to move his bowels more frequently than usual. He said his legs felt "heavy" and "sore," complaints that persisted from one training session to the next.

Another runner reported that three weeks after his best marathon, he ran one 30 minutes slower, had a persistent sore throat, slept poorly, and lost his zest for life.

Once a runner gets that stale, he or she needs complete rest for up to six weeks. Continuing to train will only prolong the time the athlete needs to rest. I recommend using the hour a day usually spent in training to take a daily nap. The object is to reestablish homeostasis—to return all body systems to equilibrium. Although we are not sure exactly what body changes cause staleness, it does appear that the body is in negative nitrogen balance (that is, tissue is being broken down rather than built up).

Another mark of staleness is a cortisol deficit that occurs in response to running-induced hypoglycemia, apparently due to exhaustion of the hypothalamus, not poor adrenal response. The hypothalamus is partly responsible for producing many

133

other hormones, accounting for the many and varied symptoms experienced by athletes run down by overtraining.

Staleness can't be treated, but it *can* be prevented. The best way to do that is to closely monitor symptoms and body rhythms. A drop in afternoon weight, drinking more liquids in the evening, and going to bed later and awakening earlier are all warning signs. A rise in the morning pulse and respiratory rates, or an increase in training heart rate, also suggests the runner is on the verge of overtraining.

Another test is a comparison of the pulse rates when lying and standing. When you stand, pulse rate always increases somewhat. But it goes up considerably more if you're overtrained. (This measurement dates back to the 1930s, when it was part of the Schnieder Test, designed to diagnose fatigue in fighter pilots.)

CAUSES OF CHRONIC FATIGUE

Mild fatigue should respond readily to rest. Any accompanying symptoms—insomnia, muscle ache, lymph gland enlargement, and lack of sex drive—usually subside. Running can be resumed in 2 or 3 weeks (6 to 12 weeks for more serious burnout). At times, however, fatigue is persistent and not due to overtraining. In these instances, diagnosing the cause of the fatigue can be tricky. A physician who treats a runner must be aware of conditions to which runners are prone. And he or she must remember that runners react differently to diseases or drugs than nonrunners do.

I can cite classic examples of the various conditions that can cause chronic fatigue and poor performance.

Iron deficiency. A young female runner who had been a state champion as a junior in high school ran poorly and complained of fatigue as a senior. Routine blood tests were all normal. She didn't have anemia, but she *was* iron deficient. Her serum ferritin—a measure of iron stores in bone marrow—was extremely low, a clear sign of iron deficiency. (More on iron deficiency later in this chapter.)

Mononucleosis. A 52-year-old male runner with chronic fatigue had extensive laboratory tests, all within normal limits.

Symptoms of Overtraining

Training conscientiously is one thing; *over*training is another. If you are experiencing a fair number of the following signs, you may be staler than you think. Take a few weeks off and *rest*.

Emotional and Behavioral Changes

- Loss of enthusiasm and drive
- Desire to quit
- Lethargy, listlessness, or tiredness
- Peevishness, irritability, or anxiety
- Depression
- Inability to concentrate at work, or poor academic performance
- Changes in sleeping patterns (awakening at night, difficulty staying asleep)
- Low sex drive

Physical Changes

- Drawn, sallow, and dejected appearance
- Drop-off in performance
- Inability to complete training
- Gradual weight loss
- Increase in early-morning heart rate of more than five beats per minute
- Abnormal rise in heart rate on standing and during and after a standard workout
- Slower recovery in heart rate after exertion
- Feelings of dizziness when standing from a seated position
- Feelings of heaviness in the legs
- Sluggishness that persists for more than 24 hours after a workout
- Muscle and joint pains
- Persistent muscle soreness, increasing from session to session
- Swollen lymph glands
- Gastrointestinal upsets (especially diarrhea)
- Increased susceptibility to infections, allergies, headache
- Minor scratches that heal slowly
- Absence of menstrual periods (amenorrhea) in menstruating women

He had no fever, weight loss, or loss of appetite. But a test for mono was unmistakably positive.

Thyroid deficiency. A 45-year-old man with persistent fatigue and poor performance was found to have hypothyroidism. Thyroid medication promptly improved his performance.

Thyroid overactivity. A world-class female runner noticed a drop in her performance. Running a 6:30 mile felt like a 5:30 mile. The cause? An enlarged, overactive thyroid.

Eyedrops. A middle-aged runner was putting in considerably fewer training miles for almost three years. He finally suspected the cause might be the eyedrops he was using to reduce ocular pressure. When his physician changed the drops, he returned to his original training distance. (Note: Runners should never stop taking a prescription medicine without checking with their doctors for alternatives.)

Beta blockers. Any number of runners receiving beta blockers for coronary artery disease, hypertension, or mitral valve prolapse have experienced fatigue and exercise intolerance. One runner said, "Putting me on beta blockers was like putting on lead boots." If you suspect your heart medication is affecting your performance, check with your doctor. Perhaps the dosage can be adjusted.

Coronary artery disease. In runners with known coronary disease (or several serious risk factors), exhaustion should be treated with great respect. It warns of impending disaster.

Anorexia. A world-class marathoner who was racking up high mileage plus eating a low-calorie diet experienced a rapid deterioration in performance. She lost a lot of weight, stopped menstruating, and virtually retired from running. After returning to a more sensible diet, her performance picked up.

Sinusitis. Runners who develop colds they can't shake usually have sinusitis. In my view, this is the most easily missed diagnosis in medical practice. To get a good picture of what's going on, the sinuses have to be transilluminated in a dark room—something rarely done during a physical examination.

Exercise-induced asthma. Persistently poor performance, especially during cold weather, can be due to exercise-induced bronchospasm. I experienced this myself some years ago, 6 to 10 minutes into a race. Using prerace medication resolved the problem. (More on exercise-induced asthma later in this chapter.)

Unlike nonrunners, the runner who develops fatigue almost always has a physical reason for flagging energy. Rarely is runner's fatigue due to depression, boredom, or inactivity, as is common among the general population. Doctors who treat runners for fatigue and exercise intolerance need to pursue the problem vigorously. Because unless a specific cause is found and treated, fatigue will probably persist.

GOING FOR THE GOLD, WITH OR WITHOUT ASTHMA

About two years ago, I had just passed the mile mark in a 10-K when I felt some tightness in my windpipe. I had some difficulty getting air in and out, as though my throat was somehow closing down. I tried coughing, but the feeling persisted. I continued running, coughing intermittently, and after a few minutes the tightness went away. I finished the race with no further difficulty.

From then on, this sensation occurred regularly when I raced. It always came on early in the race and cleared before the finish. Eventually, I realized that I had exercise-induced asthma (called EIA for short).

My experience with exercise-induced asthma is increasingly common among athletes, much to the surprise of people in sports medicine. Surveys indicate that *one out of ten* athletes has EIA, and this estimate may be low, since symptoms vary from one person to another and doctors don't always suspect the problem exists. My guess is that the 20 percent of our population with hay fever includes plenty of prime candidates for exercise-induced asthma.

No doubt many runners and athletes who cough or hyperventilate when they run never suspect that the problem is really due to exercise-induced asthma. In some runners, the only symptom may be "inability to improve." But even if they suspect they're experiencing asthmatic episodes during races, by the time they see a doctor, the symptoms will have passed, and they'll be breathing normally, even on pulmonary function tests.

Asthma is due to what doctors call "transient bronchoconstriction"—that is, temporary spasm of the bronchial tubes. Between attacks, the condition is undetectable. Therefore, the only way to diagnose exercise-induced asthma is to induce it with exercise. Running at race pace for 6 minutes (on a treadmill or outside the doctor's office) should and usually does trigger bronchoconstriction that can be detected in pulmonary tests.

Doctors know a lot more about what triggers exercise-induced asthma attacks than they used to. Cold, dry air is a frequent culprit. When running in cold weather, susceptible runners should take steps to heat and, if possible, moisten the air they inhale, such as wearing a ski mask without a mouth opening. This will also protect the face against cold air, which can trigger an attack even if not inhaled.

"Cold" is relative: It doesn't have to be freezing out to cause bronchoconstriction. So I start wearing a mask when I run as soon as the weather turns cold. I also make a few flat-out sprints before a race, to be sure I take enough time to warm up and (I hope) desensitize myself to asthma. I have a hunch that a brisk 440 would do the trick, but I'd hate to do that before the race.

Mainly, I rely on medication, a beta-agonist inhalant (a drug that relieves bronchospasm by relaxing bronchial muscles). I position the inhaler several inches from my open mouth, exhale normally, then take a deep breath of the inhalant, which I hold for 10 seconds. I wait a few minutes, then take a second puff. I do this 2 hours before a race, again 1 hour later, and then once more, 15 minutes before I go to the starting line.

If I follow this routine, asthma doesn't bother me during the race. When I don't use the inhaler right on schedule, I have difficulty breathing. I'm lucky: These simple measures work for me. I've met other runners with asthma who have had to do much more. Some are on cromolyn (a drug that reduces sensitivity to inhibiting histamine release), with or without the beta-agonists. Some are on daily oral therapy with theophylline (a muscle relaxant derived from substances found in tea leaves). Others may need cortisone by inhalation or even orally to resume normal running.

Asthma is extremely difficult to treat if the individual also has persistent sinusitis. Food sensitivities, irritants in air pollution, and airborne allergens can *also* contribute to the problem. Runners with EIA almost always need help from an allergist with considerable experience treating exercised-induced asthma in athletes, especially if they take cortisone.

Rest assured, exercise-induced asthma can be controlled almost 100 percent of the time. You shouldn't have to stop running. You shouldn't even have to settle for diminished performance. After all, some of the athletes who won medals in the Olympics have asthma!

The most difficult step in treating this condition is making the diagnosis. After that, the athlete should be home free. Effective therapy is available. All you need is a physician who knows how to handle the problem. (Note: Doctors warn against overdependence on inhalers. See your physician if you need more than two canisters a month.)

IRON, FOR WOMEN WHO RUN

My daughter, who exercises regularly, was in her early thirties when she began to feel tired and washed out. Instead of finishing her workouts with increased energy, she noticed increasing fatigue.

Tests showed her red blood cell count was normal, but her serum ferritin (an indicator of bone marrow iron stores) was only 10 micrograms, a level almost always associated with the absence of available iron in the bone marrow. She began to take iron supplements, and within a week, her strength and stamina returned.

What my daughter experienced was a typical case of iron deficiency. It's very prevalent, but it's also easily diagnosed and easily treated. It is *also*, in all likelihood, the most frequently missed diagnosis in female athletes. A red flag should go up when a woman runner complains of deteriorating performance.

I learned this years ago when I attended a symposium at Yale Medical School. The speakers that day emphasized four points:

1. Iron deficiency can be present without anemia. In fact, iron stores have to be almost totally depleted for anemia to occur.
2. Iron deficiency without anemia can cause a variety of symptoms, including excessive fatigue and exercise intolerance.
3. Correct diagnosis of iron deficiency depends on a bone marrow test to confirm a decrease in iron stores.
4. Iron deficiency without anemia is very common in women.

Since that convention in New Haven, droves of women have taken to athletics, particularly running. And they need more iron for the increased muscle mass, increased red cell mass, and the red cell breakdown that occurs with training. Otherwise, the result is deficiency or depletion of iron stores.

According to a review of the current medical literature, anywhere from 50 to *100 percent* of female athletes have this condition. One researcher has even suggested that *all* female athletes at the collegiate level take iron supplements.

One reason for this almost universally low level of iron stores (and the drop in performance that may ensue) is inadequate diet. Estimates suggest that 80 percent of American women are on iron-deficient diets. Surveys show runners' diets are particularly low in iron, especially the better-absorbed heme iron, which is found in meat, fish, and poultry but not in plant foods. One study of female runners put their daily intake of iron at 70 percent of the Recommended Daily Allowance (RDA) and their consumption of heme iron at only 50 percent of the national average.

Fortunately, as iron deficiency has become more prevalent, the diagnosis has become much easier. The serum ferritin test has replaced the less convenient bone marrow examination as a ready indicator of a person's bone marrow iron stores. Virgil Fairbanks, M.D., a hematologist at the Mayo Clinic, states, "In our experience, the serum ferritin assay has proven to be the most sensitive and specific diagnostic test for iron deficiency. Often it identifies iron deficiency when all other tests are normal."

Serum ferritin levels of 10 micrograms per milliliter or less are almost always associated with greatly reduced—*or totally absent*—bone marrow iron. But even levels below 50 micrograms should raise suspicions of iron deficiency, especially in men and postmenopausal women. If levels exceed 100 micrograms, it's unlikely the athlete's symptoms are due to inadequate iron stores.

Even if the diagnosis is uncertain, people with iron deficiency respond so well to iron supplements that they're worth a try. In one experiment, rats on an iron-deficient diet were able to run only 3 minutes on a treadmill, compared to a normal 16 minutes. When given an iron supplement, they were able to reach a normal running time within four days.

Why this profound effect on performance without any anemia? We are only beginning to discover how many metabolic functions depend on adequate iron supplies. During exercise, for instance, lack of iron results in an accumulation of lactic acid, our dreaded antagonist in seeking peak performance. Inadequate iron supply also leads to a decrease in the release of thyroid hormone. When that happens, metabolism slows, and energy levels plummet.

Unfortunately, it's difficult to get enough iron through diet alone, especially for athletes, who need higher-than-average quantities of this nutrient. Simmering sauces, soups, and stews in iron pots can add considerable amounts of iron to the diet. Doctors also recommend eating iron-enriched cereals. (Check for 100 percent of the RDA for iron on the box.) Or you can take iron tablets.

The important thing to remember is that anemia is the *last* stage of iron deficiency. By the time the red blood cell count and hemoglobin are affected, vigor and endurance will long since have vanished. My daughter's case is typical: deteriorating physical performance with a normal blood count and low serum ferritin. Diagnosis: iron deficiency. Response to therapy: prompt.

A CASE OF MUMPSIMUS

I've been racing for over 25 years. Almost every weekend, I compete at distances ranging from a 5-K to a half-marathon. Over these past two decades or more of running, I've never felt the need to cool down.

In college, I was taught to keep moving after a race. Seeing me lying supine and breathless on the ground always upset my coach. If I refused to move, someone was dispatched to get me up and walk me around.

When I became my own coach, I realized that both approaches were wrong. Walking does not help that terrible distress after a race. But lying flat is not the answer either. It's better than walking, but not much. The best position, I discovered, is kneeling with my elbows on the ground and my head between my hands. This prevents fainting (from low blood pressure) and promotes blood flow back to the heart. When the gasping and the pain subside, I put on a dry T-shirt, preferably a turtleneck, and my sweat suit. In all these matters, I follow my body's instruction. It chooses to rest. It prefers a certain position. It wants to stay warm.

Elite runners are masters of the cool-down. Front-of-the-pack runners tend to *continue running* after finishing a race. They're animals who take delight in further effort. I, too, am an animal, but a much less gifted one. I take delight in getting warm, then sitting in blessed peace and watching *other* people cool down.

If a case is to be made for cooling down, it has to do with reducing lactic acid in the blood. The difference in clearing this waste product of exertion is a matter of minutes, however, not hours or days. When I'm doing interval quarters, I keep moving, because it removes lactic acid and gets me ready for my next interval in a shorter period of time. When I'm not going to train again for 24 hours or race again for the week, subtracting 4 minutes from my lactic acid recovery time is of no importance.

The real and ever-present danger in the postexercise period is chilling. It is much more important to get into some warm, dry clothes after completing a race than to worry about movement. Even when I'm in peak condition, a chill can do me in. The next morning I wake up with a sore throat, a runny nose, and the prospect of a ten-day battle with a cold.

To me, the obligatory cool-down is a clear instance of mumpsimus—the migration of error from textbook to textbook. Mumpsimus originally described those changes in church liturgy that were inserted without authority or reason and then passed from one group to another to become accepted as sacred writ. The cool-down is one such ritual that has become part of conventional wisdom. Every manual on exercise states the need for cooling down as a given, so now it's one of the canons of exercise, although the original work substantiating this practice cannot be found.

Two reports on cooling down make for interesting reading. The first is from a Boston group on what they called the "Post-Exercise Peril"—serious arrhythmias that occur immediately following a workout. Presumably, these arrhythmias are triggered by elevated adrenaline levels, which the investigators noticed were considerable at the conclusion of exercise. This rise in adrenaline lasted for several minutes and was considered the vulnerable period. To minimize danger, the authors suggested two courses of conduct: (1) lie down, or (2) keep moving. Under no circumstances stand still. Blood will pool in the legs, and fainting may occur.

What this report suggested was that position was more important than motion. Staying put is fine, but being supine is not the answer. Lying flat speeds the venous return of blood and increases the load on the heart. Cardiac patients who complete exercise stress tests without experiencing chest pain frequently develop pain immediately if they lie down afterward. If they sit up, the pain disappears within seconds. Sitting reduces the load on the heart.

The second report corroborated the first. A Texas group also noted elevated postexercise adrenaline levels. Then they took note of what happened if subjects (1) kept walking, (2) remained standing, or (3) lay supine. Lying down lowered the supposedly dangerous levels of hormones immediately. Standing was not quite as effective, and walking was least effective. Five minutes of lying down was best, followed by walking, then standing.

So, what *is* the best way to recover from exercise? The answer is, Rest. This allows elevated adrenaline levels to drop to normal more rapidly. The next question is, Rest in what position? The answer is, Any position that prevents fainting and, at the same time, doesn't overload the heart. Sitting fills the bill. But if you feel really bad, nothing gives relief faster than the knee/chest position.

8

Running to Win

Doing your best is all it takes to be a real champion.

CREATED EQUAL?

The Declaration of Independence states unequivocally that all men are created equal. Yet every day I find reason to believe this to be untrue. I run a race, and half the field beats me. I attend a seminar and can't follow the reasoning of the speaker. I read a book, and I can't understand what is evident to others. Daily, I am instructed in my deficiencies. I do something, physical or mental, and realize how far I fall short of what other people accomplish.

Despite the Declaration, we apparently are not born equal. I can no longer aspire to win the Boston Marathon. I most certainly will not receive the Nobel Prize for literature. I am surrounded by people who know more, do more, and make more than I do. But like many others, I identify with *my* performance, not theirs. I *become* my marathon time. I become my latest book. I become the last lecture I gave. And of course, I see my failures.

I am all those things, of course. They are part of the self. They are the various ways I have of expressing who I am and what I believe, the manifestations of the mind/body machine that I am.

But I am more than a mind/body complex. I am a soul as well. I share with everyone on this planet one power infinitely more important than talent—*will*power. In this power of the soul, all of us are created equal. Each one of us is capable of the ideal or moral action that philosopher William James defined as "the action in the line of the greatest resistance."

Anyone who's so inclined can decide on ideal action. The will considers the question, "Will you or won't you have it so?" And in that decision, you can be the equal of anyone else. "Effort is the measure of a man," wrote James.

How well we know that. I am never content with contentment. I am uneasy when things go easily. "Don't take things easy," said Paul Dudley White, the great physician, "take things hard." Doing one's absolute best becomes the criterion.

"I am writing the best I can," said the author of some best-selling popular novels. "If I could write any better, I would. This is the peak of my powers." It matters little that she cannot write any better. It matters, more than life, that she is doing it with all her might.

Running in races has made this whole subject plain to me. I am thinking now of Palmetto Drive, the long, steep hill at the 5-mile mark of the Bermuda 10-K Run. For most of the race, I am running in the lee of a gentleman my age who's wearing plaid shorts. Just before the hill, I pass him, which puts me second in my age group. It's a short-lived moment of triumph, though. The hill suddenly puts urgent demands on my body. I forget the imperative of beating anyone in my age group (especially someone in plaid shorts!). Now it's just me and that hill. My legs are heavy and filled with pain. My breath comes in short gasps. I am bent almost double. The battle shifts. It becomes me against *me*, my will in a duel with my mind and my body, a contest with the part of myself that wants to stop.

All around me are runners engaged in the same struggle, pushing themselves as if their lives depended on reaching the top of this hill. The leaders have already finished. The race, you might say, is over. But not for us. A spectator who could see this race for what it truly is would see not bodies but wills straining to reach the crest. Here indeed is "action in the line of the greatest resistance," as James put it.

In speaking about the champion horse Tom Fool, jockey Ted Atkinson said, "He makes the effort and makes it more often." The uncrowned champions at the back of the pack do the same. Unconcerned with what others are doing, driven by the need to do our best, we make the effort, and we make it more often. And for those few moments, we become the equal of anyone on this earth.

WINNERS ALL

As I pass the 4-mile mark in a 10-K in suburban Chicago, the volunteer armed with a stopwatch sings out my time: 29:59. I am on a personal best pace, on a flat course, on a perfect day for running—46°F and no wind.

This is my maximum steady pace. My throttle is pushed to the floor. I am red-lining my way through these tree-lined streets. I will, I know, be able to sprint in the last 100 yards, but until then, this is the best I can do. I am at the edge of productive effort. There is a barrier of pain and fatigue and shortness of breath that propels me just this fast and no faster.

An exercise physiologist would tell me that I'm running at just about 95 percent of my maximum oxygen capacity. In fact, virtually every runner in this race is running close to his or her max. Whether at the head of the pack or farther back, every one of us is using the same level of effort and undergoing the same ordeal.

The difference is this: As I pass the 4-mile mark, the leaders are being cheered as they cross the finish line. I must endure this suffering for another 2 miles or more, while they sit around in their sweat suits. They are now comfortable and enjoying refreshments, while I have almost 20 minutes of torture remaining.

When I think of a race this way, I realize that those of us in the rear are more to be commended than those up front. The elite runners are excused after their relatively brief run, while those of us lagging behind have to fight the agony for an additional period of time. If effort is the measure of a man, as William James claimed, we "also-rans" more than measure up.

Viewed this way, the saying that everyone in a race is a winner becomes more than a cliché. It becomes an actual fact. If every runner is charged to give the maximum and *does,* the criterion is no longer where you placed but whether you stuck to it. Winning is being able to say "I didn't quit." When runners do their best, they all are equal. But the paradox is that those far back in the pack exceed the designated winners in the time they must endure the forces that would make them quit. So everyone is a hero. And none are more heroic than those deep in the flow of this struggle against time and distance and self.

This is why every finisher warrants applause, *especially* those farthest back. How does their 95 percent effort differ from the winners'? It doesn't—not in pain, not in fatigue, not in shortness of breath. In every respect, I race at the very edge of what I can handle, *and* I do it longer. Those of us who ran along with the leaders in years past and now are in the bottom third of the finishers know this firsthand. Today in Chicago, everything about the race is as it always was. I am in the terrible duel with the self, responding to the wordless information flooding my brain, intent on doing my best. But today, unlike years back, I must not only endure, but endure *longer.*

When I finish, I will stand at the end of the chute and watch as those who ran behind me come through. And I'll see that all are spent, some near collapse. No one has done less than their best. And their best is, in a real sense, better than everyone who finished ahead of them. They are winners and heroes all.

THE CALL TO HEROISM

This Monday night at Lake Takanassee, there is a 1500-meter race before the customary 5-K event. Eighteen runners have entered. I am one of them.

The oldest of the other runners is almost 40 years younger than I. But as we stand at the starting line, no one comments on the absurdity of my competing against them. No one remarks about my aging body. No one questions my reasons for entering a race in which I will finish far behind the person next ahead of me. No one asks, "To what purpose?"

They don't ask because they already know my answer, and theirs as well: "To be a hero." Whether 22 years old, 32 years old, or 72 years old, a runner enters a race to be a hero. But seeing a 72-year-old in a race elevates one's consciousness about the absolute connection between athletics and the heroic.

The writer who told us that and told it best is the Spanish writer Miguel de Cervantes. In *Don Quixote*, he took the epic, the story of the hero, and molded it into the novel, the story of the common man. He took the myths buried deep in the subconscious and placed them in the dust and dirt of the plains of La Mancha. He joined the reality of the present with the tales that go back to Achilles and Arthur and El Cid. In his saga, reality is represented by the people who regard Don Quixote as mad. They see an aging, infirm man on an aging, infirm horse, tilting at windmills. And they recognize that his supposed squire is a peasant, who himself realizes his knight is out of his wits.

The epic is the life Don Quixote is leading. The windmills are giants, and he heroically attacks them. The flour mill is a castle with an imprisoned knight, whom he attempts to free. Time and again, he performs valorous deeds. He is a bona fide hero.

In *Meditation on Don Quixote*, fellow Spaniard Ortega y Gasset points out how much Quixote teaches us about heroism. "It is," says Ortega, "the will to adventure—and here is the paradox. The will is real, but what is willed is not real. It differs from reality in that it has meaning."

Then Ortega scores his major point. "Granted that those giants are not giants. But what about giants in general? Where did man get his giants, because they never existed, nor do they exist in reality."

Heroes, according to Ortega, are people like Quixote who know we have to face giants, people who are not satisfied with reality. The hero perpetually resists what is habitual and ordinary. It comes out of a characteristic of human life, which Ortega calls "the will to be what one is not yet."

To lead a heroic life, we have to be, like Quixote, half in and half out of reality. The road race is my adventure. It is sport, which, like chivalry, has elaborate rules based on myths and our collective consciousness. It is an activity whose heroes are, if not superhuman, at least supernormal. By competing in a race, I become part of this myth. I leave the real world and enter another. And the person I become in the race comes back larger than life in the everyday world.

Why is it that of all the things I do this week or this month or even this year, I will remember this race the most? And why, of all the persons I have been, will I be most proud of the one who finished these 1500 meters?

There is no question that getting up every morning and doing your job is also a form of heroism. British writer W. Macneile Dixon makes that point in *The Human Situation*. For our lives to have meaning, they must pass muster, wrote Dixon. We must be loyal to ship's company. The human enterprise should not fail because of us.

At bottom, however, the call to heroism comes from the heart, not the head. Were reason in command, I would opt for passing muster and preserving the human enterprise. I would not be running this 1500-meter race. As I await the start, I know it is my heart that led me here. I am about to run a race against giants.

CHARIOTS OF FIRE

One of the early scenes in the film *Chariots of Fire* is a formal dinner for the incoming students at Caius College, Cambridge. In his welcoming speech, the head of the college tells the newcomers that they are replacing those who were lost in the Great War. Then he points to the pictures of these dead heroes lining the walls.

"Let each of you discover," he says, "where your chance for greatness lies. Seize that chance, and let no power on earth deter you."

Over the centuries, that call to the colors has been sounded by many wise men. It tells us not of the possibility of greatness but of its certainty, there for all of us. It's just a matter of discovering how we are to manifest it.

"A man must know he is a necessary actor," wrote Emerson. "Did he not come into being because something must be done which he and no other is and does?" No question about it—we are born to accomplish a certain task, bring our particular message, contribute our unique vision, bear our own peculiar fruit.

Nevertheless, the normal reaction is to put such thoughts aside. "The heroic seems too big for us," writes sociologist Ernest Becker in *Denim of Death*, "or we are too small for it." *Is* it big, or are we small? The heroic life is no more than the authentic life, one in which I take possession of myself and live by my own decisions and choices. Heroism begins with resisting the usual and habitual.

"Most people are other people," wrote Oscar Wilde. "Their thoughts are someone else's, their life a mimicry, their passions a quotation." How best to remedy this? To free one's self from this tendency? To resist good advice? To ignore the opinions of others? To refuse to pursue goals given to us ready made?

The two heroes in *Chariots of Fire* accomplished heroism through running. They defied public opinion, rejected good advice, and set their own goals. They seized their chance for greatness and attained it. This triumph of the body is not the whole story, but it tells us an essential truth: Through the body we can pursue our real and total self.

Most runners have made that discovery. The rewards of running are not merely physical. Training the body leads to training the mind and heart as well. The effort I expend in running is matched by the effort I devote to every other area. So running has narrowed the distinction between what I am and what I can be, between the actual self and the ideal self, between goal and reality.

What follows is the development of self-esteem. If runners possess anything to a greater degree than endurance, it is self-esteem, a most important quality. The Reverend Dr. Robert Schuller has studied self-esteem, which he calls "the human hunger for the divine dignity that God intended for us." He commissioned a Gallup Poll to determine its prevalence and effects on the American public. This survey showed that people with strong self-esteem are healthier, happier, and more productive than others.

Self-esteem results from the progressive development of the self into the heroic self we were meant to be. Wealth, ability, talent, and possessions count for little; of those, we already possess all we need. It's *effort* that brings us to greatness. My mind and imagination may have limitation, my industry need not.

The self-esteem earned through running has liberated me from the ruling opinions. It has freed me from comparison with others. I no longer think of myself as inferior or superior to anyone else, just different. My goal is the perfection of my unique and original self.

"The nature of man," wrote Aristotle, "is not what he is born as, but what he is born for." That has not changed, nor have we, since the time of the Greeks.

CLOCK-WATCHERS AT THE STARTING LINE

It's close to race time, and I'm standing at the starting line, along with a thousand or more other runners. Up ahead, toeing that line, are those who will run this 5-mile event in less than 30 minutes. Behind me are runners who will take almost twice as long to finish the race.

The starter announces: "There will be two commands!" And along with almost everyone in the race, male or female, young or old, talented or back of the pack, my hand goes to my left wrist. The gun goes off, and we all press "start" on our digital watches.

Since the late 1960s, running has evolved from a solitary activity into a mass participation sport. The ordinary individual has become an athlete. And the digital clock has become the symbol of this enormously important shift. Rarely will you see a runner, whatever his or her ability, without the obligatory digital watch.

The written instructions for runners at a recent race revealed just how universal the runner's timepiece is. The company taking photos of the runners crossing the finish line admonished: "Please don't look down at your watches—it spoils the picture."

Most runners automatically look down and press "stop" as they enter the chute. The reason is simple. The dominant concept in running now is time, so the focal point is the watch. And now the runner has the watch. That watch is responsible for the major changes we've seen in the sport over the past 25 years.

In my previous life as a collegiate runner, the coach had the watch. He told me what to do. All I had to do was respond, unthinkingly, to his orders. In races, there were no watches or mileposts to heed. In cross-country, the gun sounded, and we took off. The runner in front or behind was the only stimulus to speed up or slow down. Only the winner was concerned with finishing time. The others, like me, were concerned with placing and whether they would receive a medal.

The digital watch I wear has changed all that. Now *I'm* the coach. *I'm* in charge. I measure my leisurely endurance workouts on the boardwalk in minutes, not miles. I measure my high-intensity intervals in seconds, not quarters. As I've emphasized in earlier chapters, time and intensity have become the two important elements in my training program.

During a race, I now know my time at each mile marker and can alter my speed to match my ability and goals. I am truly a runner/coach. I can avoid the stupid mistakes I make when guessing my pace. A glance at my watch toward the end of a race tells me how much longer I have to suffer.

In many ways, I'm ruled by the watch. There was a time when I rebelled against this tyrant. For a short while, I refused to have anything to do with this instrument that had taken control of my life. Eventually, I surrendered and resumed the intimate relationship that has helped me achieve my personal best.

Sisyphus had his rock, and I have my clock. Every day in training, every weekend in the race, I face an unforgiving foe. If there is a difference between the runner I was and the runner I have become, it's due to a shift in my standard for success from the award ceremony to the watch on my wrist.

As I age with the sport, my running time becomes more important to me. I like to place among the leaders in my age group. I enjoy getting a trophy or a coffee mug. (*Especially* a coffee mug!) But what I remember most about a race is my time. And given the option of two different outcomes—one in which I would run poorly and still get a trophy, the other in which I would do a personal best but finish out of the money— I would choose the latter.

The watch has made me realize that the true competition is with myself. I run against the absolute best I can do, and my digital watch tells me whether I have done it. The other runners hold no terrors for me. By surging past me when my determination flags, they spur my battle with the clock.

As a consequence, running has become a positive sum game. Everyone can be a winner. I am not diminished in any way by runners ahead of me or increased by those behind. Everyone is locked in combat with their own watch.

Running also becomes the sport of the populace. Age, gender, disability become irrelevant to the final outcome. The contest, as Plato told us so long ago, is with the foe that is not only inside of us but part of us. The emphasis has changed from the running elite, competing for titles and trophies, to runners competing with themselves. Along with this shift has come a wavelike change in attitude, from an agonistic relationship with other runners to an agonistic relationship with the self— all brought about by the digital watch.

The late Charles McCabe, a longtime columnist for the *San Francisco Chronicle*, once said that the reason he became a columnist was that even in school, he wanted an immediate mark for whatever he wrote. So it is with me and my digital watch. It is my ever-present scorekeeper, ready at every moment to give me a grade for what I have done.

The digital watch is a guide to my training, a monitor in my race, and finally, in big numbers on the giant clock at the entrance to the chute, the judge of my efforts.

BACK TO THE TRACK

Now that I am a seventysomething runner, I've come face-to-face with a harsh reality—a severe drop in my performance. I am no longer the runner I was only a few years back. Exercise physiologists who study aging runners are well aware of this sudden decline in powers. Even the best are victims. A world-class runner, also in his seventies now, told me that every race he ran was a "personal worst."

My races are now the same as his. Quite abruptly, my unchanging life as a middle-aged runner changed. Moments into every race, the people I usually run with are far ahead. And as I get slower, the races get longer. The 10-K events seem interminable. And I now know clearly that the marathon is not an event for an old man.

The fact is, the longer the race, the older I feel. So I have taken that fact and come up with a logical corollary: The shorter the race, the *younger* I will feel. In this "crisis," the solution is to begin at the beginning, to return to what I did as a boy and become the runner I first was—a sprinter.

Later, in high school, I ran a respectable quarter-mile and even anchored a winning mile relay at the Penn Relays. So I had some speed. In college, I was deemed too slow for the shorter distances and eventually ran the mile.

When I once again took up running at age 45, I found that everyone was entering long-distance races. The marathon was the common goal. The great English runner Nick Rose once remarked about this phenomenon, saying: "Americans begin by training for a 5-mile, and as soon as they run one, start thinking, 'Marathon.' In England, we start with the 100-meter dash and then build on that speed."

I remembered Rose's comments as my times got slower and slower. Perhaps age, which had sapped my stamina, has left me with some speed and sufficient strength from my youth to make it last for a minute or two.

As a test, I entered a masters track meet and ran in the 100-, 200-, and 400-meter sprints. In the 100, I had to run against two gentlemen considerably older than I. This added to my prerace tension. I felt a hint of the excitement and not a little of the fear that preceded my races when I was in school. Suddenly, there was a sense of drama, with a very real possibility that an *81-year-old* would beat me.

He did—and so did the 76-year-old, who ran second! But I didn't care. I had felt that quiet before the gun and then the easy start—*too easy*, because I let them go and lost the race there. And even though I was two yards back at the finish, I knew that I still had some speed.

In the 200-meter event, I was positioned next to the 81-year-old, who was in the outermost lane. Again, I felt the tension concentrating in the pit of my stomach, peaking as the starter said "On your marks!" and receding with "Set!" This time, I went off with the gun, quickly attaining speed I had not known since my college days. Within a few yards, I passed my elderly rival, and the race became me against the clock. My aged colleagues were not up to this distance. That gave me a big boost, but not as much as the competence I felt and the speed with which I recovered.

Finally came the 400 meters—and another experience. "Work the first turn," a friend told me, "relax through the stretch, then turn it on." I followed instructions, not thinking that I was "turning it on" with another 200 meters to go.

Midway into the last turn, I knew I had made a mistake. My legs were already tightening up, my breathing too rapid, my arm action ineffectual as I headed down that final stretch. It was just as W. R. Loader described in *The Sprinter:* "Ahead of us stretched 150 mortal yards . . . I thought the race would never end. A boundless gray cinder desert seemed to lie in front of me. The finish was so far away it simply had no relevance." I felt all that. And fought all the way down those final yards, trying desperately to retain form and efficiency. "Would the finish ever come?" Loader asks. "Would the legs tie up first?"

And of course, the finish *did* come, and my legs tied up before I reached it. Again, recovery was swift. Within 2 minutes, I was comfortable. In 5, I thought I might even try it again. That's the wonderful thing about the sprints, the compression of experience and time. Toward the end of each race, I feel as though I'm running in slow motion, each second capturing some significant and memorable action of my body.

These races are great fun: the competence, the sensation of speed, the expending of total effort, the quick recovery. In less than 2 minutes, I experience all the rewards of a 5-mile race, with few of its drawbacks. Only in the final 50 yards do I feel the type of discomfort that predominates most of the road races I enter. My loss in speed is indeed less than my loss in stamina. On the track, I feel as fast as I was in my youth. But more than that, I feel at home.

155

How to explain this? The philosopher Paul Weiss once remarked that sport was man's effort to deal with time, space, and causality. As I see it, the sprints have to do with time, the distance races with space, and the field events with causality.

It's appropriate that both the young, who have all the time in the world, and the aged, who no longer have enough time, both turn to the sprints. There, time is compressed into an unforgettable moment. Old age, which appears to be a matter of survival (and therefore endurance), is not that at all. Time, not distance, becomes important. Life is no longer a marathon; it has become a 100-meter dash.

American poet Marianne Moore once wrote of the Harvard sculling crew, "Win or lose, their speed is marvelous." Sprinters of every age, be they 7 or 70 years old, live that truth in every race.

THAT TOUGH LITTLE MILE

Noel Carroll, a former Irish Olympian and still an outstanding masters competitor, has called for a return to "the mile."

"We have tried the marathon and the 10 kilometers, so why not the mile?" he writes in *The Irish Runner*. "The mile is, after all, shorter, easier, and quicker to measure. It seems a more immediate challenge. The classic nature of the mile run has all the glamour a runner could ask."

I have great admiration for Noel Carroll, but I must admit I've never heard a suggestion farther off the mark. The racing world is divided into two groups: those who have run the mile, and those who haven't. Neither is interested in making the mile a focus of its running program. Most runners who haven't run a mile race consider it pretty small potatoes, a "fun run" for out-of-shape, overweight beginners. *Real* runners run real distances. Given a choice of two races, veteran runners will always select the longer one. I doubt that more than a handful have ever competed in a mile on the track—nor, at this point, do they ever intend to.

On the other hand, those who have tried the mile are never too eager to try it again. As for me, I've found it best to race the mile infrequently and never in practice. The ordeal is too clearly remembered when I stand at the starting line. And along with that dread of the distance is the fear of the lean, lithe athletes waiting beside me for the sound of the gun. What follows is almost always worse even than what I anticipated. On occasion, I have run a comfortable tactical mile behind inferior opponents. In these instances, I led for a slow first quarter and then shadowed the front-runners until a final sprint that gave an easy win.

Almost always, however, the race is the exact opposite. Roger Bannister, the man who broke the 4-minute barrier in the mile, said the mile was "an almost preeminent sporting achievement." In the marathon, one endures, no matter how slow one runs. In the mile, I also endure, but while running as fast as possible.

"The appeal of the mile," continues Bannister, "lies in its very simplicity. It needs no money, no equipment, no particular physique, no knowledge, no education." It is also the classic battle with the self. It is the ultimate race, demanding equal portions of speed, strength, and stamina.

When I run shorter races, the 220-meter or the quarter- or half-mile, there's a predictable point (usually three-quarters of the way through the race) where I start losing control. Somewhere in the homestretch, my arms and legs tighten. The smooth flow of energy degenerates into an uncoordinated stagger through the final yards.

Even so, these races are short and quickly over. I run them on instinct. (A local high school runner told me he preferred the half-mile race because "I don't have to think.") In the mile, thinking begins where the half-mile ends, and the thought is "How will I ever be able to finish this race?"

I've often said that the third quarter of the mile is the most difficult stretch in competitive running. After the second lap, I'm completely spent, and I still have two laps to go. In shorter distances, the ordeal, however severe, is short-lived. Recovery is swift. In longer races, I come to a point where I know I will never feel worse than I do now. And although I'm 10 minutes away from the finish, I can live with that. Only in the mile do I face a continuing escalation of discomfort and fatigue and shortness of breath. Only in the mile do I accept and even seek the oblivion that can attend the drive around the final turn and down the homestretch.

"The magic of the mile is there to be grasped," writes Noel Carroll. But only if you are determined to come home either with your shield or *on* it.

A RACE WITHIN A RACE

Although racing may be the ultimate test of my talent, training, and willingness to stand pain, it requires very little planning. It is an elementary and uncomplicated confrontation with myself.

In the battle against the clock, my basic strategy is to set out at an even pace, try to hold it steady through the last mile, and then use whatever is left of the fast-twitch fibers (muscle tissues used for short, powerful effort) for a final sprint. This puts me close to collapse, but at least I can walk away from the finish line under my own steam.

At times, things go amiss. I run the first mile 30 seconds faster than I planned, and my lactic acid level (a change associated with sustained effort and fatigue) continues to rise throughout the race. The last mile seems interminable. Runners pass me—not in great numbers, but in a steady stream. There is no question of a race-saving sprint. When I cross the finish line, someone invariably appears at my side and offers help.

On rare occasions, certain races put even greater demands on me. In such instances, I enter the later stages of the race focusing on beating someone up front. In the distant past, that someone was anyone ahead of me. Now it pertains only to someone in my age group. The word of honor I gave myself at the starting line demands that I do my absolute best against any runner over 60 years of age.

This is not the same as struggling against the clock. One can run a reasonably painful 5-K in reasonably respectable time and endure only a short spell of what could be termed agony. However, in a struggle with another runner, the agony increases exponentially for the few seconds you gain on the clock. Albert Einstein once said that the faster we go, the longer it takes—a paradox that certainly seems to apply to races.

When I'm just behind the runner I'm following (or just ahead), the race becomes tactical, a matter of timing my sprint. I pretty well know the point at which I can hold a sprint right to the finish—when that point comes, I "pull the trigger," so to speak. Then it's a case of which of us is faster—or who made the first move. But when the runner is too far ahead for me to catch—or is obviously too strong for me to compete against—matching his pace is impossible. The runner may pass me "big," as they say, with a half-mile to go. Of course, there's always a chance that this is a ploy and that he is as played out as I am. So I don't immediately assume I'm out of it. Nevertheless, when a runner passes me, I almost always know if he has too much stamina left for me to challenge him. And then I'm back once more to racing for time rather than place.

The worst test, and one I hope will not present itself, occurs when someone with an insurmountable lead begins to slow down with a half-mile or so to go. I recall just such an experience in the last stretches of a 5-K race. A stranger apparently in my age group had quickly taken a 200-yard lead—well beyond contention—and late in the race, he was still out of reach.

By that time, I had given up on first place and had become content with the thought of coming in second. Then I noticed he was beginning to slow down. I was cutting into his lead perceptibly. I was consternated at this turn of events. I was then at the familiar limit of pain that marks the finish of every race.

This fellow was slowing down, yet catching him—if indeed I could—would mean pushing into pain that only the deepest recesses of my body remembered from the past. The distance between us continued to narrow. "Oh, no, don't do that," I implored him under my breath. "Please, don't slow down." I knew if I closed to a makeable distance, I would have to suffer beyond belief trying to catch him. If he would only hold his pace, I would be excused from going through torture I didn't want to contemplate.

But he kept dropping back. The finish was getting closer, but so was he. It was much too soon to start my sprint to the finish, but if I was to catch him, it was now or never. There was no way out. I began my all-out run, going as fast as I could. I caught him, but now both of us were completely expended, and there were still 50 yards to go. The finish came just in time. Both of us were in near-collapse.

When I recovered, I said something to him about how we 60-and-over runners are a little too old for this. "I'm only 55," he replied. "I'm not in your age group."

Aarrgh!!

FINDING THE PROPER PACE

As I stood at the line awaiting the start of the Ocean County Park 5-Mile Race, I knew conditions were right for setting my seventysomething personal best. I was well trained and injury-free, and the weather and running course fulfilled two of the four remaining requirements for setting a PR. To begin with, it was a perfect day: low humidity. No wind. The temperature in the 50s. And the course was ideal: flat and fast. Two loops on a 12-foot-wide strip of asphalt circling through this forest of tall trees.

The other two essentials, pace and economy, were up to me. The early pace is critical. Run too fast, and I tire in the final stages. Run too slowly, and I find it difficult to make up those precious seconds. The first mile must be run under conscious control. For the first mile, I'm the pilot. After that, I can relinquish the helm to the body. It knows unerringly just how much energy it can expend.

This time, my brain did a good job. I ran well, at a pace that seemed to correspond to what I usually do in the middle miles. I resisted the contagious desire to go with the pack. I refused to match the early speed of most of the other runners. I settled in and hit the 1-mile marker on target—7:15.

Now came the final ingredient, economy. Now I had to maintain that level of performance with the least expenditure of energy. Up until then, everything was right. The day, the course, the race plan were coming together for what could be a memorable run. I needed just one more thing: someone to use as a pacesetter, someone doing 7:15 miles whom I could follow.

I looked around and spotted just the guy I needed. He was a nationally ranked race-walker doing 7:15 miles, operating on cruise control, and I knew he would hold this pace right to the finish line. I got in behind him and told my body to match that speed. My body took over, and I became a spectator. Without interference or direction from me, the immensely intricate and complicated processes that occur during running were taking place. My body was attaining an efficiency that my brain could not command. And this mindless, automatic running was almost effortless.

I've experienced this phenomenon on other occasions as well. Setting one's pace apparently involves effort above and beyond the mere act of running. Distancing my mind from the act makes the running easier. Running in the wake of someone doing 75-second repeat quarter-miles requires no more effort than running 80-second quarters alone. Similarly, when running uphill, a situation where the body demands to be heard, it automatically adopts the best running form and an optimum stride length and cadence. Indeed, there are times when I need give no more thought to the mechanics of what I'm doing than a dog does when chasing a rabbit.

There are some who claim you can program yourself to improve your running economy. However, Dr. Peter Cavanaugh, an expert in the biomechanics of running, claims that there is no specific running form and combination of stride length and cadence that will work for everyone. "You will probably locate your own optimal stride lengths subconsciously," says Dr. Cavanaugh.

And sitting in behind my fast-paced friend, I let my body do just that, subconsciously settle on a specific stride length. My body was also discovering, quite on its own, its individual and idiosyncratic most economical running form. And although I didn't check, I suspect that I had a little more forward lean and that I was running a little closer to the ground, with knees slightly bent at impact.

According to Dr. Cavanaugh, some distance runners are 20 percent more energy efficient than others. It's also likely that from one race to the next, many runners differ in their own running economy. The more they turn the running over to the body, the more automatically and the more economically they run.

This strategy worked for me. The other runner and I finished the first 2½-mile loop in 18:06, right on target. We held the same pace for the second lap. The last mile hurt, of course. It always does. But by running in tandem, I was able to dissociate from the pain. My body was "attached" to the other runner and would not let go.

With 200 yards to go, I slipped the leash and expended everything I had in reserve. I stormed across the finish line, seeing the time on the digital clock: 36:10. It was my best time in three years.

I give all the credit to my seventysomething body, not my seventysomething brain.

A BIG RACE
WITHOUT BIG-TIME HASSLES

I was jogging the mile or so from my hotel to the starting line of the Bolder Boulder 10-K, surrounded by hundreds upon hundreds of runners converging toward the same point. At every intersection, more would join the march. I could see that race director Steve Bosley was not exaggerating when he predicted that 19,000 runners would run today. "The Bolder Boulder," the *Boulder Daily Camera* would say the next day, "is big time."

I felt a rising apprehension. Would success spoil the Bolder Boulder? I had been in races where it had. Great races tend to become great events. A race is held. It gets more and more popular, until it becomes more than just a race. It's a happening, *the* place to be on a particular weekend. It turns into a festival. The race itself becomes secondary. What begins as a local event becomes a national attraction.

I am not interested in happenings and festivals and national attractions. I am a racer with roots in the days when 100 runners was a large field. I want an unimpeded start, plenty of running room, mile splits, and a report on my time and place at the finish. An "event" is unlikely to produce any of those requirements.

I have run in several of these extravaganzas and know the difficulties firsthand. The crush at the start. The hordes of people moving en masse, and only those favored few up front, running freely. The hemmed-in feeling of being unable to settle in to your individual pace. The unsure feeling when there's not enough space to see changes in terrain and surface. And then the mass finish, much like a routed army, that makes any attempt to record the time and place impossible. Even at their best, these events leave me unsatisfied and determined not to return.

As I trotted toward the staging area, I thought to myself that the Bolder Boulder was one of those races to which I would never return. It had the crowds and the atmosphere of a giant folk festival, not a race. But I was completely wrong. Steve Bosley had solved the problem of the Bolder Boulder's enormous popularity. By scheduling a staggered start, he had converted the race into 27 separate races: a Citizen's Race with 25 sections, and two World Class Races (one for men, the other for women) to be held an hour later.

My bib was color coded, with my number, a large C, and the time I predicted on my entry blank (43 minutes). In the starting area, I was directed to the C group as others sought out their own letters. We were thus divided into 27 sections, arranged in alphabetical order and each containing 700 or more runners, to await the gun.

Arranging runners according to ability is not new. To enter the Boston Marathon, you have to submit your qualifying time, which puts you in a certain starting section. Guards monitor these cordoned-off sections to prevent slower runners from stationing themselves up front. At other races, such seeding is voluntary. Large placards indicate expected average time per mile—5 minutes, 6 minutes, 7 minutes, and so on. But where there is no enforcement, there is not much compliance. Slow runners up front interfere with the fast ones and cause all sorts of difficulty.

In any case, such starting protocols are unfair. Those in the back are penalized. They may have to spend several minutes jogging and pushing and shoving before they even *reach* the starting line. In a short race on a flat course with an enormous field, the start can become a race director's nightmare.

Not so in Boulder. Shortly before race time, with the press of runners extending back two city blocks, the A group was called to the starting line. High above, a man in a cherry picker flanked by a huge digital clock waited until the runners were ready and then fired the gun. Next he summoned the B group. The rest of the alphabet moved up one position. Again he waited until the runners were ready and then gave them the starting order.

We were next. At first, I thought there was a prescribed time between groups. But there wasn't. At each interval, the starter waited until he felt everyone was ready. Each unit started as though it constituted an individual race. The computer kept track of each group's waiting time, so that it could be subtracted from the runners' finishing times. Later, I heard that it took about 40 minutes to get the 25 individual races under way.

As a result of this brilliant strategy, I found myself in a race with 700 people instead of 19,000. Up ahead were runners who were presumably a minute better than we. Those a minute or so behind were presumably not as good. That presumption stood. During the race, I saw very few Bs and no Ds among my fellow runners.

The race had everything I wanted: a good start, no interference from other runners, mile splits (using some mental arithmetic), a wonderfully steady pace, and a finish in the University of Colorado stadium in front of 20,000 spectators.

Two weeks later, I received a certificate from the Bank of Boulder, where Bosley is president. It had my official finish time, my average pace per mile, my place in the race, my place in my age group, the total number of finishers, male and female, with winning times.

Would I return to Boulder? You bet. If you can achieve the wonderful benefits of making it big *and* retain the wonderful elements of staying small, you have yourself a great event that is also a great race—the particular place to be on that particular weekend.

RACING WITH THE CURRENT

With 3 miles to go in the Gasparilla 15-K Run, in Tampa, Florida, I began to have trouble moving with the flow. There is a current at every point in the river of runners that forms the race. That current moves at different speeds—from a sub-5-minute-mile pace to over 10 minutes per mile. But after a mile or two, I am usually with people I will be near up until the finish.

Staying with the current means passing a fellow runner now and then. At every moment, from beginning to end, are people who find the current pace just too fast. Those maintaining speed keep picking up on those who falter. The runner has to be aware that keeping on the pace means moving with the faster runners as they go by.

In longer races, like a 15-K, this is particularly true. Past the halfway point, only an occasional runner should pass you. By then you should have settled in with a group running at pretty much the same consistent, steady speed.

A hill is one element that will slow the tempo and change the pattern. By the time I reach the top of any hill, I'm with runners who were formerly in the pack behind me. At times, I can rejoin my group by flying down the other side.

At Tampa, there were no hills, just a small bridge a half-mile into the race that I would have to cross again a half-mile from the finish. Otherwise, the 9.3-plus miles were absolutely flat: a little more than 4.7 miles out along the bay, and about 4.7 miles back. I held with my platoon until I was down to the final 5 kilometers, feeling the distance and the pace—and the wind. We had gone out with the wind at our back—apparently not strong enough to make a difference (probably somewhere around the 12 miles per hour we were averaging). But going *into* the wind certainly was making a difference. Now I was continually reaching for just a little bit more. I began to fine-tune my running, to refine my form, trying to get the most with the least effort. I moved in behind a runner to use him as my pacesetter. That allowed me to forget about what the speed should be. I just hung on.

Time passed. I remained on the very edge of what was possible for me. I was trying to stay with that flow—a speed that would equal my time in this race last year.

Suddenly, I thought about how I would feel after the finish. I would wonder why I hadn't run faster coming up to the bridge and the final half-mile. I resolved then that *there would be no regrets*. I would leave no doubt that I had tried as hard as I could. Now, anyone who was moving away from me or anyone who came to my shoulder *was* the current. I was determined that from here on in, I would hold nothing back. I was not going to save anything for the crowd in downtown Tampa.

It was an odd feeling. I have always, it seemed, done as well as I could in a race—my best at the moment, or at the most, a best that fitted in with a strategy that ended at the finish line. This was the first time I had run answering to a judgment to be made *after* the race was over, by the most demanding of all judges—myself.

And there, with 3 miles to go, I knew I had nothing to fear. There was no way I could run the final 5 kilometers any harder than I was now. The verdict was already in. I did my best and could walk away from the finish line content with that effort.

THE SAVING GRACE OF THE 10-K

"The marathon is the acme of athletic heroism," writes Roger Bannister. The marathon allows ordinary people to do extraordinary things. It admits common, garden-variety runners into Valhalla, that great hall in Norse mythology populated by the souls of slain battle heroes. In the marathon, thousands pursue their individual perfection—and attain it.

But what of the runners who come to watch, unwilling to accept this challenge? What of runners not disciplined enough to do the necessary training and afraid of what might happen in those terrible last miles? What of those who must greet these heroes at the finish line without having done something heroic themselves?

Nonrunners at a marathon are unaware of this chasm between runners who have entered the race and runners who have not. Other spectators do not see the guilt that consumes us. Only runners, and more particularly those of us who did not compete, can know the feelings of being a noncombatant in running's greatest battle.

The runner reduced to watching the marathon is like Coleridge's Ancient Mariner approaching and seeking forgiveness from all who will listen to his tale of woe. "Shrive me" is the plea. Blot out my sin. Wipe the slate clean. But even when pardoned, the guilt is too great. The runner is still a sinner, at least in his or her own mind. Only through some atoning deed can wholeness be restored. Only through penance can the runner be cleansed.

When a 10-K race is held along with the marathon, as often happens, it's an opportunity to do penance. Running it is the exonerating act. In those 6.2 miles, reparation is made. I redeem the fallen creature who failed to enter the marathon. The 10-K race is the purgatory in which I pay the temporal punishment for that sin. Through that suffering, I set things right. And I find, as an Irishman said, that I'm equal to anyone else and maybe better.

I'm not going to pretend that a 10-K run is as demanding as a marathon. Yet in its own way, this shorter race can be even more painful. For one thing, the pains incurred in the two races are quite different. The pain I have felt in the final stages of a marathon is one of exhaustion. My legs are gone. I am trying to find muscles I have not used. The supreme act of heart, mind, and body is to keep running, however slowly. Keep running, no more than that.

In the 10-K, simply running is not enough. Right from the gun, I have to push the throttle as far as it can go and still allow me to finish. The torment here is global: chest, belly, legs—all protest. There is never a moment that I am not at the very limits of what I can do.

On the other hand, the first half of a marathon can go by as if I were sitting in a train watching the landscape. When I run a marathon rationally—admittedly a tall order—I can finish with a smile on my face. This is something I've never been able to do in a 10-K race. If I analyze the 10-K, I can easily see that short of the marathon, it is the toughest race on my yearly schedule.

It has been said that the 20-mile mark is the halfway point of a marathon. You could also say that the 5-mile mark is the halfway point in a 10-K. Almost always I run my first 5 miles as though the race were going to end there, then have to find reserves of strength and stamina to cover the final 1¼ miles at the same speed. The last stages of a 10-K, therefore, are filled with a prolonged and escalating pain and exhaustion and shortness of breath unequaled in longer or shorter races.

Having endured this world-class suffering, I am no longer an outsider. I am again one of the saved. It is as if I have gone to confession ("Bless me, Father, for I have sinned, it's three years since my last marathon"), been given penance, and received absolution. I can then leave the "confessional" in a state of grace.

Thank heavens, then, for 10-Ks and other races held at marathons like Charlotte and Houston and the Twin Cities. Having paid my dues, I can then savor the whole event. I can join the communion of saints who ran the marathon.

IN QUEST OF T-SHIRTS

I once asked Fred Lebow, president of the New York Road Runners Club, how he enticed hundreds of volunteers to work for him. "Never underestimate the power of a T-shirt," he replied.

I know the power of the T-shirt. I have been in that horde of runners in the Peachtree 10-K in Atlanta chanting "T-shirt! T-shirt!" as we approached the finish line. I have been among the thousands at the Bloomsday Run in Spokane getting our shirts only seconds after completing that grueling course. The T-shirt is a reminder of a great event, a seal on some great personal effort. It's a status symbol, as much for myself as anyone else's esteem.

The T-shirt shows how high I've gone in the hierarchy of races. There are T-shirt equivalents of a Mercedes or Alfa Romeo. T-shirts are presumed to reflect the ability and experience of their wearers. At the very least, someone jogging to the line in a Boston Marathon shirt is judged to be a veteran, a runner to be taken seriously.

The appeal of the T-shirt lies in its scarcity. Not everyone can get one, only those who enter the race. It's a one-time race, with a one-time prize. When I wear a T-shirt from a particular race, held in a particular year, I'm saying "I am one of the favored few. Your chance for this shirt has come and gone."

At races, the T-shirt also rescues me from anonymity. I stand on the line in nothing but shoes and shorts and a running shirt, indistinguishable from hundreds of others runners. The shirt establishes my personal identity, the only way I have of being a person instead of a number.

Of course, once the race begins, the T-shirt becomes of little importance. What I am wearing no longer attracts attention. I recall passing two spectators at the Bix Seven, an extremely tough race, and hearing one say to the other "There are so many faces." Before the race, I am a T-shirt. During the race, I am a face. My T-shirt is a remembrance of agony past, but my face shows agony present.

The poet who wrote "Hope springs eternal from the human breast" might well have had the T-shirt for tomorrow's race in mind. The runner who is looking for the perfect race is also looking for the perfect T-shirt. I have enough T-shirts to last years, yet every week I am waiting eagerly on line for yet another.

Race directors know the power of the T-shirt, and the entry blanks frequently tout "long-sleeved" shirts, to lure those who might otherwise go someplace else. Sometimes, the T-shirt is used as a threat, assured only to preregistered runners. The form ominous warns, "Post-entrants will receive T-shirts as they remain available." Race directors sometimes pressure runners even further, announcing that only the first 200 to submit entries will get a T-shirt. One such time, I called the director to find out if I would make the first 200. "Send in your entry," she answered glibly, "and you'll find out."

I read these entry blanks closely. T-shirts are very important to me. I don't want to arrive at a race and find that I'm not going to get a T-shirt or that the only ones left are small or extra large. So I pay attention to the fine print. But beyond caveats concerning limited availability, I remain in the dark to what the T-shirt will look like. I have no idea of either the color or the design. When race day arrives, I may find I have gone to great pains to acquire quite an ordinary-looking T-shirt.

A few years back, there was an enterprising race director who would display his T-shirt in advance. For weeks before a race, he would attend other races and distribute flyers while carrying a pole displaying the T-shirt for his race. His race no longer exists, but it invariably drew a large number of runners because they saw and liked the T-shirt they would get.

I usually arrive at a race early. For one thing, I like to allow time for a long, slow warm-up. But arriving early also allows me to select a T-shirt before the big crush. I am assured of getting one, in the size I need. (I have the misfortune of being an "in-between." Medium is too small, large is too large.) Then I examine the label for fiber content. Is it all cotton or a blend? After all that, I may be stuck with a quite ordinary T-shirt that I am unlikely to wear anyway.

When that happens, I do one of three things: Get a small for one of the grandchildren, a medium for the women in the family, or an extra large to sleep in. Unfortunately, as I have become selective, so has my family. If I don't like a T-shirt, no one else wants it either. That's because another part of a T-shirt's attraction is that it's an object of art. The color, the graphics, the material, the styling make it a thing of beauty. Now beauty may be in the eye of the beholder, but there is a consensus as well. When I assemble a supply of my rejects for my friends and family, there are few takers.

9

Exercising Your Training Options

*When the running gets tough,
the tough start walking.*

STRIDE FOR STRIDE

I was jogging in the middle lane of an indoor 16-laps-to-the-mile track at a health club in Detroit. The inside lane was reserved for walkers, the middle lane for slow runners like myself, and a few fast runners were using the passing lane, on the outside.

After spending about 10 minutes in this swirl of differing orbital speeds, I noticed that a runner rushing by me was taking about the same number of strides per minute—about 85—as I was. I let this sink in for a while and then turned my attention to a woman walking briskly in the inner lane whom I had lapped several times. *Mirabile dictu!* She was taking the same number of strides as well. Every one of us, walker, jogger, and runner, was doing close to 85 strides per minute. The light bulb went on. I had a "Eureka!" experience.

Later that week, I met a cyclist and asked him what tempo he used on his bike. His answer was about 90 revolutions per minute. Apparently, both running and biking involve about the same number of repetitions per minute. The muscles don't care what they are doing, as long as they're doing it 80 to 90 times per minute. I am accustomed to performing a specific number of repetitions to develop strength. What I didn't realize was that a prescribed number of repetitions of a low-intensity effort helps to develop endurance.

Experienced drivers know the most important instrument on the dashboard is not the odometer or speedometer, it's the tachometer (a device that measures engine speed in rotations per minute, or RPMs). So fitness, too, can be measured not in speed or miles covered but RPMs. Thirty minutes of running, walking, or cycling involves anywhere from 2,400 to 2,700 repetitions ("rotations") per leg. These repetitions are the key to endurance. They bring about the changes in the muscle that increase our physical work capacity (PWC), which is another way to describe fitness.

We now know that 95 percent of the effects of aerobic exercise occur at the muscle level. *Aerobics* leads to very little increase in heart function and virtually no increase in lung function. The muscle cell (which is the "motor" of the body) becomes more and more efficient. These thousands of repetitions trigger changes that enable us to go farther and faster on less and less fuel.

When I made this discovery, it seemed so simple, I knew it must be true. I recalled Einstein's remark: "When the solution is simple, God is answering." That's the way the Creator works. Great truths are stated in small sentences: $E = mc^2$; *cognito, ergo sum* ("I think, therefore I am"); "Less is more." Fundamental principles can be expressed in simple formulas.

Physiologists have done that for fitness. The formula: Exercise for 30 minutes at a comfortable pace four times a week; and select any activity that involves large muscle groups (legs, back, shoulders, buttocks, and so forth). It doesn't matter whether you walk, jog, cycle, dance, or whatever, as long as you do it for the prescribed time at the prescribed pace.

I have spent the last decade preaching this dogma. But one day, jogging along the boardwalk, I started to have some doubts. How was it possible for walkers going half my speed to get the same benefit? And how could a half-hour of easy running profit me as much as the runners passing me and disappearing up ahead? This nagging doubt has pursued me through the years. Every creed contains some beliefs that are difficult to swallow. There were times I choked on this one.

If my notion about repetitions holds up, the fitness formula could be reduced to a specific number of repetitions (say, 2,500), performed four times a week. The time you put in would vary with your RPMs. As the RPMs get progressively lower, more time would have to be spent at the activity. But when walkers, joggers, runners, cyclists, or recruits who march in boot camp maintain their RPMs in the 85 range, they all reap the same reward.

The distance covered in 30 minutes of walking or running is irrelevant to fitness. It does, however, have an effect on metabolism. It takes 100 calories, more or less, to move a 150-pound body one mile. Running, therefore, is more cost effective than walking in losing weight and lowering coronary risk factors. To lose excess weight, a person has to walk two or three times as long as they would have to if they ran. To lose weight and keep arteries free from disease, the odometer becomes important.

As noted in chapter 4, however, fitness is independent of coronary risk factors. (Fit people *can* and do have heart attacks.) In fitness, *tempo* is all-important. I suspect that most runners have learned to run at a certain cadence. Arthur Newton, one of the all-time great runners, certainly did. In their book *The Lonely Breed*, Ron Clarke and Norman Harris have this to say about Newton: "He reasoned that rhythm was all-important to running and that music would sustain this, so he sent tunes spinning through his head as he ran." According to Clarke and Harris, Newton decided that the 4/4 tempo (common time) of marches was unsuitable for running, and the 3/4 (the waltz time) was superior.

That may be the simplest formula of all: Waltz for 30 minutes, four times a week. Waltz, that is, whether you are running or jogging or cycling or on a treadmill or stair climber at a health club. Slip into those 85 RPMs, and get fit.

WALKERS ARE ATHLETES, TOO

I was in Thomasville, Georgia, to speak to various groups about health and fitness, then participate in a 5-kilometer walk. The talks went well. I emphasized that running might only be for the few, that there are many other ways to exercise, and that walking would help a person become fit and healthy.

My audiences varied. I spoke to physicians, corporate executives, the Kiwanis Club, hospital personnel, and the general public. I tried not to be condescending about walking. Runners do not generally regard walking as real sport, nor do they regard the walkers they pass on the roads as real athletes. Until my visit to Thomasville, I shared that opinion.

The race Saturday morning had 1,014 entrants. The starting line resembled some of the better-supported road races held every year, although most of the entrants did not have the lean, gaunt look I associate with runners. There were very few whippets in the field.

I decided to start in the rear and work my way through the field, although I realized that in a short race of little over 3 miles, I might not get very far along. Initially, I did fairly well. I found that walking at a fast pace was more demanding than expected, but I was passing people regularly. Soon, however, I reached a point where I was just going with the flow.

Meanwhile, up ahead, I could see the flashing lights of the lead police car and a lengthening stream of walkers far faster than I. Soon came the first mile split. "15 minutes," the official called out.

It was difficult to believe. I was at flank speed and doing exactly 4 miles per hour. Despite pumping my arms, using my hips, and keeping my tempo as high as possible, I was barely able to keep up with the people around me.

It didn't get any better. A little farther along, I heard someone say, "We're at the halfway point." I looked at my watch, and so far my time was a little over 21 minutes. I suddenly knew how long a 5-kilometer walk was. If I'd been in a 5-kilometer *run*, using this much effort, I'd be nearing the finish line. I was in the process of discovering that a 5-kilometer walk is equal in effort to a 10-kilometer run.

I now regarded my companions with new respect. I'd be satisfied if I could just keep up with a group of middle-aged, somewhat overweight women just ahead. Try as I might, others who seemed to be out for a Saturday stroll crept farther and farther ahead.

Sometimes the reason for this competence became obvious from conversations around me. One young man was telling a young woman with a dog on a leash that he spent 40 minutes a day on the StairMaster. She, in turn, told him that her dog set a pace that was difficult to match.

Still, I was mystified. If allowed to run, I am certain I would have been close to the leaders. As it was, almost 400 walkers completed the course before I did.

I had seen a report extolling the merits of walking 12-minute miles. My first reaction was to doubt that such a program would come into general use. How many people can walk that fast? Evidently, more than I suspected. Certainly, a large number of those who walked in Thomasville could do it.

My 4-mile-per-hour pace (equal to 15-minute miles) seemed a reasonable substitute. Harry Andrews, the great turn-of-the-century track coach, was a strong advocate of walking as training for runners. And those who simply wanted to get fit, he said, needed no other exercise. He encouraged his pupils to seek their own pace, which almost invariably turned out to be 4 miles per hour.

I know from doing stress tests that up to about 4 miles per hour, walking was comfortable, but after that, it was much more comfortable to jog. Except for an accomplished race-walker, walking faster than 4 miles per hour was difficult. It became inefficient and tiring. On the other hand, at slower speeds, walking is more efficient than jogging. When I took a stress test with a pulse recorder in front of me, I found that jogging raised my pulse ten beats higher than walking at the same pace. But as one nears 5 miles per hour, the opposite is true.

Fortunately, most of this information is academic. If you walk 12-minute miles instead of 15-minute miles, you simply save a little time. Walking the same number of miles, whatever the speed, burns up roughly the same amount of calories. Put another way, it takes up to twice as long for walkers to move their body 1 mile as it does a runner. So in a given period of time, walkers use about half the calories that runners do. But having made that adjustment, walkers become fit and healthy athletes—and masters of their own sport.

I met a thousand of them in Thomasville, Georgia, and became a believer.

TRI, TRI, AGAIN

When people used to ask me why I didn't do triathlons, I had a ready answer: "Swimming is boring, and cycling is dangerous." But these were merely excuses for avoiding activities that held little interest for me. Running was my specialty. However, my downtime as a runner is considerable. I rarely go three months without some problem that prevents me from running. Most often, I'm sidelined because of overtraining or overracing.

Eventually, I became a triathlete—by chance, as a way of filling these downtimes. I remain a triathlete by choice. I now swim, bike, or run for training, and I combine the three in triathlon races. My new program minimizes injuries (or at least their disruption of my life). Compared to running, swimming and cycling produce few overuse injuries, and when I can't run, I can usually continue to work out in the water or on wheels.

Long before I decided to attempt a triathlon, a friend had urged me on. "You can swim," he told me, "so you will do well in your age group."

He was right. But neither of us realized how difficult it can be to return to swimming. Swimming is like many experiences from youth. It gradually becomes fantasy, and only the good parts remain in the memory. I remembered myself as an excellent swimmer. In my mind's eye, I was an undiscovered star with the potential of Buster Crabbe or Johnny Weissmuller. As my friend coaxed me on, I relived these dreams of glory. I forgot that water was never my element. I was built for endurance activities on land, but I could not endure in the water. Low body fat does not suit a swimmer, nor are matchstick arms a natural advantage. In a matter of minutes in the water, I was not only cold but also exhausted. I no longer wondered why

Olympic champion Frank Shorter, a former high school swimmer, had avoided the triathlon. With our low percentages of body fat, distance swimming was like exercising in the freezer.

But finally, after two weeks of swimming, I stopped thrashing desperately. I swam my quarter-mile in the ocean, but at a slow pace. I came to realize that I was not an undiscovered Crabbe or Weissmuller, and I accepted my limitations.

I also learned that swimming does have its great moments. The all-out short sprints of interval training are an exhilarating challenge, a way to test how fast I can go and how much pain I can stand. When I finish, my mood lifts, and my ego expands—in direct contrast to the boredom I once associated with swimming.

As for bicycling, it can indeed be dangerous. I found that out the day of my first fall, which wasn't some minor, run-of-the-mill topple into the weeds. I collided with the rear wheel of another cyclist during a group ride and landed sprawled on the road. This flip left me bruised and bleeding.

Several cyclists stopped to check my condition, and one went to get a car to pick me up. Meanwhile, I stood there holding my bike and assessing the damage: nothing broken, no major injuries, only minor pain.

So I remounted the bike and, still bleeding, set out riding again. Five minutes later, the cyclist who had gotten the car caught up to me and yelled out the window, "You're a certified nut."

Perhaps he was right. But by then, I had forgotten the fall and was enjoying the bike, pumping away at amazing speed and actually passing other bikers. Picking myself up and continuing was a mark of *something*.

Later, I told a veteran cyclist "Perhaps it's a defect in my value system, but when I fell, I wasn't worried about myself. I was scared that my bike had been damaged."

"At that moment," he replied, "you became a true biker."

RUN FASTER AND FARTHER, *WITHOUT* ADDING MILEAGE

Not everyone trains for a triathlon. But many runners cross-train in some fashion, adding biking or strength training or any one of various other activities to their training program. But are they better off than dedicated single-sport athletes?

"There has never been a definitive study," a prominent exercise physiologist told me, "that showed that cross-training improved one's performance in a particular sport." Yet rarely does a week go by that I don't hear of some runner setting personal bests after adding cycling and/or swimming to a running program.

My physiologist friend suggests that is due to decreasing running mileage and doing quality work instead of what some call "junk" miles.

"Someone backs off from a difficult training schedule through cross-training, and this allows muscle to recover. Then performance improves," he explains. And that certainly is true in many cases. Nancy Tinari, a world-class runner, dates her success to the time she began cross-training and reduced her running to 40 miles per week. And biathlete Liz Downing, another top performer, is proving to be almost unbeatable, despite limiting herself to 20 miles per week. In fact, most runners who run better while training for a triathlon experience this paradox. Lowering mileage raises their performance.

Could there be another explanation for this improvement besides preventing overtraining? I think so. If you overtrain, you've reached your peak and passed it. Yet these triathlon-trained runners tend to surpass anything they have done previously. So it seems logical that the beneficial effect of cross-training must occur in the muscles *not* used during running. And this is precisely what a study from Pennsylvania State University suggests: Fundamental changes in nonrunning muscles may account for improved running performance following cross-training. More specifically, the researchers found that training muscles not used for running lessened blood lactate accumulation during running and speeded up its removal during active recovery after running.

Minimizing the accumulation of blood lactate enables a runner to maintain a faster speed—or to keep going when he or she would otherwise be forced to stop. The major predictor of running ability, aside from maximum oxygen capacity, is the anaerobic threshold, which could roughly be described as the runner's maximum cruising speed. Running any faster creates a buildup of blood lactate and forces the runner into oxygen debt and a state of acidosis (a disruption of the acid-base balances in the blood and body tissues). Although there is some disagreement about cause and effect, the onset of blood lactate accumulation (OBLA, for short) is the commonly used marker for the anaerobic threshold. *In short, it limits performance.*

It would be simplistic to say that the OBLA is the whole story to anaerobic threshold. Still, there is enough evidence to suggest that controlling blood lactate is important. Exercise physiologist Fritz Hagerman once described the anaerobic threshold as "the speed at which a good runner slows down and a poor runner stops." Hence, the faster the speed you can maintain without blood lactate levels rising, the better.

And that is just what happened in the Penn State experiment. Runners who added arm training to their program had a delay in the OBLA. They also had lower peak lactate levels (58.2 milligrams, compared to 71 milligrams) and a 35 percent quicker return to normal values during active recovery (working at 50 percent of maximum oxygen capacity). *Apparently, these trained muscles were better able to clear away blood lactate, whether they were being used or not.* Venous blood being pumped back to the heart by the arms while running had much more blood lactate than arterial blood pumped from the heart. This did not occur in runners who had not trained their arms.

A multi-sport program begins to make sense then. Our entire muscle mass can contribute to improving our 10-K time. I find that much more reasonable than any other explanation. Yes, a specific event trains specific muscles. It also trains the oxygen delivery to those muscles to the limit. How, then, can swimming and cycling benefit my running? This experiment provides the answer. The triathlon-trained muscles slow down lactate accumulation, which may well be *the* major limiting factor in running performance. So it's reasonable to assume that all else being equal, the more *non*running muscle mass we train, the better we will run.

This report may not be the definitive study that my physiologist friend would like. Its relevance to running performance requires further investigation and field trials. Blood lactate may not turn out to be as important as a shift toward acidosis or other metabolic changes brought on by a flat-out 10-K race.

Still, if you've hit a peak and found that increasing mileage seems to be getting you nowhere, performance-wise, cross-training may well trim off enough seconds to turn your usual weekly effort into a personal best.

CROSS-TRAINING WISDOM

The triathlon is the ultimate cross-training event, involving distance greater than many serious runners normally cover, however. Is the triathlon a safe pursuit for the injury-plagued runner?

Anecdotal evidence says "yes." Triathletes constantly corner me, bearing witness to a life free of the injuries that bedevil runners. Formerly sidelined runners reappear with a bounding stride, the smile of health, and T-shirts proclaiming their participation in some one or other of these swim-bike-run events. I have a friend whose sciatic pain was his sole topic of conversation while he was running. Now he's a triathlete and only mentions his sciatica to say that it's gone for good. He and others who formerly concentrated on distance running encouraged me to join in a sport they said would cure whatever ailed me.

Despite these testimonials, the case for triathlon training may not be all that strong, however. A study done at Mount Sinai Medical Center in New York questions how much of an advantage the triathlete has over the single-sport runner, cyclist, or swimmer. The researchers were surprised to find that triathletes have a significantly *higher* incidence of injuries per year than do single-sport athletes, including runners.

The investigators surveyed four different groups (31 triathletes, 39 runners, 31 cyclists, and 39 swimmers). In one year, 90 percent of the triathletes had suffered an injury, compared to 61 percent of runners, 51 percent of cyclists, and 33 percent of swimmers.

What's more, both runners and triathletes tend to have much longer and more severe injuries than cyclists and swimmers. The runners' injuries took an average of 40 days to heal and resulted in a loss of approximately 25 training days. For triathletes, injuries lasted 28 days and cost them 19 training days, on the average. For cyclists and swimmers, injuries averaged 12 days and cost 8 training days.

What's the answer, then? Should a runner embark on triathlon training in order to reduce injuries? Or should an injury-plagued runner *avoid* the triathlon? The authors conclude that a runner-turned-triathlete will suffer fewer and less severe injuries, but *only* if he or she trains the same total number of hours per week. Cross-training works *only if total training time is not increased.* Otherwise, the additional training time will result in *more* overall injuries, and the runner who becomes a triathlete will have *more* injuries, not fewer.

As for cyclists and swimmers, these statistics indicate that becoming a triathlete definitely increases both their risk of injury and its severity. What it comes down to is that whether you are a runner or a triathlete, running is still the main cause of injury. Cyclists or swimmers add the hazards of running to their previous exposure to injury. Runners, on the other hand, are now subject to the lesser but still present injury potential of cycling and swimming.

My triathlete friend who overcame low back pain trains exclusively by cycling and swimming. He runs only in the triathlon itself. This is a compromise few triathletes will make, but he finds it acceptable. He's fit, injury-free, and competes regularly.

If the triathlon is to be a haven for the "running wounded," I suspect this sort of compromise is essential. Because the fact of the matter is, injury rates are directly related to the mileage a runner puts in. Using alternative training to substantially lower that mileage should reduce a runner's downtime with injuries to a considerable degree. However, using alternative training *while* maintaining mileage would have an opposite effect: You'll spend more time on the injured list.

One of the interesting findings in this survey was the total time put in training by each of the four groups. The cyclists trained 14 hours a week, and the triathletes, 13 hours. Swimmers and runners put in about equal time—7 hours a week.

The 31 triathletes split up their training time, devoting 5 hours to cycling, 5 to running, and 3 to swimming. Twenty-four were injured while running, 13 while cycling, and 5 while swimming. Here again, running proved to be the chief hazard to the healthy triathlete, just as overtraining is to the healthy single-sport runner. And again, the apparent conclusion is that cross-training works *only* if overall training time remains the same.

SPEED FOR A PRICE

It was evening at Sandy Hook, on the Jersey coast. The sun was setting over the bay. A friend and I were enjoying a cold beer and the satisfying fatigue that follows our weekly practice sessions with our triathlon group. We call it practice, but we swim, bike, and run as if it were a race. My friend had done especially well, finishing up close to the leaders. It was his best performance since he had joined the group.

When I congratulated him, he said, "I went out and bought some speed." I could not imagine what he meant. Even at my age, I'm still a little naive and, at times, quite slow on the uptake. My first thought was that meant drugs, or perhaps some new ergogenic aid. Was there finally some supplement that lived up to the claims of its merchandiser? Was there something you could take to give you an edge?

Then he pointed to his bike. "I paid $300 for those wheels," he said. "They're worth almost 2 miles an hour." I looked at them. They had fewer spokes than the wheels on my Miyata 310 and had odd-looking tires. The tires, he told me, were made of cotton, with a thin ribbon of rubber for contact on the road. They cost $50 apiece.

In biking, less is more. Less also costs more. Each decrease in weight is expensive. Every improvement in aerodynamics raises the sticker price. This new equipment had helped him average 24 miles per hour going downwind and 18 miles per hour on the return.

As I finished my beer, I mulled over the question of these advances in design. My first reaction was to relegate this high technology to the top-drawer competitors. Why should my friend, a middle-of-the-pack athlete, or I, bringing up the rear, go out and buy the best? For all the gains in open competition, it would not be worth it.

But I'm new to the triathlon. I am a runner and have spent decades in a sport where equipment is minimal and has little effect on performance. Initially, the triathlon seemed the same. The triathlon is a test of total fitness, arms and legs, quadriceps and hamstrings, coordination and strength, speed and stamina. The triathlon is a difficult event that becomes more difficult as it progresses. I never believed I would see a runner walking during a 4-mile race, yet this occurs, even during our pre-triathlon training sessions.

One would not think technology was important in the triathlon. It is, after all, a kind of trench warfare. (Perhaps not as primitive a struggle as the marathon, but close to it.) Why should $1,000 bikes and $300 wheels have a place in this battle with the self?

Then I remembered my father. He was by any standards a poor golfer. I am sure he never broke 100. Yet he stepped out onto the green outfitted like a touring pro. He used Ben Hogan clubs and the best balls for distance and accuracy. He vacationed at Pinehurst and Sea Island, Georgia, so he could play the most challenging courses. He thought of himself as a good golfer and bought whatever a good golfer would need. And his game, however awkward and at times embarrassing, was the better for it.

There will always be plenty of human interest stories of athletes doing astounding things with pickup clubs or a borrowed bike. There is always someone ahead of me wearing the wrong gear and pedaling away on a heavy-duty bike. No matter. I am happy with my Miyata 310. It cost more than I care to say, but this is now my art, and I do it just a little better because I have a good bike.

Technology does not spare me the effort. These aids that scientists give cyclists are not, as they might appear, energy-saving innovations. After all, my 310 is not self-propelled. But it *is* engineered to reduce any effort that is useless in propulsion. It is designed to minimize every factor that interferes with the interaction between the biker and the bike. Effort now translates more directly into performance. Less energy is consumed in overcoming wind resistance. The union of bike and biker becomes closer and closer, until they become almost one.

Pure energy becoming pure speed. The bike now becomes the extension of the biker's body, and the cycling, the expression of the biker's personality.

This is as it should be—the artist-engineer creating the perfect vehicle for the artist-athlete. The ability of the cyclist is of no concern. All that matters is doing what it takes—no, what-*ever* it takes—to achieve one's personal best. All one's speed, strength, and stamina being directly translated into one's art.

Don't believe for a minute that my friend is looking to make things easier. Whatever changes can be made in one's bicycle, there will be no fundamental changes in one's sport. It will always be a matter of the human machine, the mind/body complex with which we express our soul attempting to go faster, farther, and higher. My friend would ride himself to near-collapse, whether he was riding a Columbia resurrected from his youth or a Greg LeMond special. Buying speed simply allows him to be all the cyclist he is.

CLIMB EVERY MOUNTAIN

The protocol for total fitness is simple. Lifting weights one day and jogging the next will do the job. But how long could you sustain this routine? Would the benefits outweigh the boredom? Wouldn't we start to feel like Sisyphus, forever pushing the stone, yet never arriving at a goal?

I have a friend who teaches a fitness course at a state university. His students lift weights one day and jog the next. But they rarely drop out of the class. Why? Because the daily workouts are part of a mountain climbing course that prepares all 25 students to climb Oregon's Mount Hood. Striving to climb the mountain transforms this otherwise mundane fitness program into a new and challenging experience. A challenging goal changes something boring into something quite exciting.

"All preparation is performance, or performance to be," wrote Emerson. He would have approved of this course. Implicit in the training is the climbing of that mountain. The mountain is a tangible symbol of what the students are to achieve. The thought of the mountain infuses them with a discipline and dedication quite beyond the pragmatic impulses that fuel the ordinary fitness program.

Each of us must have a mountain, even if some might look on it as little more than a hill. We need a meaningful goal, a reason for engaging in this enterprise of being fit. Otherwise, it's simply not worth the amount of time and effort we put into it.

I can't state too often that I am not merely a cholesterol level, or a percentage of body fat, or a treadmill test. Nor am I a profile of mood states or the condition of my arteries. I am, of course, all those states. What I mean is, I am all those and more. I am a living human being, seeking experience and attempting to make sense out of my life.

Our life must contain mountains or marathons or their equivalents, else we will not be sure we have reached our potential. The person who descends from a mountain is not the same person who began the ascent. Nor is the person who finishes a marathon the same person who started the race. A fitness program without a challenge is like being in the army during peacetime.

I'm not saying that anything less than a mountain or a marathon makes a fitness program routine and mundane. Not at all. But some new, out-of-the-ordinary, relatively difficult task must lie ahead of us and provide inspiration, something of sufficient difficulty to revise our self-image and increase our self-esteem.

Lifting weights one day and jogging the next can go a long way toward achieving these ends. But we need an additional element—the accomplishment of some task, the attainment of some goal. Most fitness programs have purpose, but no meaning. On the other hand, climbing a mountain has tremendous meaning, but no purpose. Still, that goal dancing in our head can convert the most boring exercise into something meaningful, to the point where we can almost taste the sweet triumph that we know will occur at the peak.

You simply need something you think yourself incapable of. Try something you've never attempted before. Whether golf or karate, wind surfing or tennis, softball or soccer, it will give you an effective goal for getting fit. I recently visited a university where the curriculum *offered 75 different ways to earn physical education credits.* You'd be surprised at how many mountains are out there waiting to be climbed.

185

Our concentration on the physiology of exercise has blinded us to the simple truth that an athletic experience represents the key to a successful fitness program. Put a mountain at the end of your program, and things will change.

ONE WITH THE WAVES

This was no day to be at my desk. The surf was up. From my third-floor window at our beach house, I could see the waves building up at least a hundred yards from shore. The board surfers at Middle Beach were performing their wizardry on combers that looked 10 feet high. To the south, the younger fry on their Boogieboards were catching rides that would provide conversation for the entire winter.

The cause of this welcome change in our ocean was Hurricane Bertha, 500 miles to the southeast. The distant storm was also responsible for the riptide, the offshore countersurge that made the waves crest abruptly and come crashing down rather than simply breaking.

I could see all this from the shore—the size of the waves and the huge foaming as they broke. But it was only a hint of what was going on under the surface. I decided to seize this opportunity to exercise a few nonrunning muscles and go in the water. As soon as I was waist-deep in the water, I knew I would have to temper the joys of bodysurfing with concessions to the awesome power of this ocean. There would be no going beyond where my feet could touch bottom.

I've been a bodysurfer since I was a youngster, and at seventysomething, it's one thing I can still do well. Some of my best days at the beach have been those with a good surf, the wind blowing from the west, and the waves just right for riding.

Bodysurfing is an art. It requires very little athletic talent. My swimming skills are marginal. I use them mostly to get out to where the waves break. Then with no more than two or three strong strokes at precisely the right time, I can catch any breaking wave. *Timing* is the key. If you catch a wave after it's broken, you're engulfed in foam. If you start too late, you miss it entirely. Experienced bodysurfers get a feel for the point in a wave when it is just about to break, the moment that offers the one and only opportunity for success.

When that happens, I am, for an instant, on the crest, looking down from an incredible height at the flat expanse of water reaching toward shore. Then I feel the power of the wave twisting me forward. It takes me out into the clear, and like the figure on the prow of a ship, I ride it in. At times, the wave reaches such an alarming height that I pull out rather than chance injury. And even when things go well, there's that instant of fear. Will I be dashed to the bottom in this turbulence?

On the way back out to catch the big ones, I am conscious of the sea's overwhelming power. As I dive under one wave after another, I feel them crashing over me as if they were depth bombs. They toss me around under the surface, and I have to struggle to get my bearings and gain control. When I come up gasping for air, I am just in time for another huge breaker that will submerge me once more.

Today, as on most days, I am almost alone in my sport. At our beach, bodysurfing is barely surviving as a sport. In my 50 years at the shore, I have seen its adherents dwindle, as younger generations take to their surfboards. It seems as if only the lifeguards, our family members, and a handful of others have any proficiency or desire to take a cresting wave, glide down its break with head and shoulders out of the water, and ride it to the beach.

Some of the more proficient bodysurfers wear fins. I have a pair, but they get little use. I prefer the contest to be between me and these breakers thundering toward the shore. Nevertheless, there are times like today when fins would be a great help. These huge waves are breaking just beyond my ability to touch bottom. And at that point, the riptide threatens to take me farther out.

I decide then to practice my art at a lower level. I take the smaller waves. But even the smaller waves are so big they drop me off in 4 or 5 feet of water. And they break suddenly, with the foaming water rising almost as high as the original crest. Time and again, I come plummeting down into a maelstrom and only occasionally get a sustained ride toward shore. I then go back to riding with my head tucked in between my arms.

Tucking my head in was the first lesson I learned in body-surfing. In this way you *become* the wave. And the roaring in my ears and the tremors coursing through my body give me a sensation of speed unequaled in any other experience.

I can say that because of a remark made by Sir Malcolm Campbell, who once held the world speed records both on land (in a car) and on water (in a speedboat). Yet he once said that the greatest feeling of speed he ever had was riding a horse over brush. Bodysurfing has another characteristic of riding a horse over brush—the stretching of time, similar to that moment perched at the top of a huge wave, looking down at the level water below. Within a fraction of a second, I see the possibilities—a ride to remember, or an ignominious wipeout, and possibly a painful and even serious injury. I am even offered the choice, no longer available to an equestrian, of letting prudence—or cowardice?—prevail. I can renege and wait for a less dangerous situation.

Bodysurfing offers more than speed and danger. It is also aesthetic. When I bodysurf, I am using a new medium—the ocean—as a dancer uses the stage. A well-ridden wave is a thing of beauty, a real joy to experience. I am participating in the flow and energy and music of the ocean by adding my own individual expression.

And so today I am not at my desk. I am out roughhousing with Father Neptune, enjoying the art and play that is body-surfing.

Mind Games

*Running tempers stress, leaving
you calm, relaxed, and confident.*

RUNNING IS BORING?

When I give a lecture addressing the general public, I'm usually
introduced with glowing accounts of my running achievements. The moderator puts particular stress on the number of
marathons I've run and how I miss training only when I'm
injured.

As I wait to speak, I can sense a growing apprehension in
the audience, as they realize that they've been trapped. They
are about to spend the next hour listening to a *runner*.

Then I come on and attempt to allay their fears. "Running
is boring," I tell them. "And runners are even more boring." The
laugh that follows indicates total agreement.

The runners in the audience understand that I speak in
jest. I am there to introduce sedentary people to the generic
drug "exercise," not to make them into runners. Running is

simply one brand of this drug. There are a host of other brands, one of which will certainly be as interesting and joyful and life-giving for them as running is for me.

Nevertheless, there is some truth in all humor. There are times when running *is* boring. Times when it is torture to drag my reluctant body out on the road. And there are runs where I can't wait to get home. Boredom has been defined as the desire to be somewhere else—and it occurs more frequently when I'm running than I care to admit.

That desire to be somewhere else also occurs in my encounters with certain runners. From time to time, I meet a zealot whose zeal makes me apathetic, whose enthusiasm causes me to yawn, whose obsession with running makes me doubt my own faith. I try, then, to dissociate myself. I am, I tell myself, an apologist for running, but not for my fellow runners.

Others besides myself take this same attitude. One veteran runner wrote to the *New England Runner*, registering his complaints about his competitors. "I have found most runners to be very egotistical, self-indulgent, and generally obnoxious," he said. "Constant talk of PRs (personal records) and past performances permeate postrace affairs."

But these are not the runners who bore me. I would be in the center of that group, matching PR with PR, past performance with past performance. People who are egotistical, self-indulgent, and obnoxious may be irritating, but they are not boring.

They are also not your typical runner. Almost all runners are interesting and fun to be with. Runners have a sense of perspective about reality. More than most people, they understand and accept the hand they were dealt in life. More than most, they understand that competition is fundamentally a struggle with the self and, with this, have acquired a sense of humor. These runners have found the formula for the good life: "Be fit, have a sense of humor, and love what you do and the people you do it with."

Bores, to my way of thinking, have no sense of humor. They lack a sense of proportion. They are preoccupied with trivia. Those with charts of daily, monthly, and yearly mileage come immediately to mind. Sometimes I receive letters from injured runners containing sheets of such data, which I immediately consign to the wastepaper basket.

Some runners use mileage to establish their identity. I recently spotted an article by a 50-year-old runner who had logged over 120,000 miles in his life. Tipped off by the headline, I was saved from the boredom of reading the details about this human odometer.

I also number among the bores the streakers (those who have run every day for months and years). Fortunately, most of the people who do this are closet streakers. They keep this behavior to themselves. My eyes immediately glaze over, however, when I am trapped by a streaker who has come out of the closet.

There's a category of bores who focus on the medical benefits of running. A few are so preoccupied with their risk factors that they rarely talk about anything else. These people are usually heavily involved in the vagaries of their pulse rates. Their happiness depends on just how many times their heart beats per minute before, during, and after their runs. My only interest in my pulse is how slow I can get it—and, of course, how I can use it in conversation to bore other people. Perhaps the most upsetting of bores is one who has approached me with his medical problem and has now heard me repeat three times what I think he should do. Yet he sails right on with another repetition of his complaints. This person is in love with his own voice, just as I am with mine.

When something like that happens, indeed, whenever a bore brings on the old ennui, I stop listening and concentrate on something interesting—like *me*, out on the road and running. If boredom is simply the desire to be somewhere else, I can pick up my mind and go there.

I am not proud of this solution. A more mature approach to the bore would be to see the value in this encounter. "There are no boring subjects," wrote the English journalist G. K. Chesteron, "just uninterested listeners." There is much to be learned from bores, even if I find it too boring to make the effort to discover what it is.

Running itself is not boring . . . usually. And I don't always have to make an effort to send my mind elsewhere. Sometimes it goes off of its own accord.

RUNNING AS A
RIGHT-BRAIN EXPERIENCE

The "runner's high" is simply one more way to alter your state of consciousness. Behavioralist Abraham Maslow described such states as peak experiences. At a more rarefied level, they're considered mystical. The runner's high is of the same order of events, which, at one end of the spectrum, produce auditory or visual hallucinations, and at the other, a oneness with the universe.

Such occurrences are not as infrequent as one would imagine. One survey, to my recollection, found that one-third or more of the people questioned reported mystical experiences. This compares with another study in which 10 percent reported having auditory or visual hallucinations. It's also interesting to note that about 10 percent of the population is easily hypnotized.

I would suggest to you that all these phenomena, including the runner's high, are related. They are manifestations of the same mental event—the elimination of our conscious control. This reduces our link to reality to pure reflex. What we are then doing physically becomes an automatic act or series of acts, much like driving along in your car and finding your mind has been on cruise control.

When I am on a running high, I'm back in my bicameral mind, as suggested by Julian Jaynes, professor at Princeton University. I'm back in the Homeric period, with the two halves of my brain conducting a dialogue between God-the-executive and man-the-follower. I am receiving my instructions from within. They are not the product of my reasoning. I am acting out what the authority in my right brain commands or suggests. This results in concepts or actions that need not be logical or even rational. (The right brain is where the emotions are and where happiness and meaning and joy reside. In contrast, the left brain deals with the cares and duties of day-to-day living, the demands of holding a job and surviving in society.)

Whether I achieve a runner's high or not depends on whether or not I reach this receptive, unquestioning, right-brain state. If my mental processes can be divorced from my physical functioning, then I can listen to my right brain. I can learn what the oracle has to impart.

This is a condition primary to education. Our ideas have to be coaxed out of us, not fed in. We must have experiences, to be sure, to make our concepts understandable. But inside of us is the inherited wisdom of the race, our unconscious heritage waiting to be released when time and experience achieve the power to make it manifest.

This same phenomenon that allows us complete freedom to discover a growing awareness of selfhood can be used to defeat it. In looking for this authority, we follow gurus, consult astrologists, or heed other, restrictive determinants of our behavior. Our life ceases to be our own.

It is between these two worlds that we would be. Avoiding the purely rational life, and the limitations of science, yet at the same time, realizing that many nonrational movements are in many ways irrational.

Jaynes is no advocate of the rejection of consciousness and a return to the right brain. There is a case nevertheless for making time each day to probe this area and plunder its treasure. And if we cannot explore this area on our own, we tend to accept the exploration of others. Hence the rise of seers and psychics, of cults and charismatic leaders. We accept the authority of surrogates who proclaim the same master's word.

A Catholic friend of mine once told me her main argument with her Catholic schooling could be put in one sentence: "They wouldn't let me think." You do not have to be a product of the Catholic schools of the 1940s and 1950s to have that experience. The truth is we don't *want* to think. We want to have our choices made for us. And with good reason. Life is not logical. Life is not rational. We must always be facing the contradictions of our immortal feelings resident in an all-too-mortal body.

The logical left brain suppresses the notion of death and goes on with business as usual. Unless directed toward a problem such as earning a living or putting a man on the moon, thinking for oneself can lead only to depression and despair.

The neurotic, said Danish philosopher Søren Kierkegaard, is the person who has looked at life full face. It is only by concealing from ourselves the true import of the human condition that we can go on living a normal life. We deny death in order to live without its presence filling every waking moment.

We come to know that science can tell us *how* to live, but it will never tell us *why*. Yet those answers must also be available in some way. So we join churches, become members of cults, look for gurus and swamis. We seek authority and accept the role of follower.

But this is as it should be. In describing the "assurance state," William James said we make a connection with a higher power, either within or without. And to do this, we must escape the reasoning mind. James filled his treatise *Varieties of Religious Experience* with testimonies of these sudden, ecstatic revelations that effected a permanent change in various individuals' lives.

Encounters within the self occur when one is detached from the everyday world, when one's contact with material reality becomes less and less. In an attempt to explore other realities, James experimented with the effects of anesthesia, specifically nitrous oxide, on consciousness. Sleep and the dreams attendant to it are yet another way to find the secrets hidden in our mind.

We have, then, this certain knowledge that knowledge is not enough. Reason alone is inadequate. Logical answers do not suffice. We feel in our bones that what we seek is beyond the efforts of our own intelligence or any human's intelligence. What we seek is beyond words—and rarely more than momentary.

It is the expectation of that brief and sudden joy that keeps me out and running on the road.

HURRY AND WORRY

Of all the lessons sport teaches us about life, perhaps none is more dramatic than the danger of focusing on the outcome. William James pointed the finger at this unfortunate human tendency in his essay "The Gospel of Relaxation":

> I suspect that neither the nature [nor] the amount of our work is accountable for the frequency and severity of our breakdowns, but that their cause lies

rather in those absurd feelings of hurry, of having no time, in that breathlessness and tension, that anxiety of feature and that solicitude for results, that lack of inner harmony and ease, in short, by which with us the work is apt to be accompanied.

In sport, this breakdown can be immediate. The pitcher who grips the ball too tightly loses the movement on his fast ball and is soon removed from his duty. Without some movement to the inside or outside, the fast ball, no matter what the velocity, becomes easy prey to an accomplished batter.

But that batter, unless free of anxiety and tension and without thought of past success and worry about future failure, is likely to lose the chance for a solid base hit.

Sport provides any number of such examples of the need for relaxation, even at peak effort. This is the theme, for instance, of *Zen and the Art of Archery*, wherein the pupil is instructed in eliminating all concern for the result.

Timothy Gallwey popularized this approach in his book *The Inner Game of Tennis* and later in *The Inner Game of Skiing*. Almost daily, we read interviews with athletes who provide striking examples of this psychological truth. We must train and prepare and plan, but once the whistle blows to start the game or the starting gun goes off at a race, we should devote ourselves to the sport, not the final result.

James put it this way:

> Prudence and duty and self-regard, emotions of ambition, and emotions of anxiety have, of course, a needful part to play in our life. But confine them as far as possible to the occasion when you are making general resolutions and deciding your plans of campaign. When once a decision is reached and execution is the order of the day, dismiss absolutely all responsibility and care for the outcome.

What brave words! And how brave they should make us. The errors in our attitude so evident in sport are the errors we have in our attitude toward life. The athlete realizes that there has to be a balance between tension and relaxation. The coach has two types of problem players: those who try too hard, and those who don't give a damn. Sport and life are best played in a state of relaxed tension or tense relaxation.

Willpower is not creative power. I can, and should, discipline myself. I can, and should, put in my hours of preparation. But unless I arrive at the point of not worrying about the outcome, the juices will not flow. There are things I must do. Just as there are occasions of sin, there are occasions of grace. I must comply with the requirements for the productive act. I must put myself in the creative situation. But only by leaving everything, in a sense, to a higher power, by living for the process and not the product, will something uniquely my own ensue.

Again hear from James:

> It is your relaxed and easy worker, who is in no hurry and quite thoughtless most of the while of consequences, who is your most efficient worker; and tension and anxiety, and present and future, all mixed in our minds at once, are the surest drags upon steady progress and hindrances to our success.

We cannot allow pressure to make us press, or tension to make us tense. The truth we see in the great athletes is how easy it all can be. The club head speed of the championship golfers is beyond me. But *the ease with which it is attained teaches the lesson.* Performance need not be sacrificed when one is relaxed. Performance is, in fact, the sine qua non of our best days in sport—and in life as well.

EXPLOSIVE EMOTIONS

"I lost my temper," said the runner next to me, "and then I lost the race."

We were standing at the awards ceremony. The winner had been announced. He was short and thin, and he moved quietly through the crowd to collect his prize. He looked smaller and weaker than the tall, muscular young man beside me.

The second-place finisher stepped forward, then two others, then my friend's name was announced. Although he had come to win, he had never been a factor in this race.

Later he told me what had happened: "I started out in front and at a good pace. Then this guy who won jumped in front of me and slowed down. I passed him right back, but he did the same thing over and over again. Finally, I got so mad that I actually gave him a shove."

From then on, the loser had more and more difficulty maintaining the pace. Other runners glided past him. After a season of fine performances, he turned in his worst effort.

It's an old lesson: Never get angry at another runner. Rage and anger are self-defeating. These emotions create overwhelming tension that makes the task seem more difficult than it should be.

When form counts and concentration is essential, a runner doesn't profit from treating an opponent as the enemy. That is not only bad psychology, it is also bad *physi*ology. Such distractions control our attention and cause us to squander energy.

Even distractions that are not hostile interfere with performance. In the New York City Marathon one year, running down First Avenue, I heard someone calling my name. I scanned the crowd for a familiar face. In less time than it takes to tell this, my speed slackened, and my form deteriorated. I had to get right back to the business at hand: running a good marathon.

Hostility has much more profound effects. All athletic activity is a combination of muscle movements—maximally contracted prime movers, guided by delicately relaxed antagonists, with the opposing muscles constantly reversing roles.

This entire operation becomes ineffective once anger sets in. Equilibrium, harmony, and efficiency deteriorate. The harder you try, the less you accomplish.

I like to compare this to a similar physical effect when muscles are overtightened, not relaxed. Timothy Gallwey demonstrates this paradoxical response in his clinics. He asks a volunteer to bend his arm at the elbow and then prevent Gallwey from straightening it. The individual usually contracts all the muscles of the arm, including the ones used for straightening, and Gallwey has little difficulty doing just that. Yet when the person simply relaxes and resists the pull naturally, Gallwey can't straighten the arm.

Attaining proper running form is difficult at best. If you become enraged, it becomes impossible. Using opposing muscles simultaneously and maximally creates confusion, and even the slightest degree of disharmony interferes with correct function and maximum output.

Critics might see temper in another, positive light. For with anger comes a surge of power, an insensitivity to pain, a disregard for danger. I wouldn't deny these immediate effects or the bodily changes that accompany these emotions. I would argue, however, that these effects are short-lived. Long-distance running events that require endurance and form cannot be dictated by irrational surges of activity that, however powerful, are misdirected.

There is a need, of course, to get psyched, whether it's for a race, a game, or just the next 24 hours of living. We need a fire burning within us to do our best. But that incentive must be directed within. Our opponents are there to bring out the best in us, not the worst.

STRESSING THE POSITIVE

What is your reflex response when under stress? A study conducted at the University of Edinburgh looked at the way people might react to life stress. The people surveyed reported using the following methods of coping:

- Talk things over with others.
- Suppress awareness of the situation by doing something else.
- Use prayer, meditation, yoga.
- Reappraise the situation, see it in another light.
- Use your sense of humor.
- Become angry with yourself.
- Become angry with someone else.
- Smoke.
- Drink alcohol.
- Ruminate about the situation.

The Edinburgh group referred to the last five behaviors as maladaptive—that is, people who exhibited negative behavior under stress were less likely to cope successfully. On the other hand, no specific coping reaction was a *guarantee* against stress-related illness—headaches, back pain, digestive upsets, and so forth.

We cope best when we have developed the basic values and virtues necessary for the good life. It is not so much what we do when under stress, but who we are. It is unlikely, of course, that anyone who has gained mastery and self-esteem would react by anger or rumination or self-indulgence. I could see, however, an initial reaction of irritation, then intense thinking, and then perhaps relaxing over a few beers.

Sometimes, you have to blow off steam. These moods, in any case, will be transient, to be replaced by a reaffirmation of oneself and one's goals. Effective stress management is effective self management. Our task is the development of the self, the attainment of those values and virtues outlined by 20th-century philosopher Erik Erikson. Stress only serves to strengthen our strengths. Enduring increases our endurance. These tests provide us with the power for greater and longer flights.

When people break down, it's not necessarily the coping techniques that have failed them. No, people break down because they have failed internally. They have not developed the necessary values and virtues for this stage in life.

Would my running, my physical and mental modes, handle my stress without internal help? Temporarily, perhaps. Certainly running will be immediate therapy, whatever my deficiencies. I will return from the run calm, relaxed, confident. But over time, will I be able to handle this adversity, close ranks, accept my losses, make a new life? That does not depend on technique. It depends on me. It is not simply a matter of time. "Time is a test of trouble, not a remedy," wrote Emily Dickinson.

We cannot depend upon time. Our life, like it or not, fortunately or unfortunately, is in our own hands. If we believe in fate, then we must love fate, love whatever happens, because all we can control is our reaction to life.

The normal life is a life of continual expansion. It is the making actual of the potential elements of our being and the continual maintenance of those gains as we go day by day. This epigenesis occurs, as Erikson has pointed out, as we master successive stages of our life cycle. We are personalities in constant evolution. We are wholes constantly wanting to be more. Success never is more than a transient satisfaction. The mastering is never complete. Success is never fully achieved. It is the spur, the great moment when one is at one's best, followed by the certain knowledge that best will never be good enough again.

We do not achieve permanently even those values and strengths we acquire. Each day is more than a battle; it is the entire war. We awake to a 16-hour journey through every stage in life. We must possess to some degree the dominant qualities of every age from birth to death—from the playing child to the elderly sage.

PUSHING ON

Finishing a marathon leads to increased energy, dedication, discipline, and a belief that you can make a difference. It's easy to see why. Getting ready for a marathon is like getting ready for combat. Its preparation is basic training.

Marathoners begin their training as raw recruits, then emerge, still untried, at the top of their physical powers. This is where dedication and discipline are born and energy results. They have gone through the purification. They have attained dominance of the body.

The first-time marathoner may be "combat ready" but has no concept of how terrible the combat will be. The veteran runner knows that the marathon takes the body to the limits—and beyond. The newcomer is in store for pain and fatigue he or she has never felt—or even imagined—before. And both the veteran and the first-timer worry that they won't have the mental toughness to carry it off.

But if the runner *does* have what it takes, a new self is born. By enduring this 26.2-mile agony, the runner achieves the physical, mental, and spiritual virtues and strengths that make a runner a successful player in life.

The runner takes the rights of life, liberty, and the pursuit of happiness and makes them obligations. We are not free to dispose of our life, cast aside our liberty, cease in the pursuit of happiness. On the contrary, we are enjoined to live the good life.

There is a battle to be fought—and fought daily. There is a victory to be won—and won continually. And there is a defeat that must be risked—and constantly overcome. We can take as our motto the words uttered by Alfred Tennyson's Ulysses: "To strive, to seek, to find, and not to yield."

BE YOUR OWN JUDGE

Man is born to be a success. When we see athletes at their best, we believe it.

On one occasion, I was speaking at an awards ceremony to honor those in the Olympic Marathon Trials. I'd been given an award and introduced. The audience expected a message. Award winners are expected to have a message, especially someone being honored for contributions to health and fitness.

"I do not have a message," I told the audience. "I *am* the message." And so were the former Olympian marathoners who had been introduced earlier in the evening, along with those vying for places on the Olympic team the coming weekend.

"What you see is my message," I said. "I am my word made flesh. My meaning in action. I tell people by my own being and becoming what is important and what isn't."

The Olympians had made their statement. The millions of Americans seeking to be their best were making theirs. In the Bloomsday Run in Spokane, Washington, some 60,000 runners were messengers who *were* the message. And the 6,000 in the Bloomsday Children's Run were indeed angels, messengers with their own message.

Our host this night was a man who builds industrial parks and develops senior citizen communities. I had never met him, never heard him speak, never read anything he said, but I knew his message. He builds each house as if it were his last. He is his truth, his knowledge, his honesty in action.

Words are cheap. Ideals cost nothing. What moves and inspires are the actions that we can later clothe in words. A life that embodies an ideal. It is only after the fact that we can translate it into universal truth.

The message of all these people is themselves: "I am what man can be. If you think well of me, think well of yourself. What you see in me is also in you." So each of us is a message. And we are in an era of messengers of all ages and both sexes telling us to aim higher and faster and farther.

Awards are a fact of life. Few of us can make it to the grave without putting up with some celebration about our contribution to something or other. And some of us even deserve such recognition. But people should be content with learning from being the living, breathing people we are. They should not expect advice that will make life easier.

In any case, God, not our peers, will sit in judgment on our life. One wonders about the estimation of people who know as little about life as you do. The only alternative is to look to people who act as if the fate of the world depended on them.

W. Macneile Dixon came to this conclusion in *The Human Situation:* "Be loyal to ship company, so that this endeavor will not founder because of you. If things fail, if we go under, it will not be because of me."

There are those who do all that in silence and inspire others to do likewise. Such messages go from heart to heart, not from brain to brain. It is the nonverbal that has the most influence. What cannot be put into words stirs us most. We are silent because the message comes from—and therefore reaches—areas too deep for speech.

Perhaps more than anyone else, the athlete is the message. We sit in the stands watching someone who, except for the moments in the arena, is unknown to us. Yet here we see why man is the marvel of the universe. "The athlete instantiates man," writes the philosopher Paul Weiss. "I am proud to be of this breed," said the poet James Dickey as he watched an Olympian in action.

We watch, and we learn. When I think of basketball player Bill Bradley, I think of moving *without* the ball, not because of anything he said but because he demonstrated what is now a basketball truth: Players can contribute at every moment of the game, whether they're carrying the ball or not. He demonstrated other truths about the athletic life that we attempt to capture in words and rarely succeed. Bill Bradley *was* his message.

So are we all. We demonstrate our answers to the great questions in life, including that most difficult one: "What it means to be a man." Do not expect it to be written in a book. We must, as German poet Rainer Maria Rilke said, "live the questions." And the way we do that is our message to the world.

The dying William James said, "There are no answers, no conclusions."

I accept that. I do not want to add my answers to that cacophony of people who think they have them. If I *do* have answers, they are mine and not yours. If there are conclusions, they are unique to me. And if I would, I could not put what matters most into words.

What I reveal of myself in speech or words is never quite the truth. If I would tell my truth, I can't. I can only live it, inwardly and outwardly. I am, for better or worse, my own message.

GIVING THANKS

A number of magazines have done features on me. Roger Kahn, for instance, profiled me in *Esquire*. When I sent a note of thanks, he told me that in his years at the magazine, I was only the second person he had profiled to thank him. In another instance, I appeared on the cover of a running magazine, which prompted me to send a note to the editor. He wrote back, "It's interesting that we have not once received a thank-you letter from any runner who has been on the cover—until yours."

My experience with my own column has been the same. I give advice to an injured athlete and hear no more until he or she is injured again. I treat ten times ten for each one who returns to say "Thank you." A year or more later, when some new difficulty has cropped up, I am told that the previous treatment worked, and I'm now asked what to do about the current problem.

Not that I find the silence of people so benefited difficult to explain. If you wish to know human nature, said Thoreau, look inside yourself. I'm no better than anyone else. We runners are a self-centered lot, high achievers who focus on doing our personal best. I am aware of my own preoccupation with performance. I accept the race as if I were entitled to it, never questioning how it came into being. And without thanking all concerned. Rightly, I should say "Thanks" at every water station, to every traffic guard, to the people at the chute, and I should end with congratulations for the race director. Yet I rarely do so, nor do many runners I know.

This extends to my other life as well. I accept hospitality on my trips and assume it to be routine. People are nice to me, and I make nothing of it. There are any number of individuals who have contributed to my life to whom I've never expressed my gratitude.

Many times we think "Thank you," but laziness and other negative elements of human nature prevent us from expressing it. For every person who writes a thank-you note, there are a hundred who intend to but don't. And many others don't even think of it. The past is soon forgotten in our push to the future. We spend little time in reflection. We do not meditate on the meaning of our experiences. Failing in that, we fail to see the people involved as well.

If lepers do not return a favor, how can I be faulted for failing to acknowledge some quite ordinary consideration? Each of us has a role we're expected to fulfill. Why, then, thank my barber or waitress or mechanic or physician? Why take pen in hand to let a writer know I appreciate what was written?

The answer, it seems to me, is that the thank-you is part of my role in having my hair cut, my meals served, my car fixed, my sickness cured. Saying "Thank you" completes the action. Without a thank-you, the person doing the favor or service feels in some way a failure. I suspect that's why the inevitable response to a thank-you is a thank-you in return.

When passengers depart planes nowadays, the pilot and flight attendants usually stand at the door and say "Good-bye." This practice is probably a public relations one—and, in any case, seems quite perfunctory. As I leave, I always say a genuine "Thank you," which provokes a quite genuine "Thank you" in response. After all, they've brought me safely through the hazards of taking off, flying hundreds of miles, and then landing. They have attended to my needs, brought me beverages and food and reading material. They have done their job, what they are paid to do, but they like being thanked. In fact, they *need* to be thanked. Giving thanks is the role of the recipient. When the donor is not thanked, a chain in human interaction is broken. The action is incomplete.

All too often, a thank-you note provokes a response that not only thanks you in return but also mentions that you are the first ever to tell this person how much he or she is appreciated. While it's true that our happiness should not depend on what other people think of us, nevertheless, happiness is undoubtedly enhanced by heartfelt good wishes and good words.

Even Thanksgiving is a day on which we thank the Lord but not his servants. But it *could* also be a day when we stop, think, then thank our fellow human beings—people who had a major influence on our life and never knew it. People we loved and left who could be told that those loving years were a gift we still treasure. There are lives that have intertwined with our own in helpful and meaningful ways. Thank-you's are never too late for all these people.

Chapter

11

Running for a Lifetime

Running generates peak mental and physical energy to help win the game of life.

ACTING YOUR AGE

When George Bush had a bout of atrial fibrillation (rapid, irregular heartbeat) while out jogging a couple of years ago, a member of the Senate suggested that Bush act his age. But he *did*. President Bush was doing what a normal 66-year-old can and should do: exercise, be fit, and put in a long, strenuous day. He was getting the most out of his 66-year-old body. As a consequence, he is able to live each day with energy and zest and fill it with productive activity.

Unlike President Bush, the average American male is sedentary and 30 years older functionally than he is chronologically. In other words, there's a 30-year gap between his age and what he can do. A trained 60-year-old can outperform a sedentary 30-year-old. George Bush's jogging has enabled him to close this gap, bringing his chronological age down to his physiological age.

Critics of Mr. Bush's exercise habits should brush up on what we've learned about the aging process. When the body exercises on a regular basis, aging is remarkably slow. So clearly, what was previously accepted as normal aging was due to inactivity. The old cliché "Use it or lose it" has proven correct.

When people use their bodies consistently, the results are illuminating. The current world record for 40-year-old distance runners is within 5 percent of the overall world record; for 50-year-olds, within 10 percent; and for people 60 years of age, within 15 percent.

You might say that these people's bodies are physical "geniuses," that these statistics don't apply to ordinary individuals. Not so. Each of us has the same potential to set our own world record—what we could have done at our peak, the age of 28, even though we didn't do it. At 40, we can come within 5 percent of that peak; at 50, within 10 percent; and at 60, within 15 percent.

People who live life fully have always been aware of how well their aging body—*and* their mind and spirit—can perform. Emerson, at the age of 62, put a note in his journal: "I look inside and don't see wrinkles or a tired heart, I see an unspent youth." Tests both in laboratories and in athletic events like the Boston Marathon and Scandinavian cross-country events have proven Emerson right.

The medical literature is now being flooded with reports on the competence of aging subjects. Anything youth can do they can do as well, or with only minor decrements in their performance. Beginners of advanced age experience the same percentage of improvement in endurance and strength as their younger counterparts.

The consensus on exercise is becoming clear. Start when you are young, and don't stop. Exercise is the only way to become fit, and it is essential in reducing or eliminating coronary risk factors. Above all, it's safer to exercise than not to exercise. And once past the age of 65, the sedentary life becomes increasingly dangerous. Study after study has shown a 50 percent reduction in heart attacks in active people over 65 years of age.

Our president is doing what every American his age should be doing—exercising regularly at something he enjoys doing. He is following nature's rules, rules that do not change as we age.

I believe that. Now that I am in my seventies, I still try to be the runner I was at Manhattan College. I want my pulse and blood pressure and cholesterol and all my physiological and metabolic functions to match what they were when I was 20. Life is not a spectator sport. All of us are athletes, only some of us are in training, and some are not.

George Bush, who was an athlete at Yale, seems to be of the same mind. As president, he needs to perform at the top of his powers. Only with a regular exercise program can he do that.

LIFE'S GOLD MEDALISTS

Behavioral scientist Abraham Maslow once recommended that we study the "gold medalists" in life. He believed that successful people ("self-actualizers," he called them) are more likely to be good decision makers. We would do well, he thought, to study their choices and benefit from them.

One group of people I would consider gold medalists is runners in their fifties who've made running part of their lifestyle. They are examples of people who are establishing new limits for our physical being. They are Olympians in their own right, individuals who are showing us what men and women are capable of.

However, I am interested not so much in their performance but in what impels them to run to begin with. What needs does running serve? What satisfactions compel them to keep at it? Other runners who are either just starting out or aspiring to a new personal best would benefit from some kind of analysis of the motives of this elite group.

Fortunately, just such a survey *has* been done. Keith Johnsgaard, M.D., questioned 180 runners, men and women 50 years old and older who had been running 6 years or more. Dr. Johns-gaard found that the reasons these people took to the roads continued to motivate them after they became confirmed runners. What's more, as running became a way of life for these people, certain factors became less important, while others became more important.

The motives listed by the runners can quickly be summarized as (in the runners' words):

- Fitness.
- Being slim.
- "It feels good."
- The "afterglow" experience.
- Centering (solitude).
- Challenge and competition.
- Identification with athletes.
- Overcoming an addiction.
- Social aspects.

Most of these are self-explanatory. Some motives—like being fit and slim, feeling good, and enjoying the afterglow—are physical phenomena. Others are psychological: centering, or the solitude experienced in running; the satisfaction of personal challenge and competition against others and of thinking of oneself as an athlete. Conquering an addiction was seldom a primary reason for running, and it became even less important after running for several years. And finally, the survey seemed to indicate that the companionship of running and associating with other runners never loses its appeal.

Men and women runners alike found that running satisfied their needs for physical fitness, mood control, and self-concept. Their decision to run was a positive factor in their success in life, reinforcing their original decision to run.

Over the years, these 50-ish runners assumed personal responsibility for both their physical and mental health. Other researchers who have studied long-term runners, including scientists from Arizona State University, observed this same phenomenon.

Both would-be exercisers and those who try to get nonexercisers moving can learn some valuable lessons from these reports on older runners. First, however, it should be said that exercise is the generic drug. Other forms of exercise can provide the same needs and satisfactions that running does.

Having said that, we must elevate our consciousness to the global effects of exercise. These gold medalists discovered that running brought about positive changes in the whole person, body, mind, and spirit. Their response to Dr. Johnsgaard's questionnaire attests to that.

Those rewards are there for us as well. That knowledge should give us the strength and stamina to persist with our own program until the rewards change us and our life in similar fashion.

LIFE SKILLS TAUGHT HERE

When you come down to it, what running does is give you the basic skills to live well. Each one of us is obliged to live our own life, without precedent or design. We arise each day to act out our own drama, write our own novel. Each of us is a unique, never-to-be-repeated individual.

In much the same way, an athlete prepares for an event. Mastering the necessary skills is all-important. Coaches are forever stressing the fundamentals. Football players must learn to block and tackle. Baseball players practice running, throwing, and hitting. Tennis players work on their serve, volley, and ground strokes.

Those primary abilities usually carry the day. True, the athlete enters the event with a game plan, a predetermined scheme of play. More often than not, though, the plan soon evaporates. Factors beyond will or control enter in. Basic ability determines who wins, not tricks, strategies, and tactics.

To win the game of life, we also have to master some essentials. Energy is one. Physical energy is necessary for whatever we do daily. Otherwise, we'll perform badly or not at all. The 24 hours we receive daily will shrink to a good deal less when we lack the endurance and stamina to use them. Running develops that energy. It can make the end of your work the beginning of your day. Running produces a fitness that allows for the full use of the physical body from sunup to sundown and beyond, until bedtime.

Why, then, settle for the fatigue and lassitude that so often set in late in the day or early in the evening? There is a cure: motion. Motion of almost any sort, provided it is vigorous and persistent. Walking, cycling, swimming, rope skipping, and, of course, running.

Running produces this fitness of muscle. But it produces another fitness, a fitness beyond that. It allows for meditation, the sine qua non of creativity, and contemplation, which provides a sense of where we fit in the scheme of things.

The game of life requires physical energy and other energies as well. Creative energy, for one. Learning how to work with the stream of consciousness. The ability of association is vital to pursuing the self. Human potential movements all stress this need to free oneself from consequences and enter the world of mind play. In running, motion becomes the mantra for this altered state of consciousness.

The game of life does not operate solely through reason. But reason and logic are necessary. One cannot go through life as pure animal. Physical energy is not enough, nor is creative energy sufficient of itself.

There is a place for discipline and self-control, for gratification denied, for the orderly actualization of the unruly, playful thoughts that come on the run. All human potential movements should instill the need for reason and order. The athlete, said Plato, grows unbalanced.

Running provides that self-control, that discipline. It prepares one for hardship. It teaches about pain and guilt. But it also demands logic and teaches how results are obtained.

In facing life, no one knows exactly what is going to happen, what is going to be needed, where the search for the Grail will lead. The best we can do is be prepared. Running makes you an athlete in all areas. Trained in basics, ready for whatever comes. Ready to live each day, fill each hour, and deal with the decisive moment.

BUY YOURSELF SOME YEARS

We know that being physically fit gives us a longer day. But will being physically fit also give us a longer life? Many studies have been done on the association between heart disease and a sedentary lifestyle. Various investigators have suggested that vigorous exercise, particularly in leisure time, protects an individual against coronary artery disease. Expending 2,000 or more sweaty calories a week, it's claimed, confers relative immunity to heart problems.

Medical studies, however, tend to measure activity itself rather than the physiological effects of activity—that is, physical fitness. A study done on successful applicants for employment in the fire and law enforcement departments of Los Angeles County has attempted to correct that. University of Southern California researchers issued a report on the relationship between actual physical fitness and subsequent heart attack in 2,779 of these men, who were followed for an average of 4.8 years.

Using a bicycle ergometer to measure physical work capacity (PWC), they found that men who were less physically fit than half of their age-matched coworkers were *twice* as likely to have a heart attack within the subsequent few years. This risk was present regardless of whether they smoked, had higher-than-average levels of cholesterol, or had higher-than-average (but not dangerously high) blood pressure. Men who had two or more of these other risk factors *and* a low PWC were more than *six times* as likely to have a heart attack.

It can be argued that some people naturally have a higher PWC, along with other factors that protect them against heart disease. PWC due to exercise may play only a minor role—or even none at all. Indeed, this report suggests that if you are a nonsmoker, have a lower-than-average blood cholesterol, and a lower-than-average blood pressure for people your age, exercising may not lower your risk further. It's *already* pretty darn good.

On the other hand, when you are in statistical danger of heart attack, being out of shape significantly increases your risk. The authors wrap up their report with this recommendation: "We believe that otherwise healthy men who smoke, whose blood pressure levels or cholesterol are even moderately elevated, or who have any combination of these risk factors should be encouraged to adopt and maintain some form of regular exercise."

Apparently being physically fit may lengthen our life—but only when there are other factors that threaten to shorten it.

KEEPING YOUR MIND YOUNG

The art of living is the process whereby the human machine, the mind/body complex, expresses the self. The science of this art is health. A sound mind in a sound body. Exercise makes for both. When we use the body with intensity to make it healthy and fit, we make the mind healthy and fit as well. As our physical work capacity rises, our capacity for mental work does as well.

"Health is the first muse," writes Emerson. I found it so. When I run, I run myself into health. I also run myself into my best thoughts. My mental life parallels my physical one. I develop mental powers that are counterparts of those my body now enjoys. Running makes me feel better about myself in every way.

Physicians who have concentrated on lengthening life through exercise tend to ignore the very important contributions that physical activity makes to the healthy mind. Dr. Roy Shephard, a Canadian physiologist, has recently written about some of these benefits. Exercise, writes Dr. Shephard, causes among other things: an increase in arousal, improvement in self-esteem, relief of anxiety and depression, better stress management, and the maximization of intellectual development.

I can attest to all of the above. I have used my running to achieve each of these effects and have rarely been disappointed. When I need to improve my psychological state, I turn to the roads and find the benefits Dr. Shephard describes.

Arousal is related to vigilance. It can be too low or too high. Maximum performance is reached when it is in the middle. Running puts my arousal in that range. It can bring me down when I am nervous and agitated, or it can stimulate me when I am bored or sleepy. Running picks me up when I am down and quiets me when I am in a hyperaroused state.

This effect is strong and immediate, but—admittedly—temporary. The effect on self-esteem tends to be delayed but permanent. My self-esteem rose with my ability to run and the coincident increase in my ability to think. A major factor was a change in my self-image. My body, as it really exists, has gotten closer and closer to my body as I would like it to be. I now see myself as an athlete in pursuit of excellence, and I'm happy with the results.

Dr. Shephard cites an 18-month conditioning program at the National Aeronautics and Space Administration (NASA) that showed major gains in the self-image of participants. These gains were associated with an increase in stamina, feelings of positive health, and a greater ability to cope with stress.

The positive effect of exercise on anxiety and depression has frequently been reported. Joggers have been shown to have low scores in physical signs of anxiety—elevated heart rate and muscle tension, for instance. Running has actually been used as a treatment for depression. In fact, in some cases, it works better than medication.

Given these excellent results in treating anxiety and depression, it is evident that exercise is also a powerful tool in stress management. I know this from my own experience in medical practice. Time and again, when I got angry or impatient with someone in the office, an hour's run would purge me of those hostile and aggressive tendencies. I would return to my work full of sweetness and light, almost incapable of anger or irritation.

A generally unrecognized consequence of exercise is an increase in the ability to learn. There is an immediate and long-range improvement in the capacity for concentration. One study was done in a Canadian school, where one group of students spent 5 hours a week on physical activity. Other students, serving as a comparison, carried on with their usual study program. Those who participated in the phys ed program scored consistently higher marks than those who did not.

Studies, of course, are only studies. You and I, each of us, are an experiment of one who must find what works for us. Will exercise do for you what Dr. Shephard claims? Will it give you a sound mind in a sound body? Will it give you the human machine you need to make your life a work of art?

You'll never know until you try for yourself.

LIMBER UP?

How old would you be if you didn't know how old you are? That question, first posed by Satchel Paige, might trigger many different answers. Some people would say, "As old as you feel." Some would reply, "As old as you look." And neither view would necessarily agree with more specific estimates of age made by a physician or physiologist. My physician would focus on the state of my arteries and tell me my biological age. "You have the arteries of a 45-year-old," he might say. The physiologist would determine my level of fitness and equate that with my functional age. "You have the maximum oxygen capacity of a man 10 years your junior," he might say.

There are, it can be seen, a variety of ways for the body to age. Some are readily observable. Some require specific testing. All are ultimately inevitable. I am bound to age.

The rate at which I age, however, is up to me. Individual behavior determines individual aging. I can age fast, or I can age slowly. And I can age in one way but not another.

One way I have aged is in my appearance and the way I go about normal activities. Carriage is important—and mine is poor. Having good posture, flexibility, and a spring in your step makes for a youthful impression. But I have poor flexibility, terrible posture, and tend to stroll rather than stride. If you saw me walking around town, you would think I was older than I am.

This form of aging is, of course, completely unnecessary. Like 85-year-old ballerinas, I could be lithe and supple, *if* I devoted some time to it. I know that doing daily yoga and range of motion exercises could take decades off the elderly way I move.

One aging agent I have escaped is tobacco. I have never smoked, so I have avoided the subtle but cumulative effects tobacco has on skin tone, texture, and appearance. If you do smoke, however, it is never too late to stop. My mother gave up smoking at 87, and it took years off of her appearance.

Alcohol also has the potential to age one prematurely. Characteristic are the puffiness of the face, particularly around the eyes, and, in women, the evident loss of muscle tone in the legs—"bird legs," a professor of mine used to call them. A dedicated drinker can age right before your eyes.

A high-calorie diet—and the extra pounds it can generate—can add years to a person's actual age. An overweight individual is often assumed to be much older than his or her calendar age.

And as with smoking and drinking, the consequences of being overweight are far more serious than the impression you make on others. As a matter of fact, one of the things doctors learn in medical school is that when making a physical exam, they should observe whether the patient looks older or younger than his or her stated age.

Merely by looking at me, an astute observer could make a reasonably correct judgment about my lifestyle. He or she could tell me that I look younger or older than my years and give probable causes for the discrepancy between my appearance and my actual age.

Some age-related changes are of little significance to longevity. I have poor range of motion, for instance, but it won't kill me. Yet they are important in other, less direct ways. If indeed I am as young as I feel and as young as I look, then the way I move will be of considerable influence on my attitude toward myself and life.

To remain young at heart, we must retain—or regain—our youthful control over our body. The late Paul Uram, once the "flex" coach for the Pittsburgh Steelers, recommended that the basic physical education in grammar school should be gymnastics. Body control, the essence of gymnastics, is fundamental to all other physical activity. Now I know now that Uram was right. I am battling age to a standstill in all departments except one. My arteries are young, and so is my performance. But my lack of flexibility and coordination betrays my age.

If I really wanted to, of course, I could change this. And I wouldn't have to take up ballet, either. A few minutes of yoga in the morning or some other kind of gentle stretching would do it. And maybe someday, I'll consider it.

NO MORE EXCUSES

Survival of the fittest is still the rule of the day. Fitness will forever be a necessity. No matter the advances in technology, we will always need the vigor and zest and stamina that go with a well-trained body. There will never be a time when these qualities go out of style.

The brightest and the best are almost invariably fit. The stories about these notables usually disclose a regular participation in physical activity. We read constantly of prominent people who exercise or jog or play racquet sports.

Further confirmation of this association of fitness with success comes from a Canadian fitness survey of unprecedented scope: "Fitness and Lifestyle in Canada." Over 22,000 Canadians, aged 7 through 70, were questioned about their physical fitness habits and activities. In general, the news was good: Over 58 percent of Canadians—both male and female, of all ages—are physically active in their leisure time.

Within this group, however, people vary. Some take physical activity more seriously and are more likely to be fit— they're predominantly young, single, better-educated managers and professionals, both male and female. These people don't smoke, and while they're not overly concerned with weight control, they like to be active. They are healthier, with greater emotional well-being and positive self-esteem. They are more likely to eat a good breakfast and get 7 to 8 hours of sleep a night.

The researchers didn't merely question these people, they tested them as well. The step test, which measures stamina, cardiovascular fitness, and muscular endurance, showed that these individuals are more physically fit. They are more flexible, too.

Among people who *aren't* fit, the most frequent excuse for not participating in a fitness program was lack of time. Almost one-quarter of the people in the study cited "not enough time" as the major reason for either not starting an exercise program or dropping out at a later date. Next came frank confessions of laziness and lack of self-discipline. Other reasons for not exercising included no access to a facility, having no one to exercise with, and cost.

When you consider the benefits of exercise, none of those excuses make sense. Lack of time? Regular physical activity gives you *additional* time—there's no better way to make the hours you work more productive. And a fitness program is *in itself* a cure for laziness and boredom. It *generates* self-discipline. It makes habitual and second nature the movement that the body needs so much.

The exercisers, the "good choosers," as Abraham Maslow calls such winners, have discovered that. They are the people who have learned how the human machine works. They have gone to school on their body. These fittest have not merely survived. They have succeeded as well.

FORMULAS FOR LONG LIFE

Minerva, the pseudonym of the woman physician who comments on medical trends in the *British Medical Journal,* had a column on the lifestyles of a group of successful octogenarians. She reported on the replies to a questionnaire sent to 15 healthy doctors (13 men and 2 women), aged 85 or older.

The answers confirm the general belief that long-lived people come from long-lived families. Many physicians came from families in which 90-year-olds were common. "The best hope of longevity," wrote Minerva, "comes from long-lived relatives."

The probability is that we are born with a genetically determined life span, which can be enjoyed to the maximum— but *only* if we follow a prescribed lifestyle. Nature, as we have found, is merciless; and breaking nature's rules will inevitably diminish our personal longevity quotient.

These older people, consciously or not, have followed nature's well-defined instructions for successful living. Their responses revealed how best to live to a fit and healthy old age.

Exercise. Fourteen of the 15 people surveyed led lives of unremitting physical activity. Half were athletes when young; and all enjoyed walking every day, even those with arthritis. Half of them were gardeners, and several went hiking and mountaineering when on vacation.

Incidentally, in that same issue of the *British Medical Journal,* investigators from the Netherlands reported that a group of Dutch skaters, followed for 32 years, lived 24 percent longer than expected. I take that to mean that people engaged in such a sport would be athletes for life.

Smoking. Only three people in the British study had never smoked in their lives. The others smoked as young adults, often heavily. Ten stopped in middle age. One smoked lightly until his eighties. One physician was still smoking a cigar a day.

Drinking. Except for four people who never drank, most of the people studied drank every day. One said that by medical standards, he was an alcoholic.

Diet. Those who detailed their diet were eating lots of fruit and vegetables and not much meat. Only one was overweight.

Marriage. All were married, and only one had been divorced. His second marriage had lasted over 40 years.

Travel and hobbies. All were travelers. Ten frequently vacationed on the European continent. Five had been around the world at least once. Several had a wide range of hobbies. All were lifelong readers.

Health. Several emphasized the happy lives they had and were still leading. One wrote, "I consider myself the luckiest person I know, and wouldn't change places with anyone." Minerva admits that this is a small, unscientific sample, yet she's prepared to make these assertions about the group:

- Smokers who stopped before the age of 40 or 50 seem to have come to no harm.
- A daily alcoholic drink or two seems compatible with a long and healthy life.
- A happy, prolonged marriage seems a good thing.
- Sustained physical and mental activity seems to be associated with not only a long life but also a happy one.

Not too many of us are likely to live as long as Minerva's octogenarians, but all of us would do well to follow their example.

THE TRUTH ABOUT AGING

Running, which has taught me many things, is teaching me how to deal with age. For one thing, running has put age beyond denial. At seventysomething, I am finally and irrevocably old. I am not and never again will be the runner I was a mere few years ago. And that runner was not the one I was a decade ago. And so on back to when I was 45 and new to this whole game.

My body is only partially under my control. I can get the most out of it. But that most is constantly becoming less. Now when I run in a race, someone is likely to ask, "What are you doing back there, Doc?" The card I'm handed at the finish line is several numbers higher. And when the results are published, I am a lot farther down on the list than I used to be.

There are other changes in my life, changes that I regard as temporary. Writer's block, the lapses in memory, the retreat into the self—they happen to people of any age, young as well as old. It is the runner I have become in races I cannot deny.

Actually, *running* a race is no different. That was the first lesson. Everything in the race is the same—the pain, the shortness of breath, the dread of what is to come, the last draining drive to the finish. The only difference is the time on the digital clock as I enter the chute.

I am racing at a pace I could have maintained a few years back, in conversational runs with a friend. Now that same pace is flank speed. I am right at the edge of all I can do. Someone passes me, and I try to keep up with her. But lungs and legs immediately protest.

Fortunately, many of the good things about a race remain. My body responding to the demands I put on it. The moments of triumph when I crest a hill. Those brief periods when I am in charge, full of speed and strength. When I am in a race where no one calls out the times at the various mile markers, I am the runner I have always been. It feels as it has always felt.

The main difference, aside from the time, is my fellow runners. I am now running, I tell my friends, with a better class of people. This came as a surprise to me. I have always described myself as a middle-of-the-pack runner, but I never was. I was an elite runner. I rarely came home without a trophy. I usually finished with people who had a chance to win something or get their name in the paper.

Now I am back with people who are known as runners only to their closest relatives. Few, if any, have ever gotten a medal or a trophy. None will make the sports summaries in tomorrow's paper. Yet all around me are runners trying as desperately as I am.

In the past, I thought those in the back were jogging along,

chatting and enjoying the scenery. But I am beginning to realize it does not matter where I finish or how fast I run. Being
a winner means doing my best. Having done that, I, and those
around me who are doing the same, can go through the chute
and note time and place with pride, not embarrassment. I ran
an annual 5-mile race 8 minutes slower than I had three years
earlier, yet I crossed the line knowing I had run a great race.
Everyone around me was putting as much into the race as those
in the top ten were. I had no doubt that those behind us were
doing the same.

When I finished, I remembered something the aging Robert Frost said: "It never gets any easier to save your soul." Fortunately, it doesn't get *harder,* either. The race asks what it has
always asked—no less and no more—simply everything over
which I have control.

FAMILIES ARE FOREVER

As I took my early-morning swim one day, I noticed a runner
watching me from the boardwalk. Later, as I was toweling off
on the porch, he approached and introduced himself as reader
of my column. Then he asked, "What is the most important
thing in your life?"

If I were asked that question at 7:00 in the evening, it would
draw a philosophic reply, like "What is 'important'?" Or: "What
do you mean by 'life'?" The sort of evasions that come after
another day of living with myself and others, leaving me full of
doubt.

But at 7:00 in the *morning,* my answer was simple and
direct as the newly risen day. Without hesitation, my head and
heart responded, "My family."

It was the absolutely certain reply of a seventysomething
male who has entered the seventh stage in Erik Erikson's eight-
stage life cycle. I have attained what Erikson terms *generavity*—
concern about the welfare of the generations to come, particularly my family.

Of the virtues and values I had to acquire in life, generavity
was the most difficult to attain. According to Erikson, this is a
rule of human nature. I doubt it. For males, perhaps this is true.

But for women, generavity is a force from the arrival of their firstborn.

When our children were born, I was primarily concerned with my self-development. My wife and family were part of that self only peripherally. They were in intimate association with me. I was responsible for their growth and development. But they were nevertheless external to the self I was making.

In my pursuit of excellence, in my profession and later in my associations, I devoted a minimum amount of time and attention to my family. At times, I wanted to be free from all the hassle of family life.

A lot of married men develop this desire to escape and pursue some idyllic life with another person. A very good family practitioner once told me, "If all the men in this town who wanted to leave their homes did so, there would be very few families with fathers."

And even when families remain intact, that life may be difficult. "The proper word for family is 'strife,'" writes Ortega y Gasset. The family is kept intact by knowing what can be said and what can't. At times, it's like walking on eggshells. This tension and its more overt manifestations have led to the concept of dysfunctional families. My own belief is that all families malfunction at one time or other. An assembly of egos in all stages of development can hardly be expected to operate friction-free.

My solution was to more or less detach myself from the group. In that position, I was not a positive influence, but at least I wasn't a negative force. I am a loner, a person interested in ideas rather than people. I liked to have people around me, but I preferred to read a book while they were there.

The antithesis of generavity is self-absorption. I was heavily involved in creativity and productivity. But I was more and more self-absorbed. The attraction of any action was what I would personally derive from it. My motivation was my own needs and satisfaction.

I was late in coming to generavity, which is no less than the virtue of caring. Its theological counterpart is charity. It is going beyond the self. One theologian described sin as "closing the ring of concern." I had closed it around myself. I now include many people inside the ring and am learning to open that ring more and more.

Growth and the attainment of a new plateau did not come simply because I was in my late sixties. In truth, it should have occurred decades back. Reaching a certain stage in the life cycle does not come automatically.

I came to this love for my family and others through a familiar life-giving force, adversity. Cancer, its attendant pain, and an awareness of my isolation brought me back to a patient, loving wife and our sons and daughters.

In giving me cancer, fortune had smiled on me. Pain was a key to opening up a new and larger life. The interests of my past are still present, but now finally seen in perspective.

That's why I was able to answer without hesitation when a stranger asked me to put my present life into one word— "Family."

Epilogue

A monastery is a place where the traditional injunctions can be obeyed. Every day, one can be born again. Daily, a person can put on the new man. Every 24 hours, one can be renewed in strength and purpose. Our everyday world convinces us of a wrongness ever present in our consciousness. The monastery replaces this awareness of evil with the ideal we hold in our subconscious.

William James called this ideal "the assurance state"— the belief that I, just as I stand, without one plea, am saved now and forever. The central characteristic of this state is a loss of all worry, the sense that all is ultimately well with one. There is a peace and harmony and what James called "a willingness to be."

There is no denying this state can occur, as it did to the apostle Paul, at any time or place. For all I know, the person sitting next to me in a plane might be experiencing this state of assurance. Or someone else in this room, a fellow writer whose typewriter is now silent, may be in the midst of such a state of faith. The Roman statesman Marcus Aurelius claimed that a man could retire into himself, regardless of the circumstances.

Nevertheless, there is a best place to repent and rejoice and know beatitude—a place like the Trappist monastery Father Henri Nouwen chose for his retreat, which attends to the body and mind as well as the soul. A place where one can go daily and become, if only for an hour, the person one was meant to be. For me, that place is running. That hour or so a day I devote to running satisfies the demands of teachers over the centuries.

This hiatus in the day goes back to Greeks in the fifth century B.C. They spent an hour every day in the paelestra, their school for athletics, perfecting their bodies. The Greeks saw man as a whole, body/mind/soul. Developing each function made a person a harmonious whole. Running develops my body and creates that harmonious whole. Running is a place where my body is at home, a place where it does what it is meant to do and does it surpassingly well. Running is where I become all I *can* be.

That same hour is also for my mind. It is the hour set aside for thinking. Out on the road, I achieve a private solitude equal to the seclusion Father Nouwen found in the abbey. I retire to my personal sanctum. I avoid my fellows. My mind is now free of distractions. I am, for once this day, alone.

Emerson recommended a daily period of such retirement. "I believe," he wrote, "a well-ordered mind has a new thought awaiting it every morning. And hence eminently thoughtful men, from the time of Pythagoras, have insisted on an hour of solitude every day to meet their own mind and learn what the oracle has to impart."

Emerson sought this isolation in his walking. "Health," he writes, "is the first muse, comprising the magical benefits of air, landscape, and exercise on the mind." These three elements inspired his work. "In the woods," he said, "we return to faith and reason. There I feel that nothing can befall me in life—no disgrace, no calamity—that nature cannot repair."

So you can see the hour is also for my soul. When I run, I am alone with myself. I have the time needed for prayer. That prayer may resemble no other prayer by any other human being. It may not even satisfy the conventional definition of prayer. But it is prayer nevertheless, a dialogue that has gone on within me since I have turned to running.

My prayer is not that of a sinner, although sinner I am. I ask neither help nor forgiveness. I simply rejoice at being whole and healthy and holy. "The proper response to the world," wrote William Carlos Williams, "is applause." On the roads, I give myself and the world and the Creator a standing ovation.

"The glory of God," wrote Ireneus, one of the early church fathers, "is man fully functioning." Find your place to do that, and you will find the peace that passeth all understanding.

Index

Note: Page references in **boldface** indicate tables and charts.